ROCKS AND MINERALS

Geology from Caverns to the Cosmos

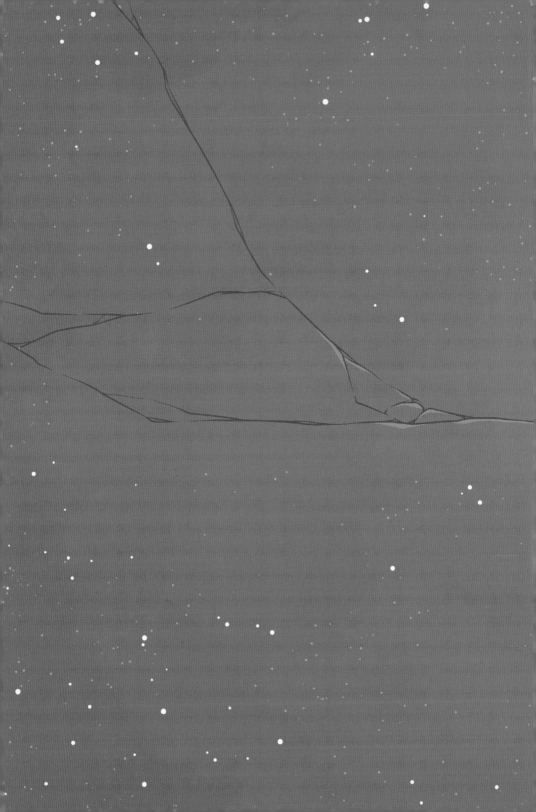

ROCKS AND MINERALS

Geology from Caverns to the Cosmos

Andy Hirsch

First Second
New York

First Second

Published by First Second
First Second is an imprint of Roaring Brook Press,
a division of Holtzbrinck Publishing Holdings Limited Partnership
120 Broadway, New York, NY 10271

Don't miss your next favorite book from First Second! For the latest updates
go to firstsecondnewsletter.com and sign up for our enewsletter.

Library of Congress Control Number: 2019903652

Paperback ISBN: 978-1-250-20395-3
Hardcover ISBN: 978-1-250-20396-0

Our books may be purchased in bulk for promotional, educational, or business use. Please
contact your local bookseller or the Macmillan Corporate and Premium Sales Department
at (800) 221-7945 ext. 5442 or by email at MacmillanSpecialMarkets@macmillan.com.

FIRST
EDITION

First edition, 2020
Edited by Dave Roman
Cover design by Molly Johanson and Chris Dickey
Interior book design by Laura Berry
Geology consultant: Andrew Bishop
Printed in China by Toppan Leefung Printing Ltd., Dongguan City, Guangdong Province

Drawn in Clip Studio Paint EX and colored in Adobe Photoshop CC

Paperback: 10 9 8 7 6 5 4 3 2 1
Hardcover: 10 9 8 7 6 5 4 3 2 1

For a geologist, a rock is never just a rock. A rock is the culmination of an amazing story that took thousands to millions of years to tell and has just been waiting for the right person to come along to unravel and share that story.

Looking back on my life, and my childhood especially, it seems as if geology chose me. One of my fondest and most vivid early memories is visiting the La Brea Tar Pits in Los Angeles, California, with my family. I clearly remember watching the paleontologists behind the glass work diligently to unearth a multitude of Ice Age fossils. After begging my parents to buy me a souvenir from the gift shop, I triumphantly emerged with a cast of a saber-toothed cat canine. This, along with an ammonite fossil given to me as a birthday present, became one of my most prized possessions and held a prominent place on my bookshelf for years to come.

This trip also solidified my desire to become a paleontologist when I grew up. While other kids were drawing pictures of themselves as firefighters, doctors, or rock stars, I envisioned myself with a hammer and chisel digging up the remains of long-extinct dinosaurs and other prehistoric animals. Like so many others, I didn't grow up to become what I had wished for in my youth, but I came pretty close. Even if I don't explore the world looking for undiscovered fossilized remains, my professional career as a geologist is rooted in the use of paleontology as a method of unraveling the history of the Earth. Paleontology is just one of the tools and scientific principles we use to help make sense of the world around us. These are the same tools and principles that the heroine of this book, Sedona, uses to explain the geologic history of the rock her young assistant, Wally, brings in for inspection.

While teaching me to skip rocks over water, my dad recounted a story from his youth about pulling layered black rocks out of the ground surrounding Skaneateles Lake in New York State. Not only were these rocks the perfect skipping stones due to their flat shape, but as they were pulled apart, a wealth of ancient fossilized marine life was revealed within. Layer after layer uncovered trilobites, prehistoric worms, staghorn corals, and other marine life that vanished from this land millions of years ago. What stayed with me about this story was how odd it seemed that fossils and evidence of an ocean environment were right there at his fingertips. How could this be when the area was clearly a terrestrial and lacustrine (or lake) setting today?

In my adolescence, we traveled to Red Rock Canyon just outside of Las Vegas, Nevada. The sprawling red-and-orange cliffs provided the perfect playground for my dad and me to scramble higher and higher in the never-ending game of worrying my mom and brother standing below. I remember pressing my face to the sides of the cliffs and running my hands along the undulating layers of sandstone and thinking how much it looked like beach sand blowing in the wind. But again, here I was standing in the middle of the desert with no sand dunes in sight. How could that be?

The answer to these questions came later, as I started to delve into the earth sciences in middle and high school, and especially as I started my studies as a geology major at Rutgers University. I learned the ins and outs of plate tectonics, stratigraphy, sedimentology, geologic time, and paleontology. It was like learning a new language because suddenly I could "read" the world around me. By applying the principles of stratigraphy and the theory of plate tectonics, I now understood that continents could move all over the surface of the Earth, creating new landscapes. What was once the bottom of the sea could now form the peaks of mountain ranges, and the processes shaping the land today can be used to understand the rock layers and depositional environments of the past.

Did you know that geologists and other scientists have discovered approximately 5,400 different types of minerals around the world? And somewhere between 30 to 50 new ones are discovered each year! These minerals combine to make a staggering number of different rock types. In fact, igneous petrologists, geologists who specialize in studying igneous rocks, have named and described over 700 types of igneous rocks alone! One might think that geologists have already discovered all the unknown rocks and minerals on our planet, but this is very far from the truth. As the Earth continues to change through the processes of weathering, erosion, and plate tectonics, new surfaces are constantly being exposed, which provides the perfect opportunity for enterprising geologists to explore.

What's more, a large portion of our planet has yet to be explored due to the difficulty of accessing and imaging the deep ocean floors. According to the National Oceanic and Atmospheric Administration, over 95 percent of the world's ocean and about 99 percent of the ocean floor have yet to be explored. This equates to roughly 343 million square kilometers, or 132 million square miles, of uncharted territory. Moreover, scientists have more accurate maps of Mars and the Moon than we do for parts of the ocean. For example, high-resolution-satellite data has allowed us to image objects on the surface of Mars that are 10 to 20 meters in size or larger. Comparatively, there are parts of our ocean that have been mapped to only a 1:50,000 scale, meaning that features less than 50 meters in size may not be visible and cannot be mapped.

All of this is to say that there is a lot more work to do. The world needs more geologists like Sedona and Wally to get out there and unravel the mysteries buried in the geologic record. These geologists will not only help find new rocks but will also help discover the mineral and fossil fuel resources needed to keep the world moving and the water resources to keep its people fed and nourished. As humans continue to push the boundaries of our own world, geologists will help lead the way as teams of international scientists explore the surfaces of new planets and moons.

So sit back and enjoy this story, and then go out and discover your own rock story!

Dr. Lauren Neitzke Adamo
Geologist, Rutgers University Geology Museum

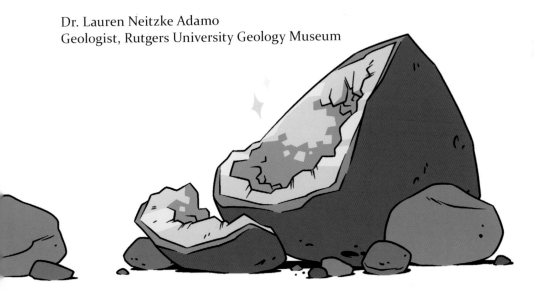

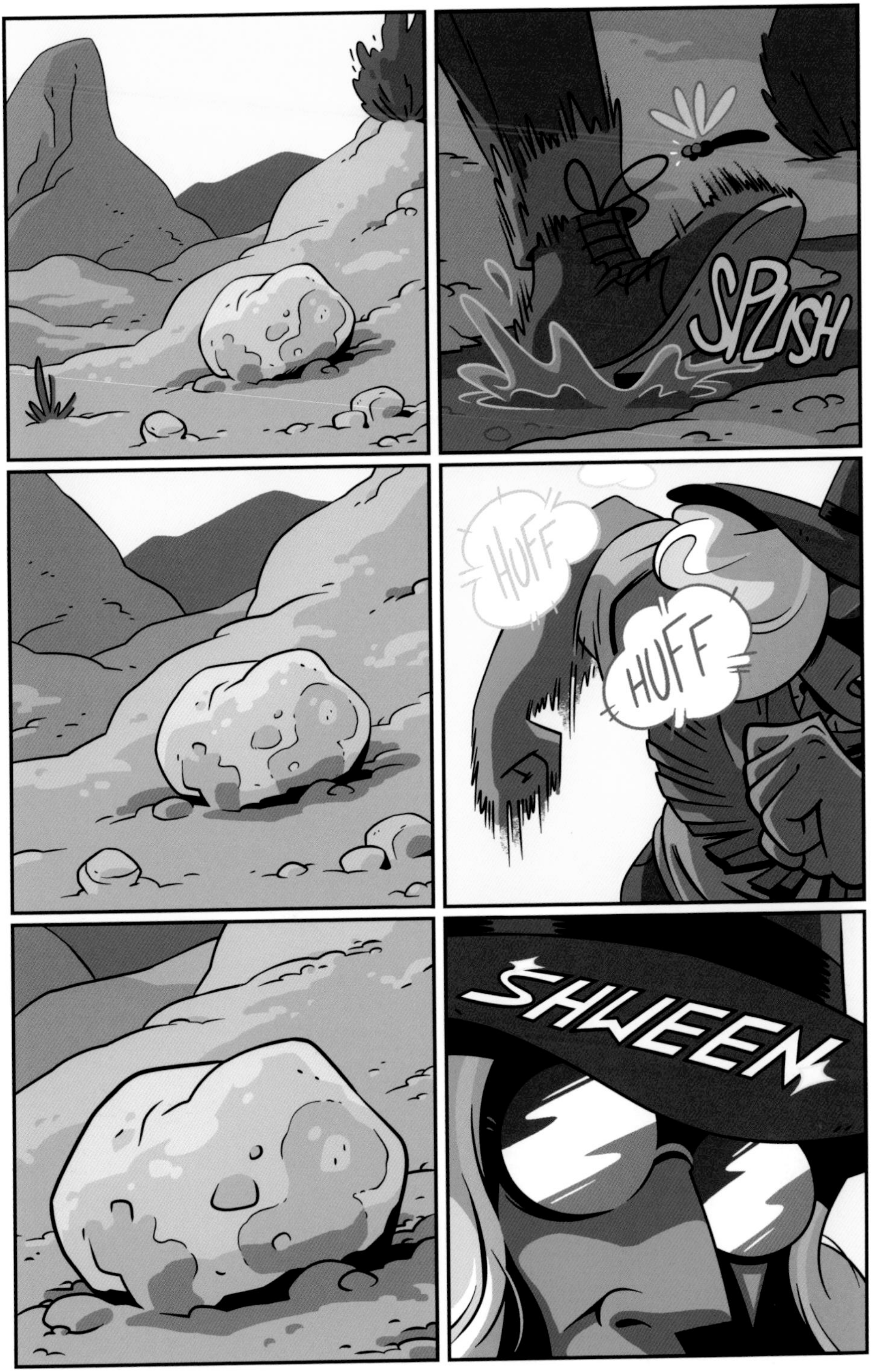
SPLISH
HUFF
HUFF
SHWEEN

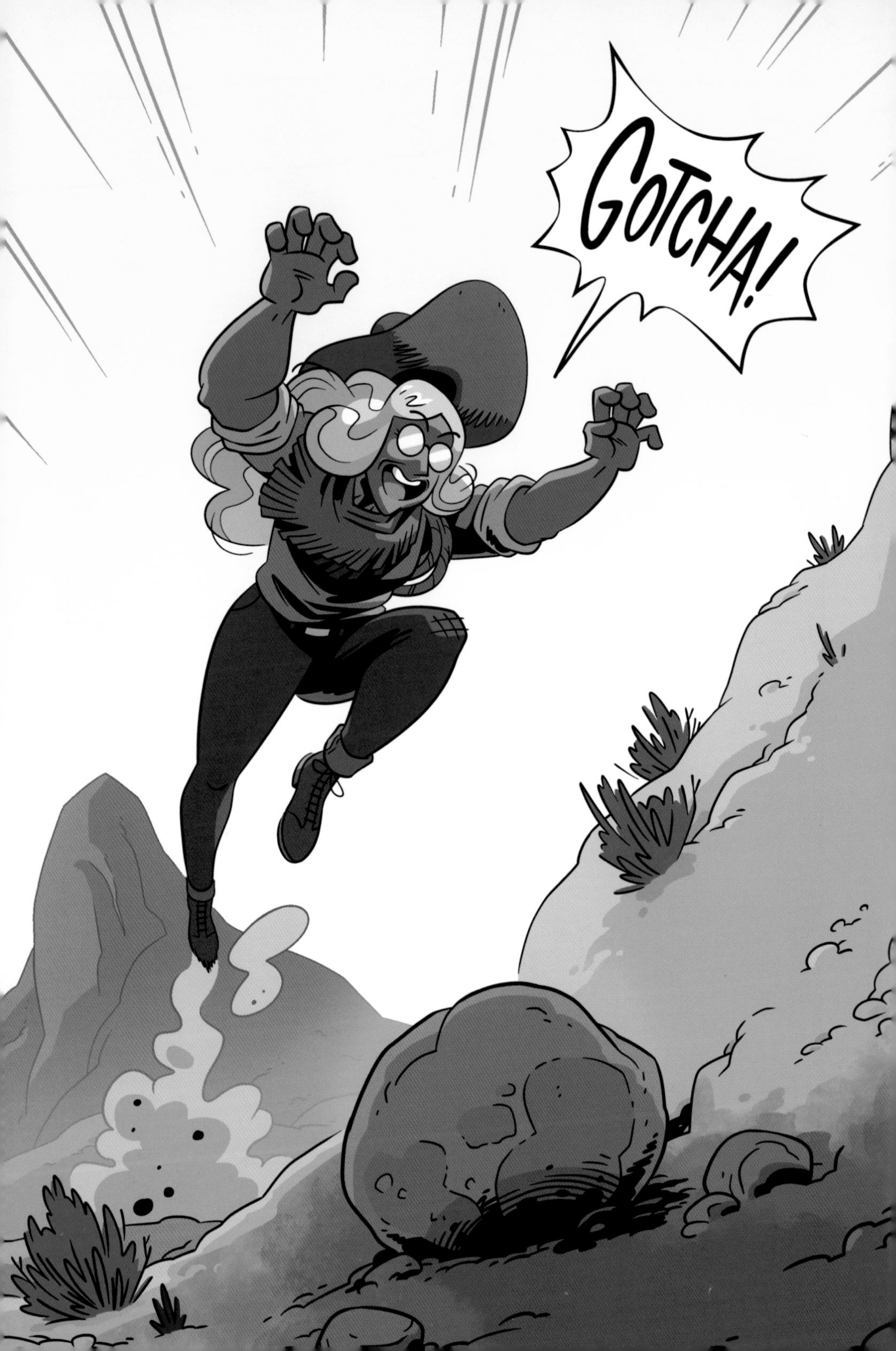
GOTCHA!

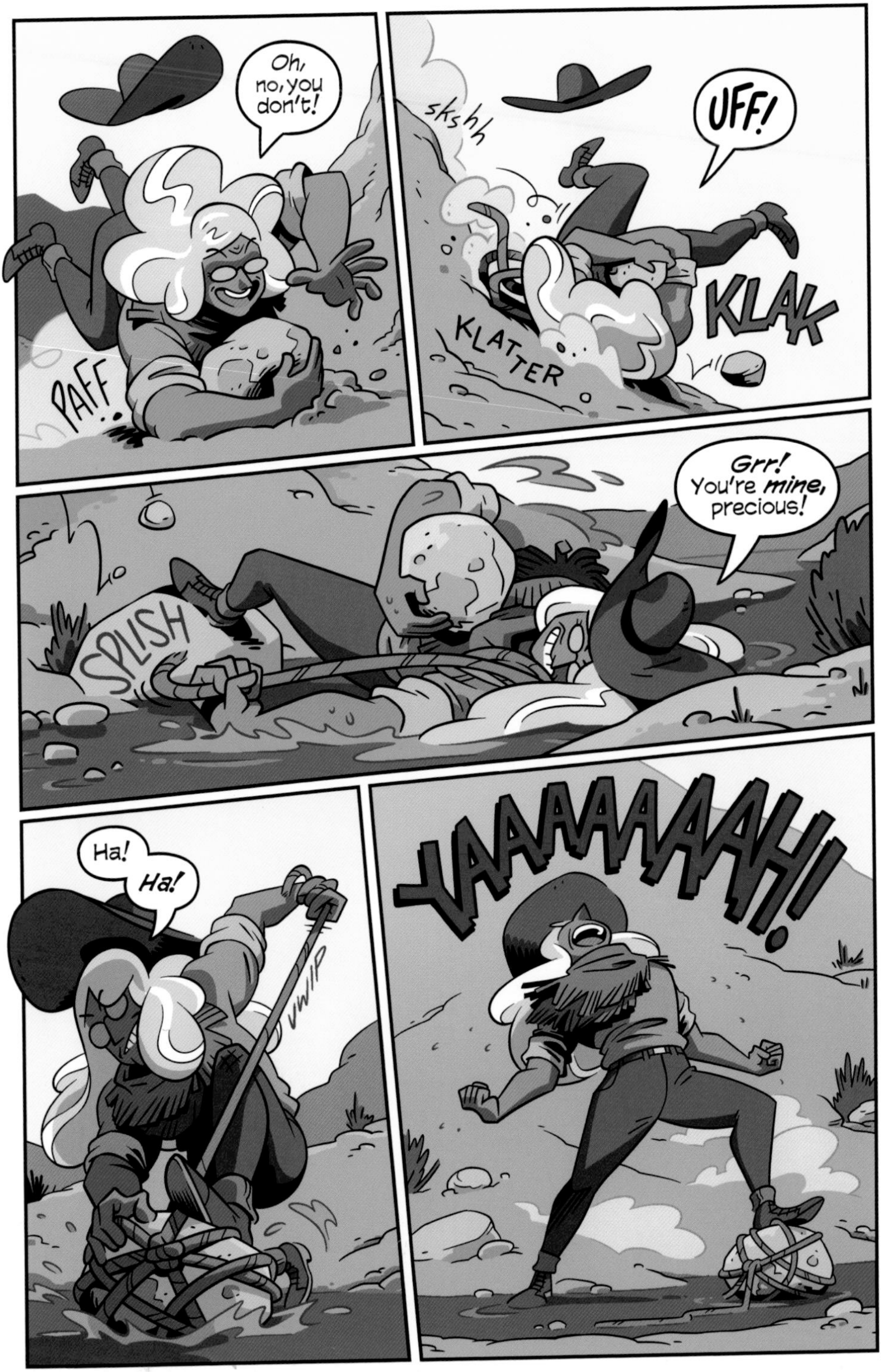
Oh, no, you don't!
PAFF
skshh
UFF!
KLATTER
KLAK
Grr! You're *mine*, precious!
SPLISH
Ha! Ha!
VWIP
YAAAAAAAH!!

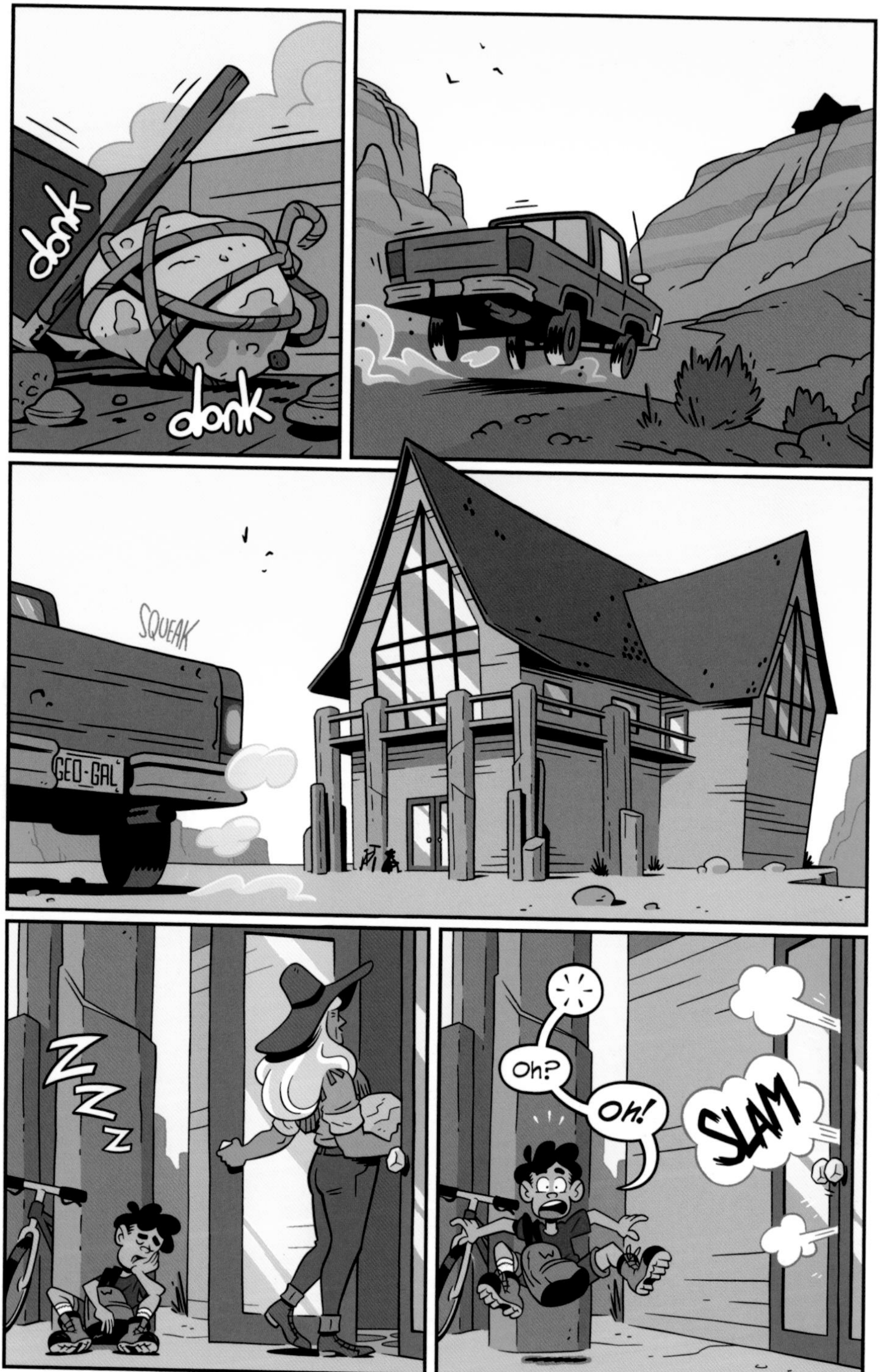
donk
donk
SQUEAK
GEO-GAL
ZZZZ
Oh?
Oh!
SLAM

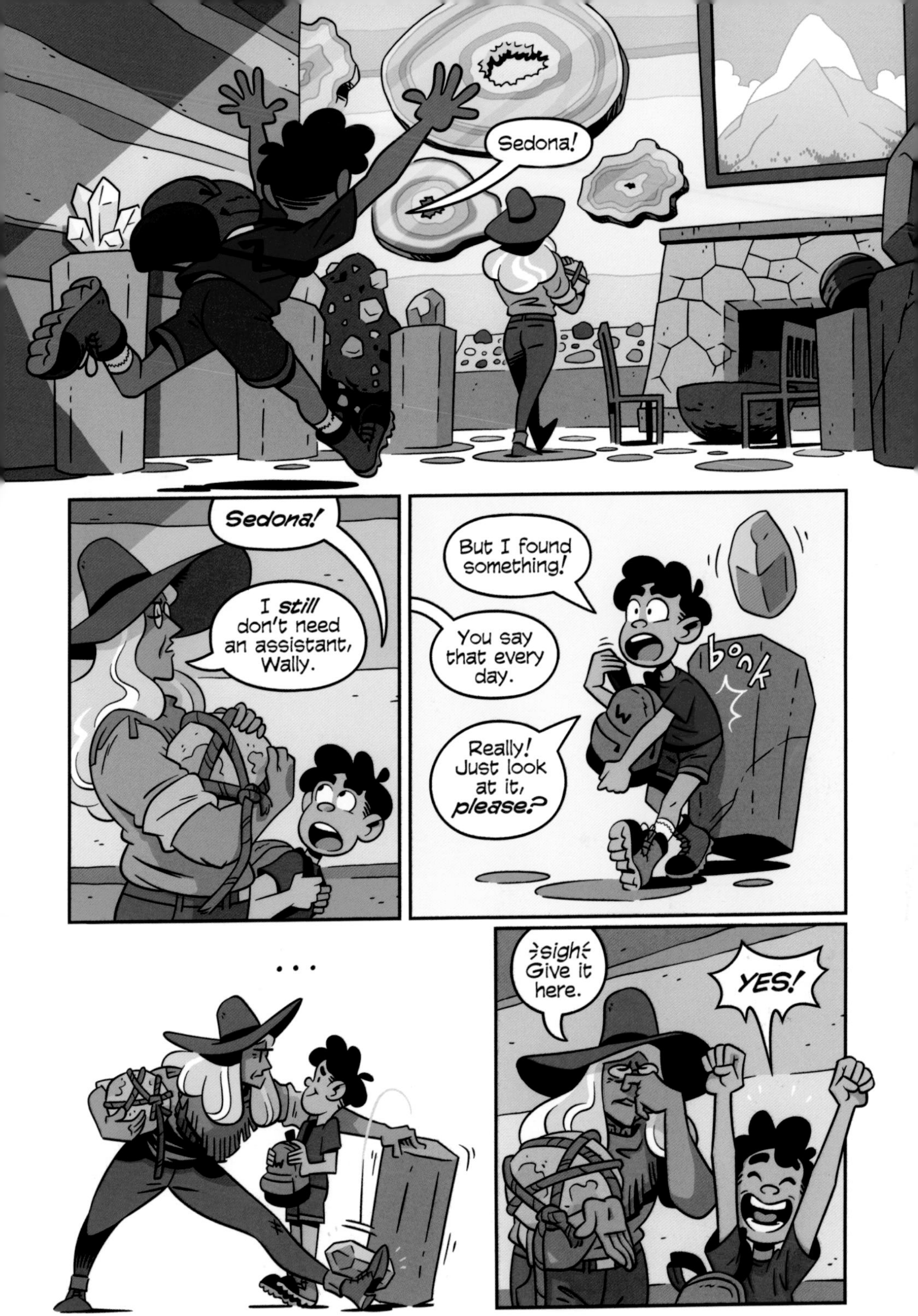
Sedona!
Sedona!
I *still* don't need an assistant, Wally.
But I found something!
You say that every day.
Really! Just look at it, *please?*
bonk
. . .
sigh Give it here.
YES!

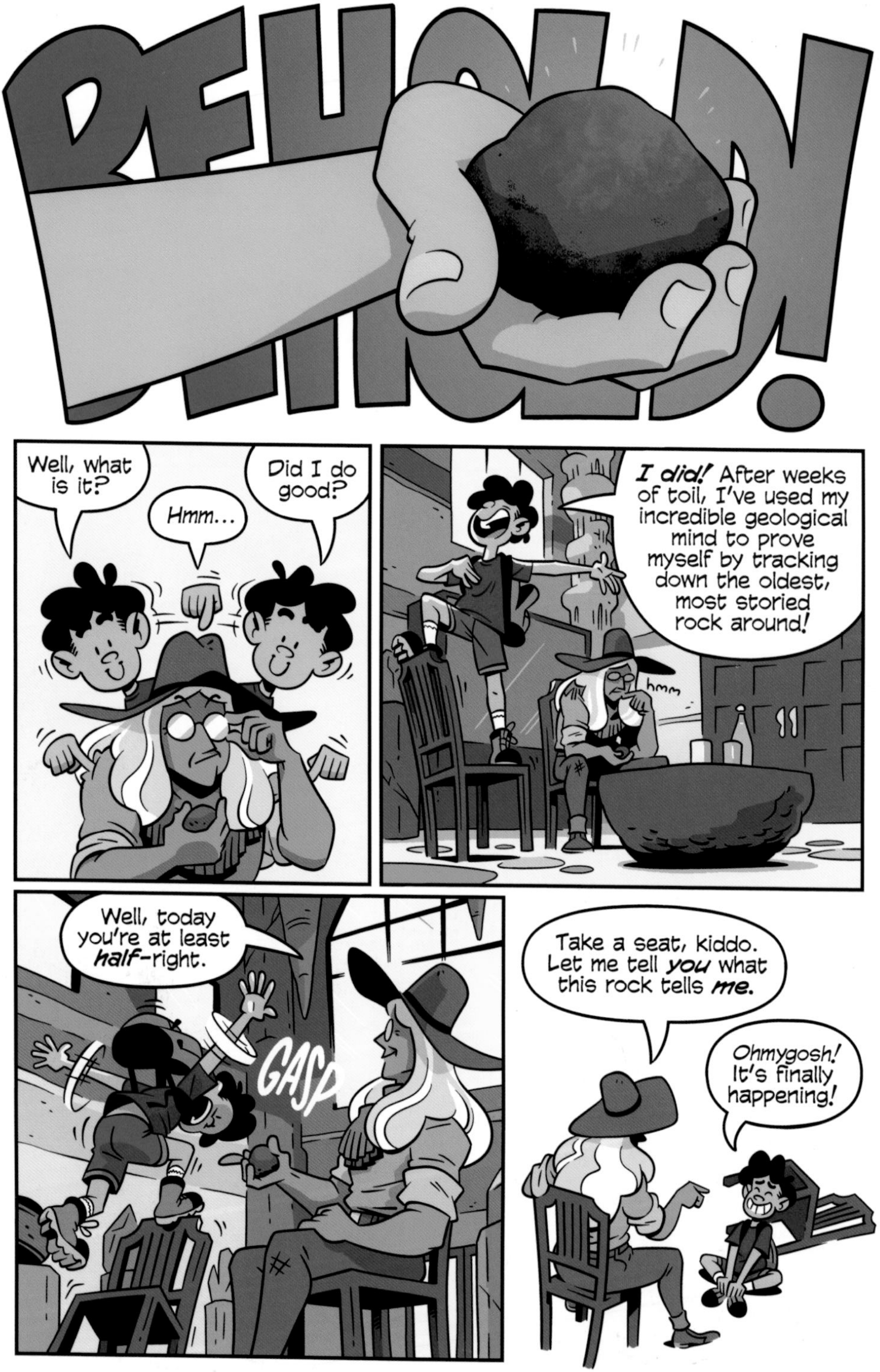
BEHOLD!
Well, what is it?
Hmm...
Did I do good?
I did! After weeks of toil, I've used my incredible geological mind to prove myself by tracking down the oldest, most storied rock around!
hmm
Well, today you're at least ***half***-right.
GASP
Take a seat, kiddo. Let me tell ***you*** what this rock tells ***me***.
Ohmygosh! It's finally happening!

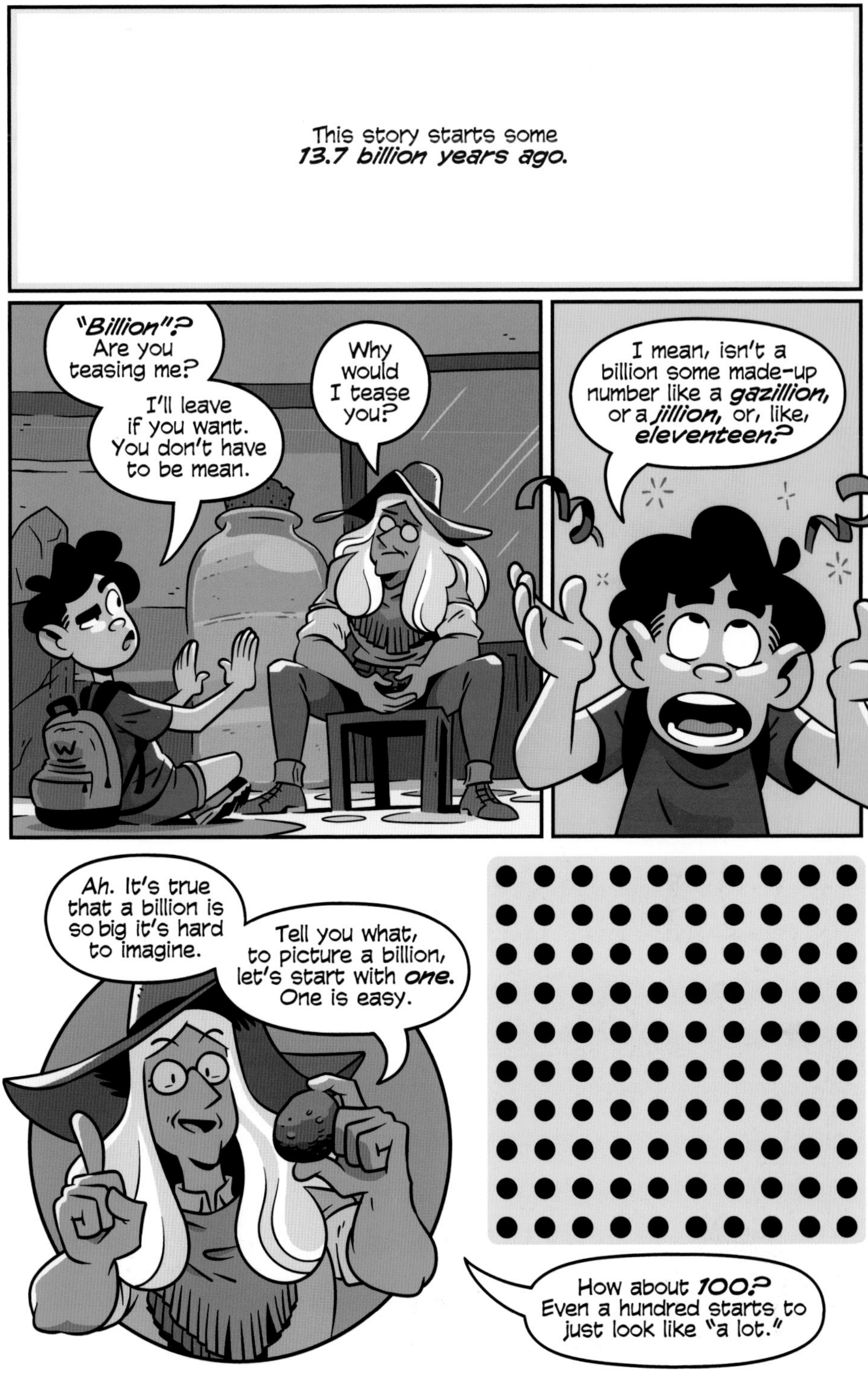
This story starts some
13.7 billion years ago.
"Billion"? Are you teasing me?
I'll leave if you want. You don't have to be mean.
Why would I tease you?
I mean, isn't a billion some made-up number like a *gazillion,* or a *jillion,* or, like, *eleventeen?*
Ah. It's true that a billion is so big it's hard to imagine.
Tell you what, to picture a billion, let's start with *one.* One is easy.
How about *100?* Even a hundred starts to just look like "a lot."

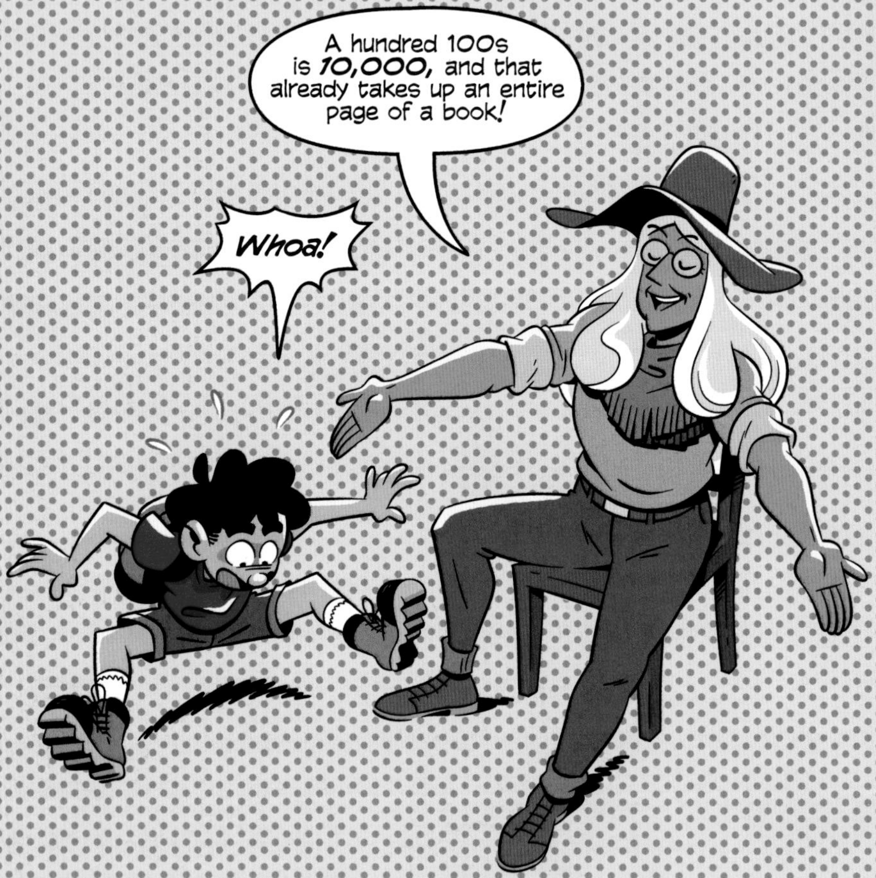

A hundred 100s is ***10,000,*** and that already takes up an entire page of a book!
Whoa!

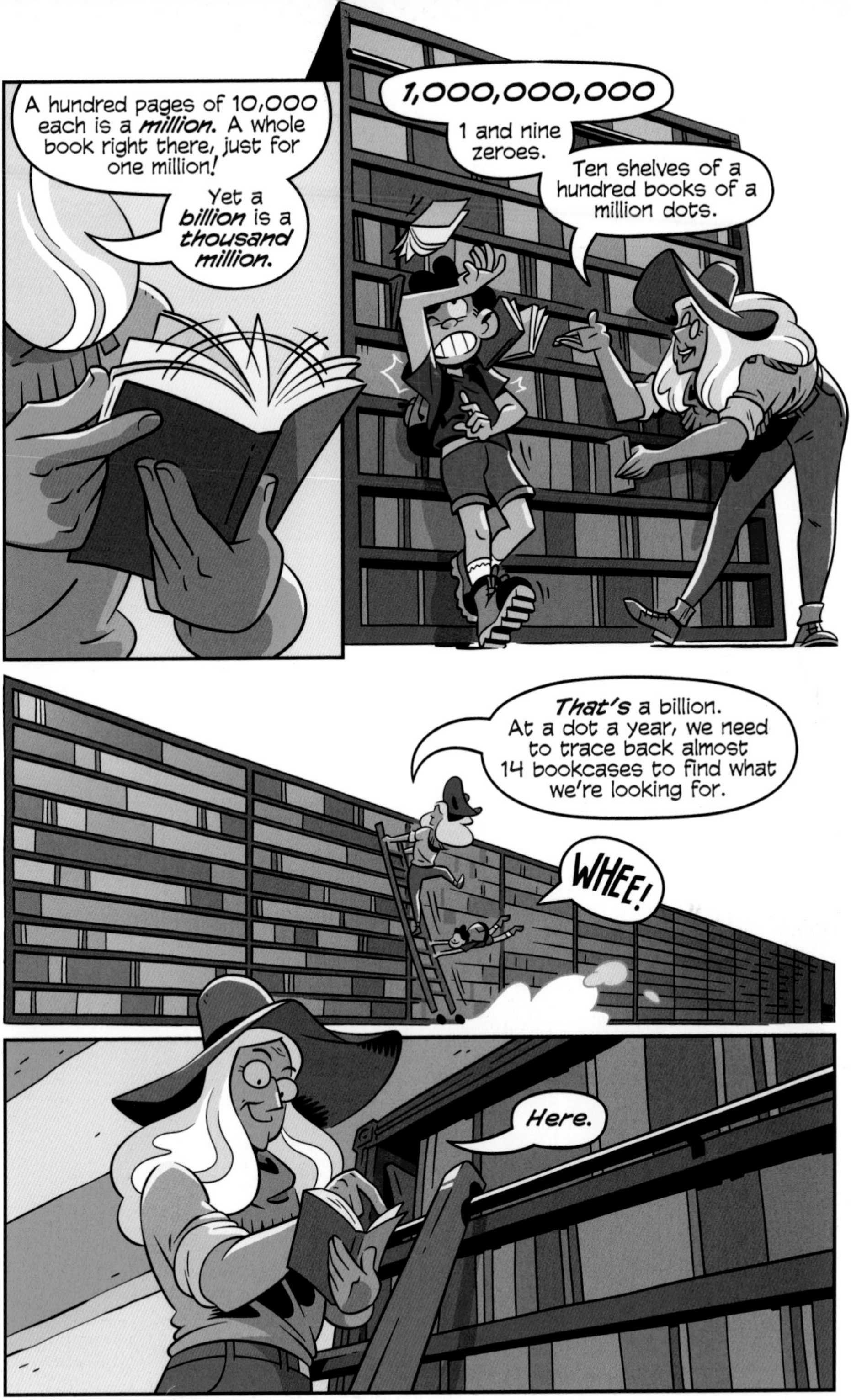
A hundred pages of 10,000 each is a *million*. A whole book right there, just for one million!
Yet a *billion* is a *thousand million*.
1,000,000,000
1 and nine zeroes.
Ten shelves of a hundred books of a million dots.
That's a billion. At a dot a year, we need to trace back almost 14 bookcases to find what we're looking for.
WHEE!
Here.

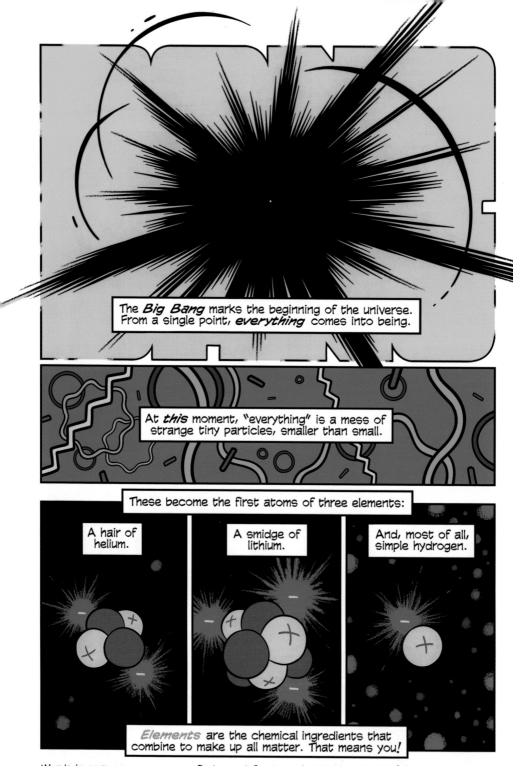

The *Big Bang* marks the beginning of the universe. From a single point, *everything* comes into being.

At *this* moment, "everything" is a mess of strange tiny particles, smaller than small.

These become the first atoms of three elements:

A hair of helium.

A smidge of lithium.

And, most of all, simple hydrogen.

Elements are the chemical ingredients that combine to make up all matter. That means you!

Words in *orange* mean you can find more info about them in the glossary!

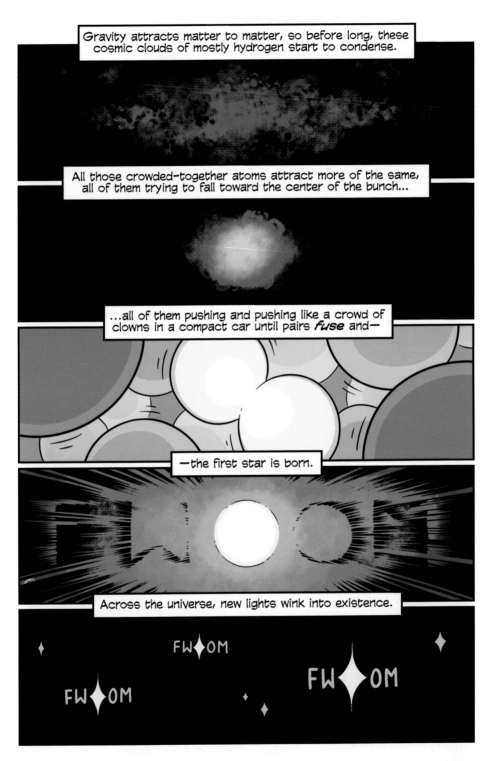

Gravity attracts matter to matter, so before long, these cosmic clouds of mostly hydrogen start to condense.

All those crowded-together atoms attract more of the same, all of them trying to fall toward the center of the bunch...

...all of them pushing and pushing like a crowd of clowns in a compact car until pairs *fuse* and—

—the first star is born.

Across the universe, new lights wink into existence.

FW◆OM

FW◆OM

FW◆OM

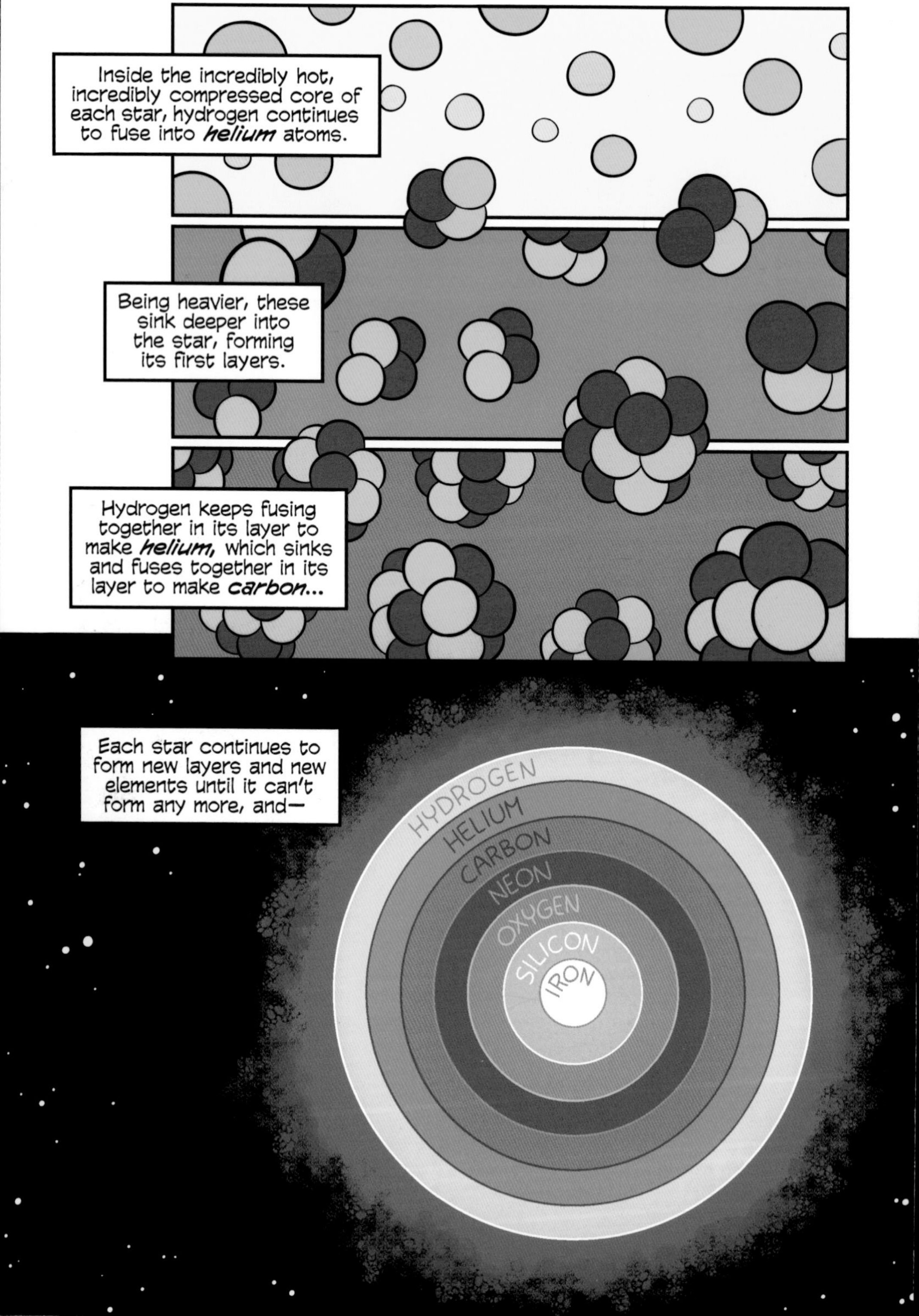
Inside the incredibly hot, incredibly compressed core of each star, hydrogen continues to fuse into *helium* atoms.
Being heavier, these sink deeper into the star, forming its first layers.
Hydrogen keeps fusing together in its layer to make *helium,* which sinks and fuses together in its layer to make *carbon...*
Each star continues to form new layers and new elements until it can't form any more, and—
HYDROGEN
HELIUM
CARBON
NEON
OXYGEN
SILICON
IRON

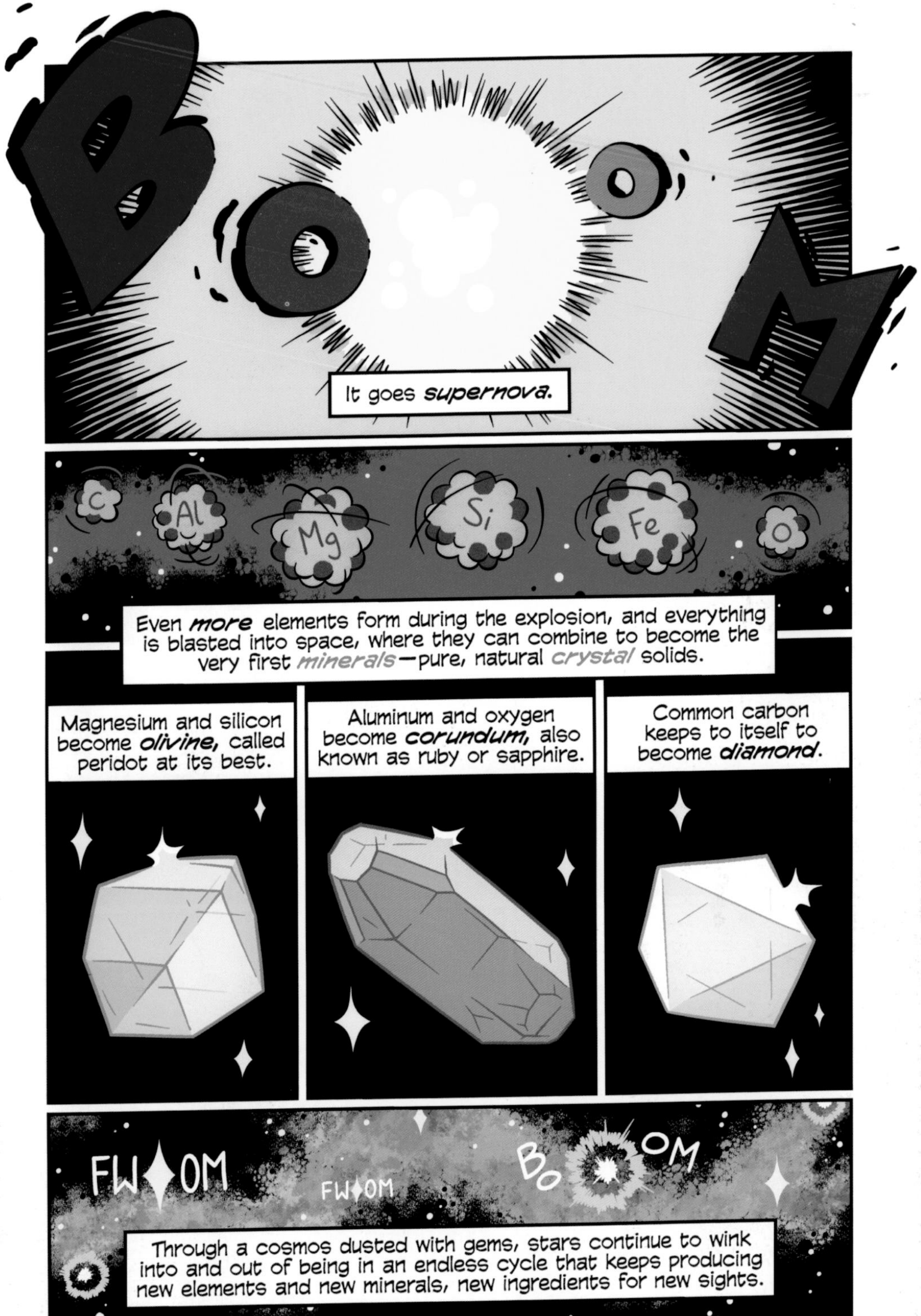
BOOM
It goes *supernova.*
C
Al
Mg
Si
Fe
O
Even *more* elements form during the explosion, and everything is blasted into space, where they can combine to become the very first *minerals*—pure, natural *crystal* solids.
Magnesium and silicon become *olivine,* called peridot at its best.
Aluminum and oxygen become *corundum,* also known as ruby or sapphire.
Common carbon keeps to itself to become *diamond*.
FWOOM
FWOOM
BOOM
Through a cosmos dusted with gems, stars continue to wink into and out of being in an endless cycle that keeps producing new elements and new minerals, new ingredients for new sights.

Nearly *4.6 billion years ago* (that's more than four and a half bookcases of ten shelves of a hundred books of a million dots) halfway out on an unremarkable arm of an unremarkable galaxy, an unremarkable star ignited.

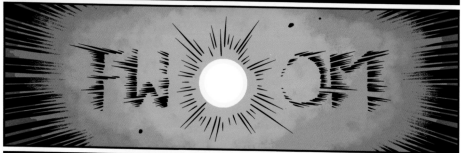

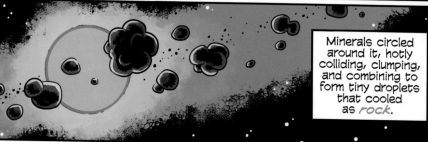

Minerals circled around it, hotly colliding, clumping, and combining to form tiny droplets that cooled as *rock*.

Those droplets make up the meteoric *chondrite* you've got here.

This... is over four and a half *billion* years old?

I... am...

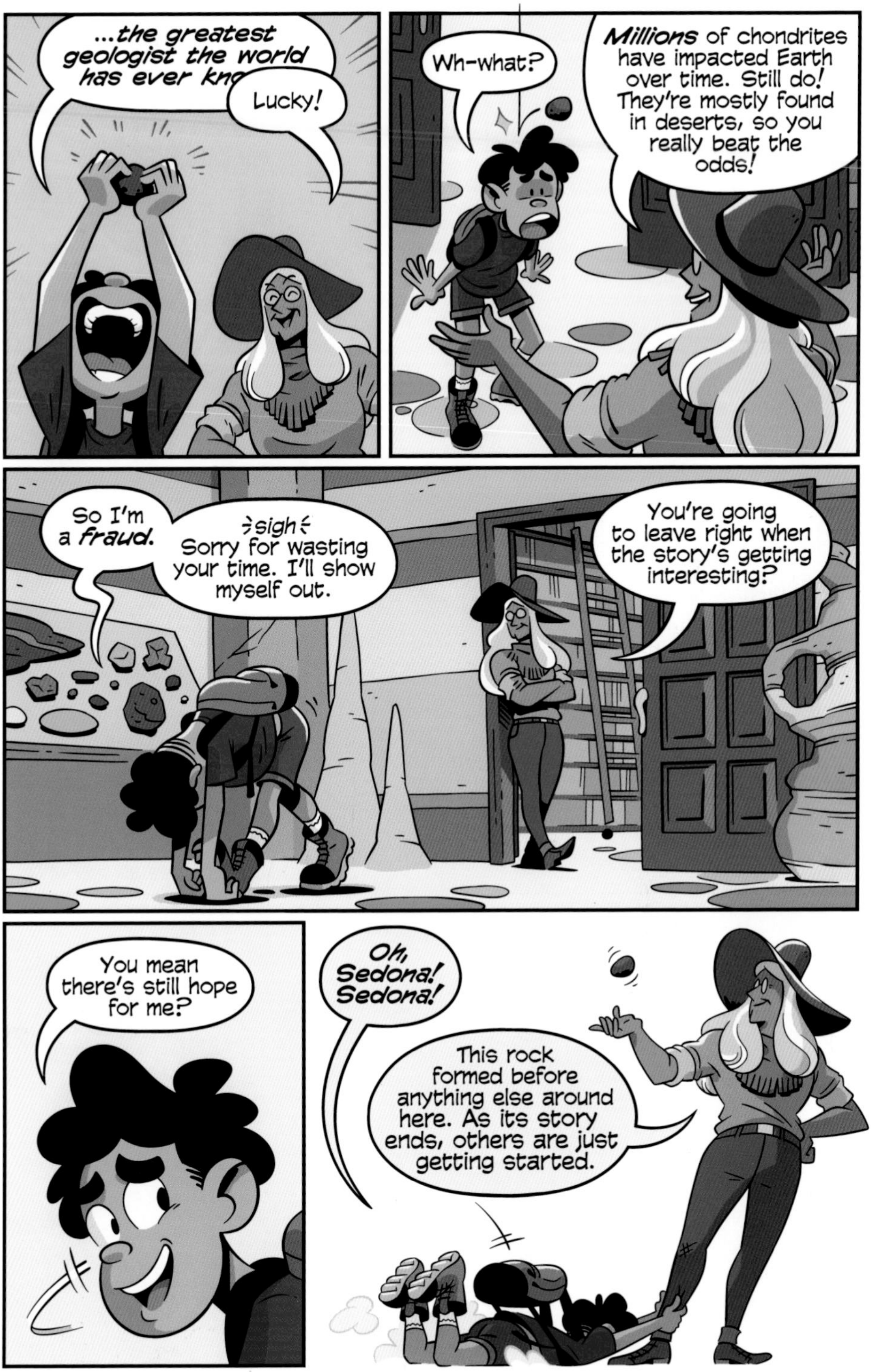

...the greatest geologist the world has ever kn
Lucky!
Wh-what?
Millions of chondrites have impacted Earth over time. Still do! They're mostly found in deserts, so you really beat the odds!
So I'm a *fraud.*
sigh Sorry for wasting your time. I'll show myself out.
You're going to leave right when the story's getting interesting?
You mean there's still hope for me?
Oh, Sedona! Sedona!
This rock formed before anything else around here. As its story ends, others are just getting started.

Remember, all we've got so far is a star with a bunch of chondrules orbiting around it, slowly gathering together from gravity and chance collisions.

A large clump is a *planetesimal*, not yet a planet.

Any that gets big enough, 80 kilometers (50 miles) across or so, starts to generate its own heat, both from pressure on its core and the *radioactive decay* of certain elements inside it that lose mass in the form of energy.

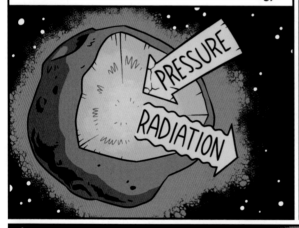

PRESSURE

RADIATION

Planetesimals come and go, smash and get smashed, mixing up their rocky recipes all the while.

Heavy elements forged in stars long ago form their iron and nickel cores, while new rocks and minerals make layers above them, all arranged by density.

IRON-NICKEL

PEROVSKITE

OLIVINE

Density is how much of something is in how much space.

A bit of matter spread out over a _lot_ of space isn't dense at all.	But the same amount of matter in a _little_ space is very dense.

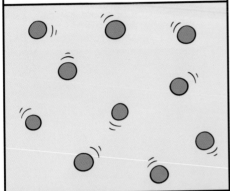

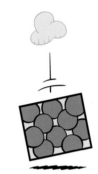

And denser material sinks beneath less dense.

Hey! My chondrite!

≥grumble≥

So knowing what minerals make up a planetesimal gives you a good idea of how it's organized.

As these bodies continue to accumulate mass, some will become proper planets. It's the third one out in this solar system that concerns us.

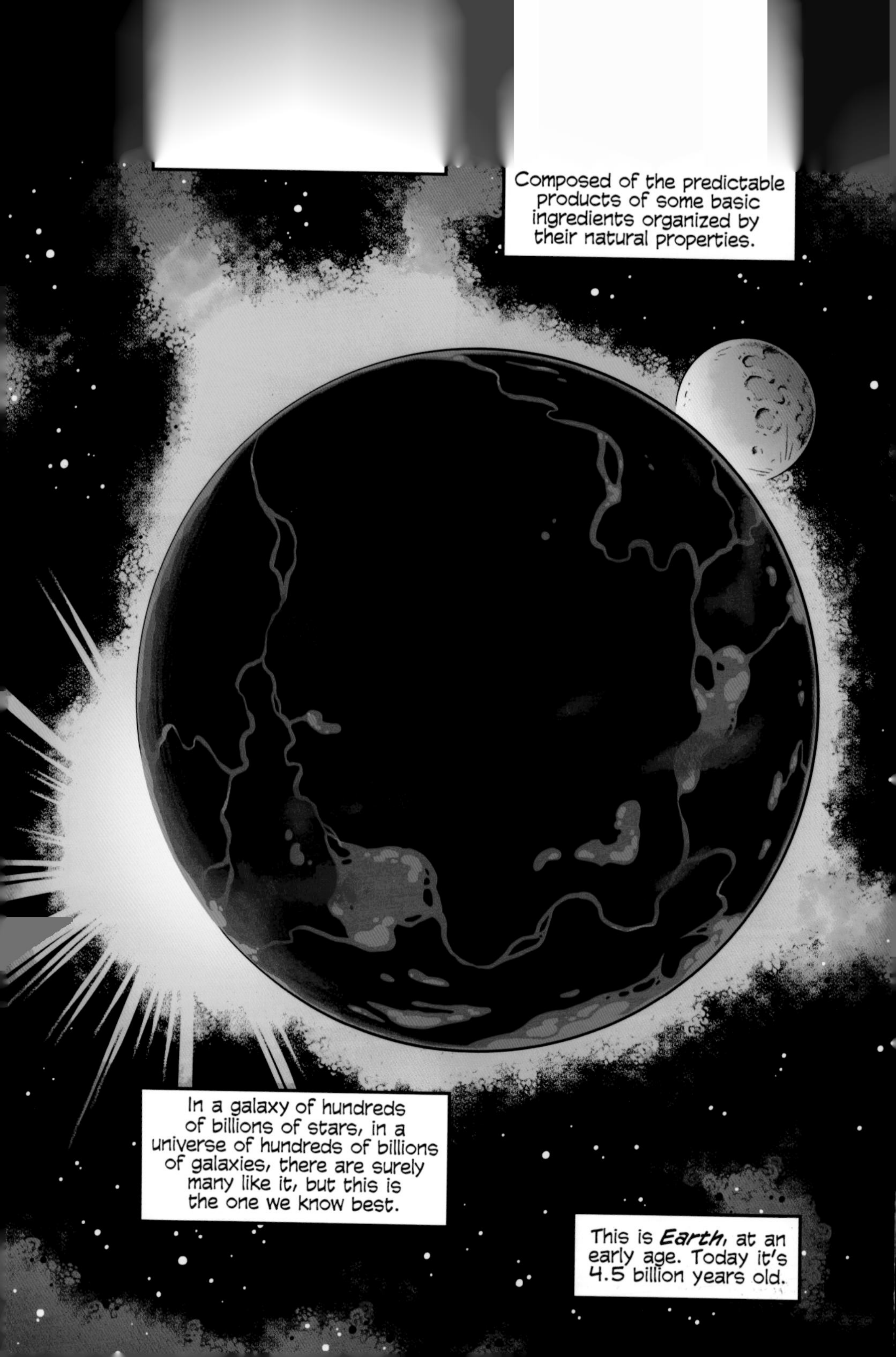
Composed of the predictable products of some basic ingredients organized by their natural properties.
In a galaxy of hundreds of billions of stars, in a universe of hundreds of billions of galaxies, there are surely many like it, but this is the one we know best.
This is *Earth*, at an early age. Today it's 4.5 billion years old.

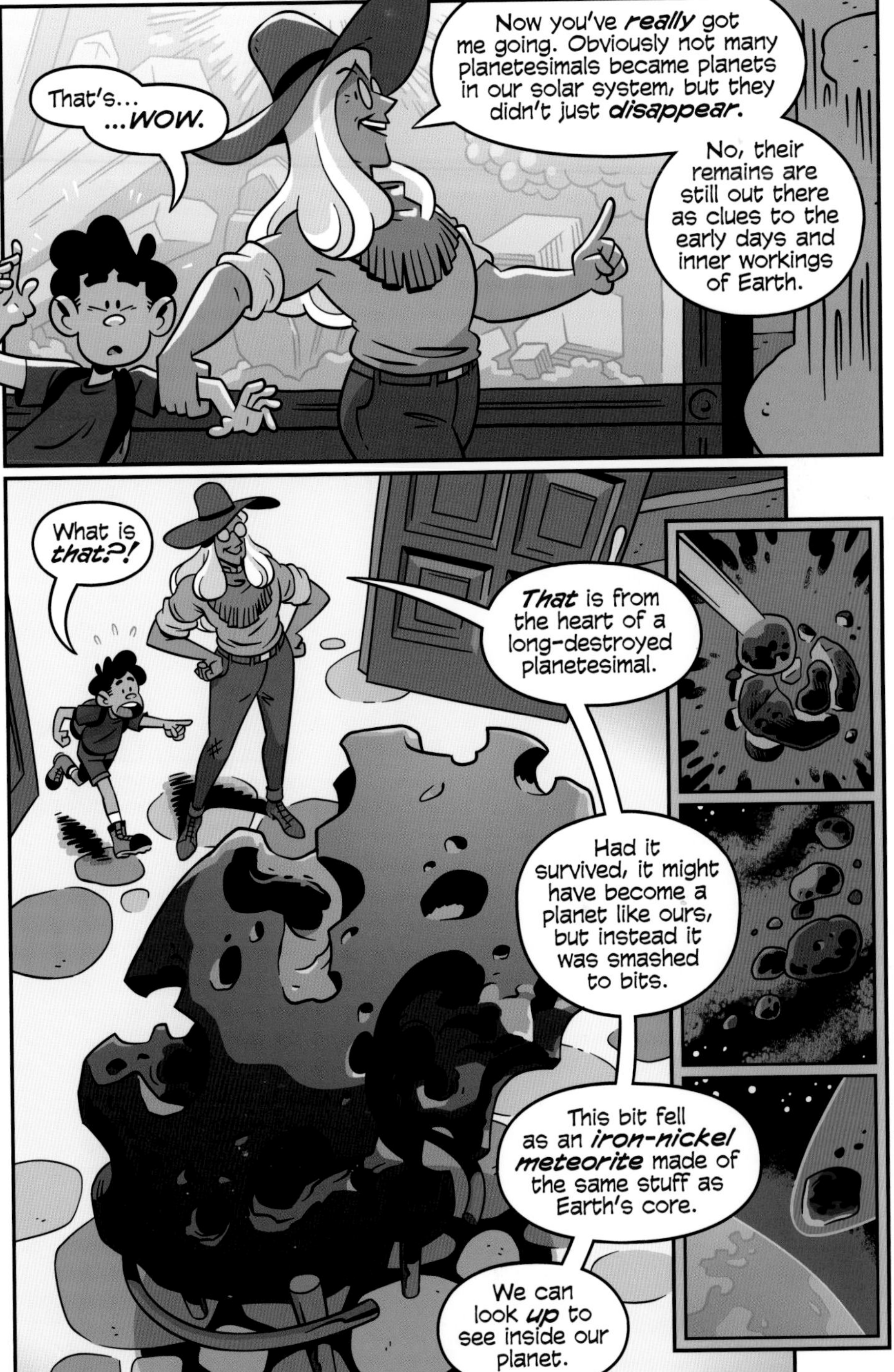
That's...
...WOW.
Now you've *really* got me going. Obviously not many planetesimals became planets in our solar system, but they didn't just *disappear*.
No, their remains are still out there as clues to the early days and inner workings of Earth.
What is *that?!*
That is from the heart of a long-destroyed planetesimal.
Had it survived, it might have become a planet like ours, but instead it was smashed to bits.
This bit fell as an *iron-nickel meteorite* made of the same stuff as Earth's core.
We can look *up* to see inside our planet.

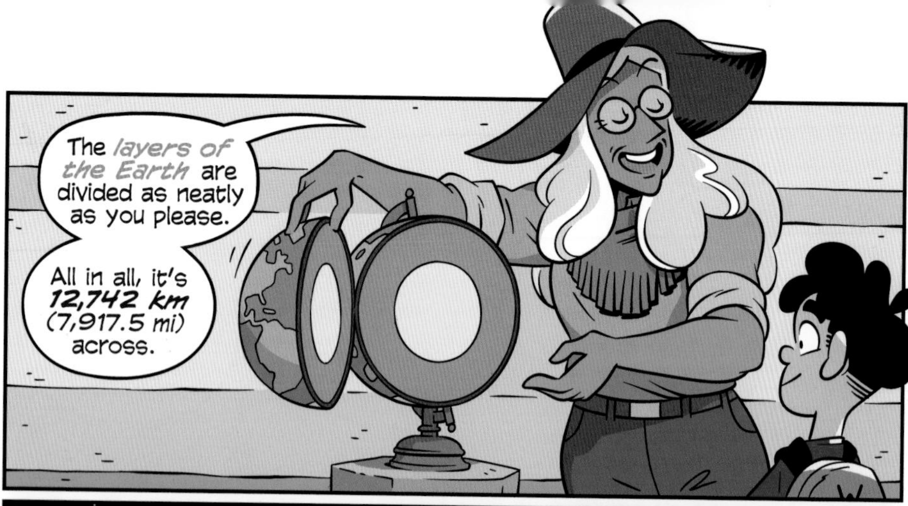
The layers of the Earth are divided as neatly as you please.
All in all, it's 12,742 km (7,917.5 mi) across.

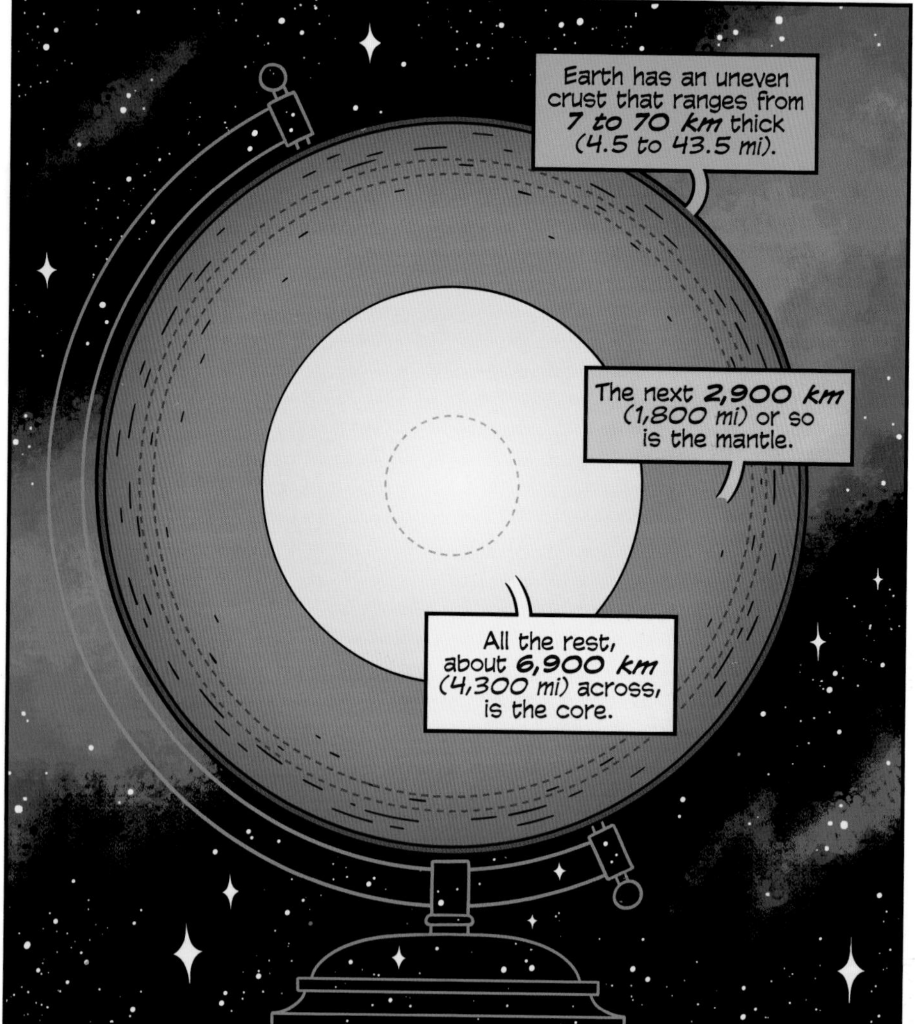
Earth has an uneven crust that ranges from 7 to 70 km thick (4.5 to 43.5 mi).
The next 2,900 km (1,800 mi) or so is the mantle.
All the rest, about 6,900 km (4,300 mi) across, is the core.

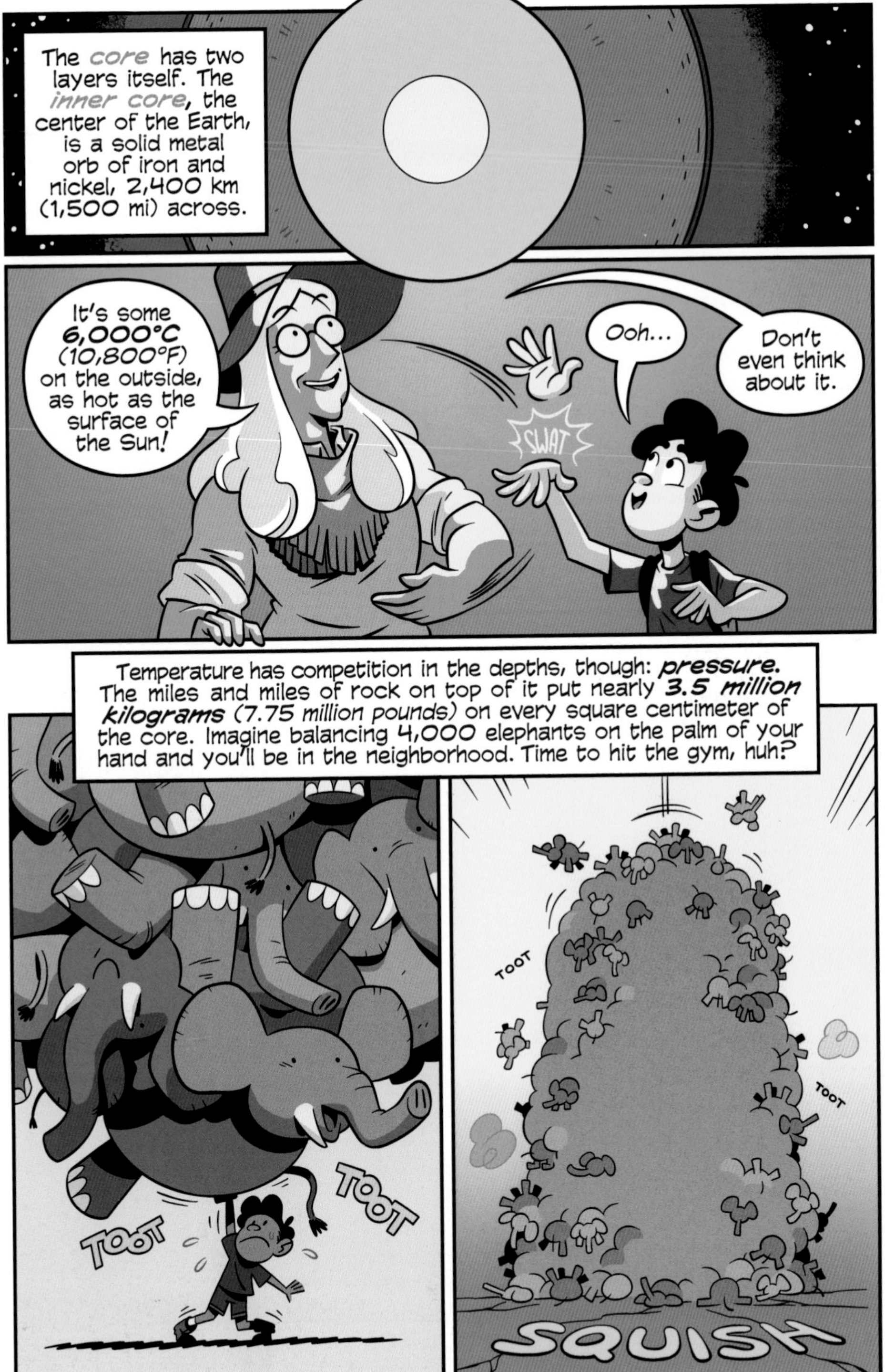
The *core* has two layers itself. The *inner core*, the center of the Earth, is a solid metal orb of iron and nickel, 2,400 km (1,500 mi) across.
It's some **6,000°C** (10,800°F) on the outside, as hot as the surface of the Sun!
Ooh...
Don't even think about it.
SWAT
Temperature has competition in the depths, though: ***pressure.*** The miles and miles of rock on top of it put nearly ***3.5 million kilograms*** (7.75 million pounds) on every square centimeter of the core. Imagine balancing 4,000 elephants on the palm of your hand and you'll be in the neighborhood. Time to hit the gym, huh?
TOOT
TOOT
TOOT
TOOT
SQUISH

Those are big numbers, but why is pressure important? Most substances expand to take up more space as liquids than they do as solids. They get *bigger* when they *melt.*

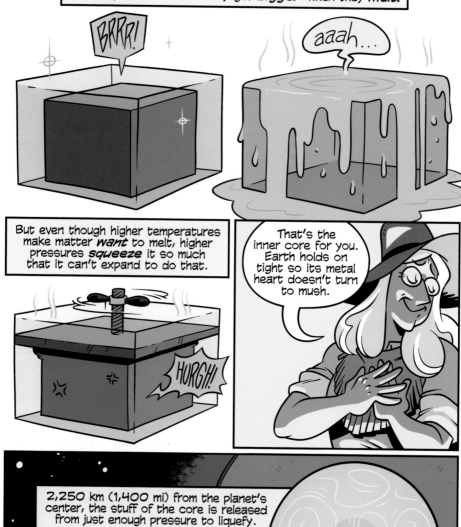

BRRR!

aaah...

But even though higher temperatures make matter *want* to melt, higher pressures *squeeze* it so much that it can't expand to do that.

HURGH!

That's the inner core for you. Earth holds on tight so its metal heart doesn't turn to mush.

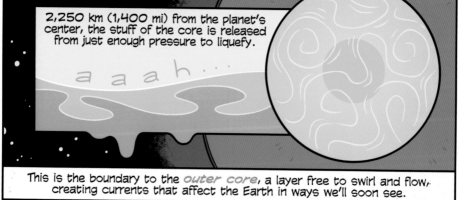

2,250 km (1,400 mi) from the planet's center, the stuff of the core is released from just enough pressure to liquefy.

a a a h...

This is the boundary to the *outer core,* a layer free to swirl and flow, creating currents that affect the Earth in ways we'll soon see.

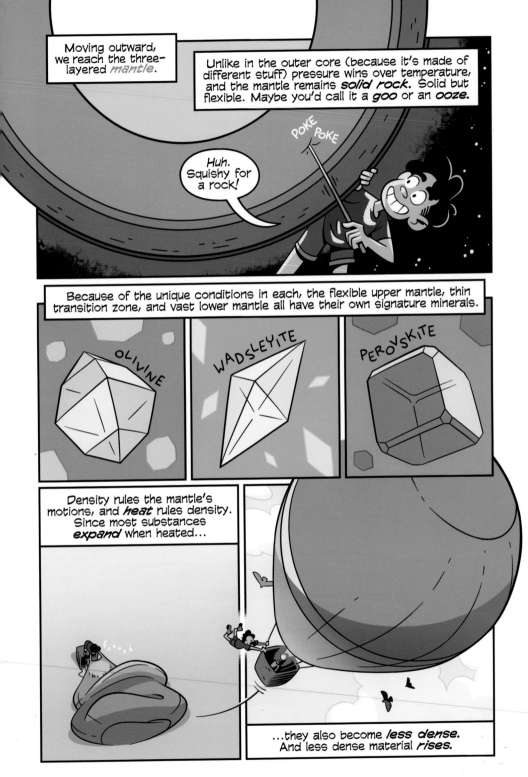

Moving outward, we reach the three-layered *mantle*.

Unlike in the outer core (because it's made of different stuff) pressure wins over temperature, and the mantle remains *solid rock*. Solid but flexible. Maybe you'd call it a *goo* or an *ooze*.

POKE POKE

Huh. Squishy for a rock!

Because of the unique conditions in each, the flexible upper mantle, thin transition zone, and vast lower mantle all have their own signature minerals.

OLIVINE

WADSLEYITE

PEROVSKITE

Density rules the mantle's motions, and *heat* rules density. Since most substances *expand* when heated...

fooosh

...they also become *less dense*. And less dense material *rises*.

Thanks to heat from the core, the mantle churns. Over and over, rock is heated, rises...

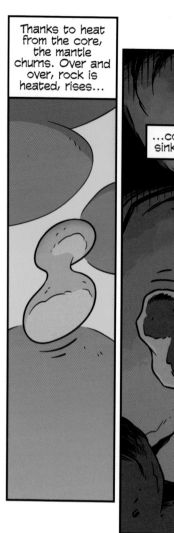

...cools, sinks...

...is heated, rises...

...cools, sinks...

This is *convection*. The mantle is Earth's gurgling guts.

Above the mantle, far from the core's heat and open to the surface environment, rock cools to become a shell known as the *crust*.

The mass of the crust is nothing compared to the core and mantle, yet it's all we humans see or have even ever sampled!

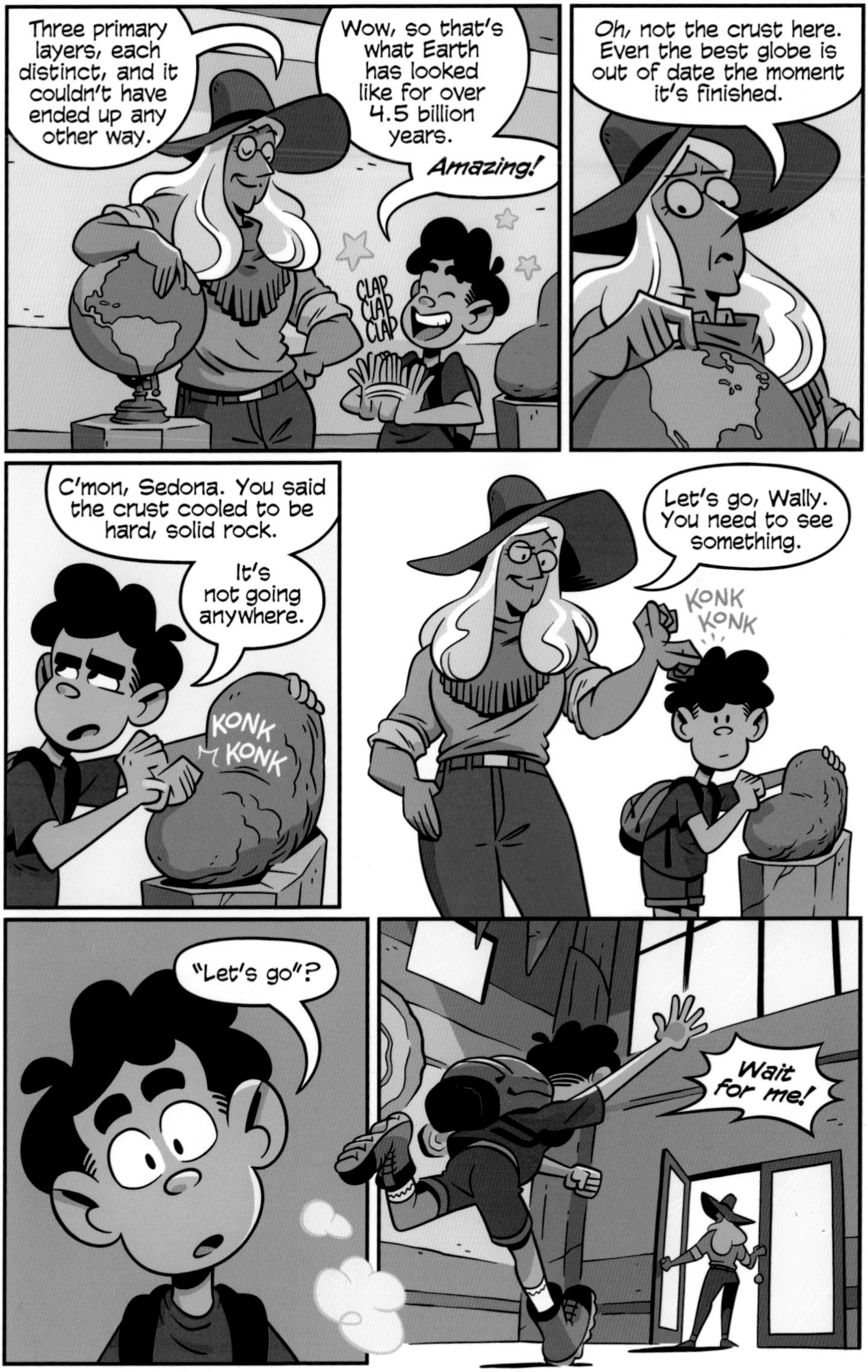
Three primary layers, each distinct, and it couldn't have ended up any other way.
Wow, so that's what Earth has looked like for over 4.5 billion years.
Amazing!
CLAP CLAP CLAP
Oh, not the crust here. Even the best globe is out of date the moment it's finished.
C'mon, Sedona. You said the crust cooled to be hard, solid rock.
It's not going anywhere.
KONK KONK
Let's go, Wally. You need to see something.
KONK KONK
"Let's go"?
Wait for me!

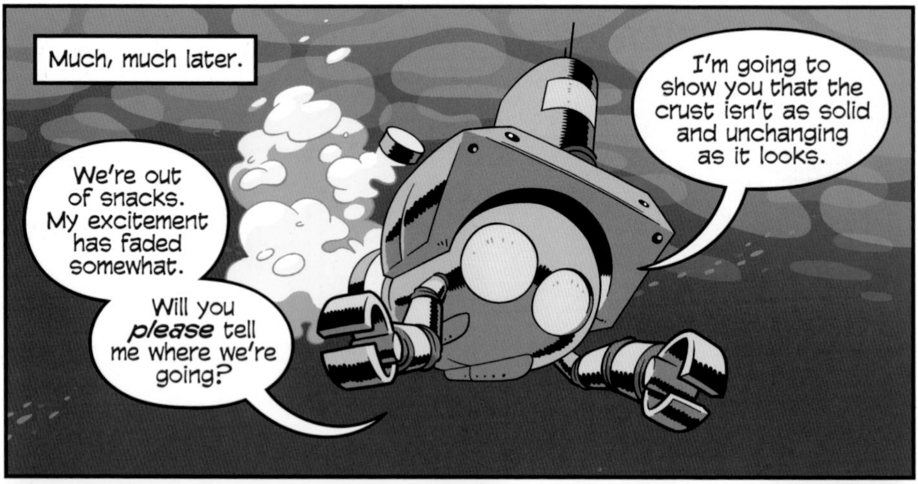
Much, much later.
We're out of snacks. My excitement has faded somewhat.
Will you *please* tell me where we're going?
I'm going to show you that the crust isn't as solid and unchanging as it looks.

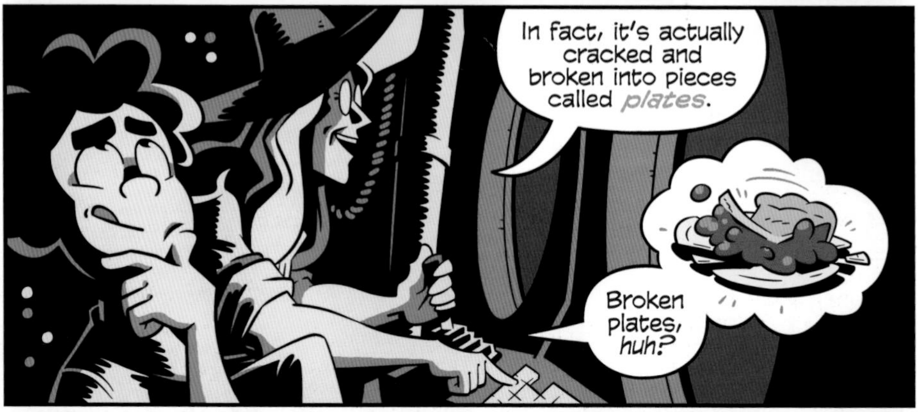
In fact, it's actually cracked and broken into pieces called *plates*.
Broken plates, *huh?*

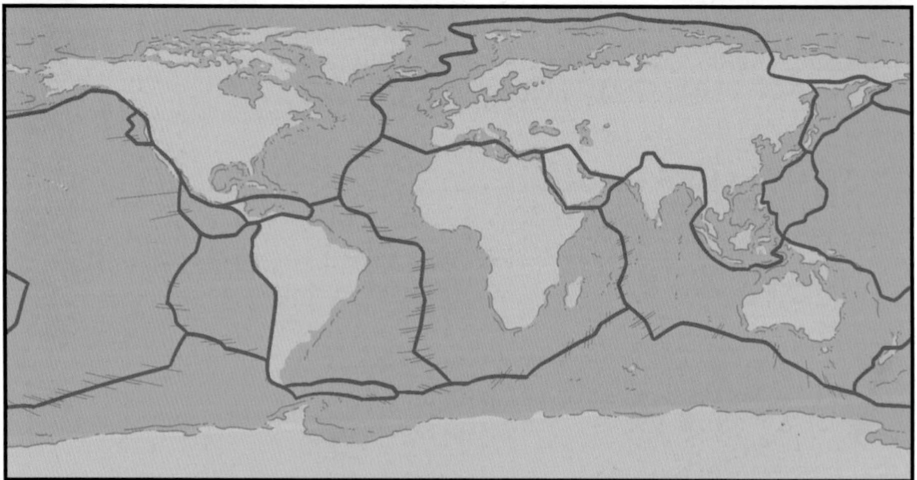
There are currently seven major plates and loads of smaller ones. Action at their boundaries reshapes the face of the Earth at scales you'd never dream of.

Plates pull apart at *divergent boundaries*, usually deep under the ocean. As pressure slides away, mantle rock can melt to become *magma* that fills the empty space with enough enthusiasm to form tall ridges of new crust.

Rift valleys run down their centers. The largest are bigger than the Grand Canyon!

Magma quickly cools to form a hard shell when it reaches the surface as *lava*. It looks cold, but inside...

...more lava is building up.

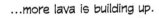

As long as the flow continues, this poofy-looking *pillow lava* will find weak spots and escape again and again.

Maybe I'll skip that nap.

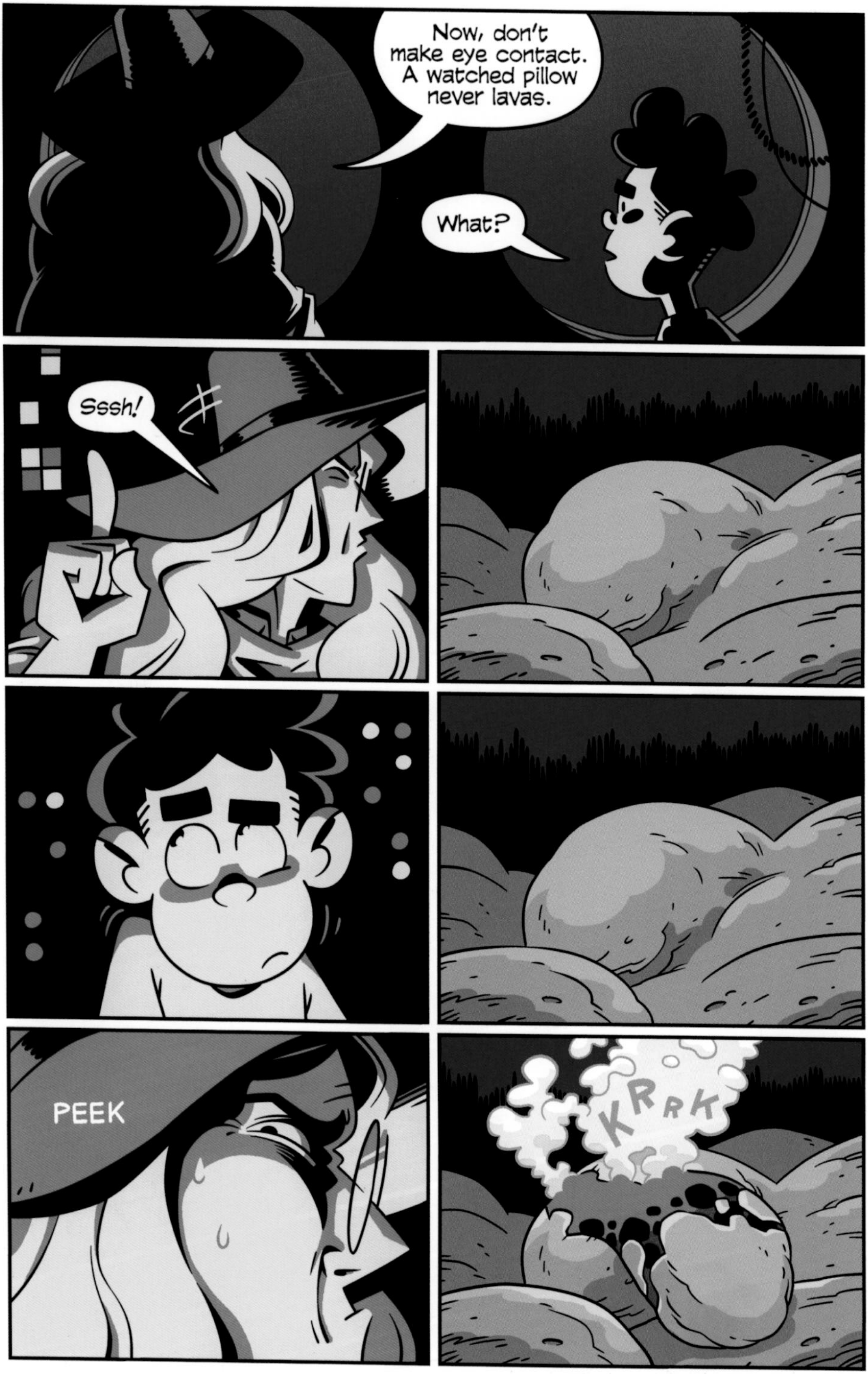
Now, don't make eye contact. A watched pillow never lavas.
What?
Sssh!
PEEK
KRRK

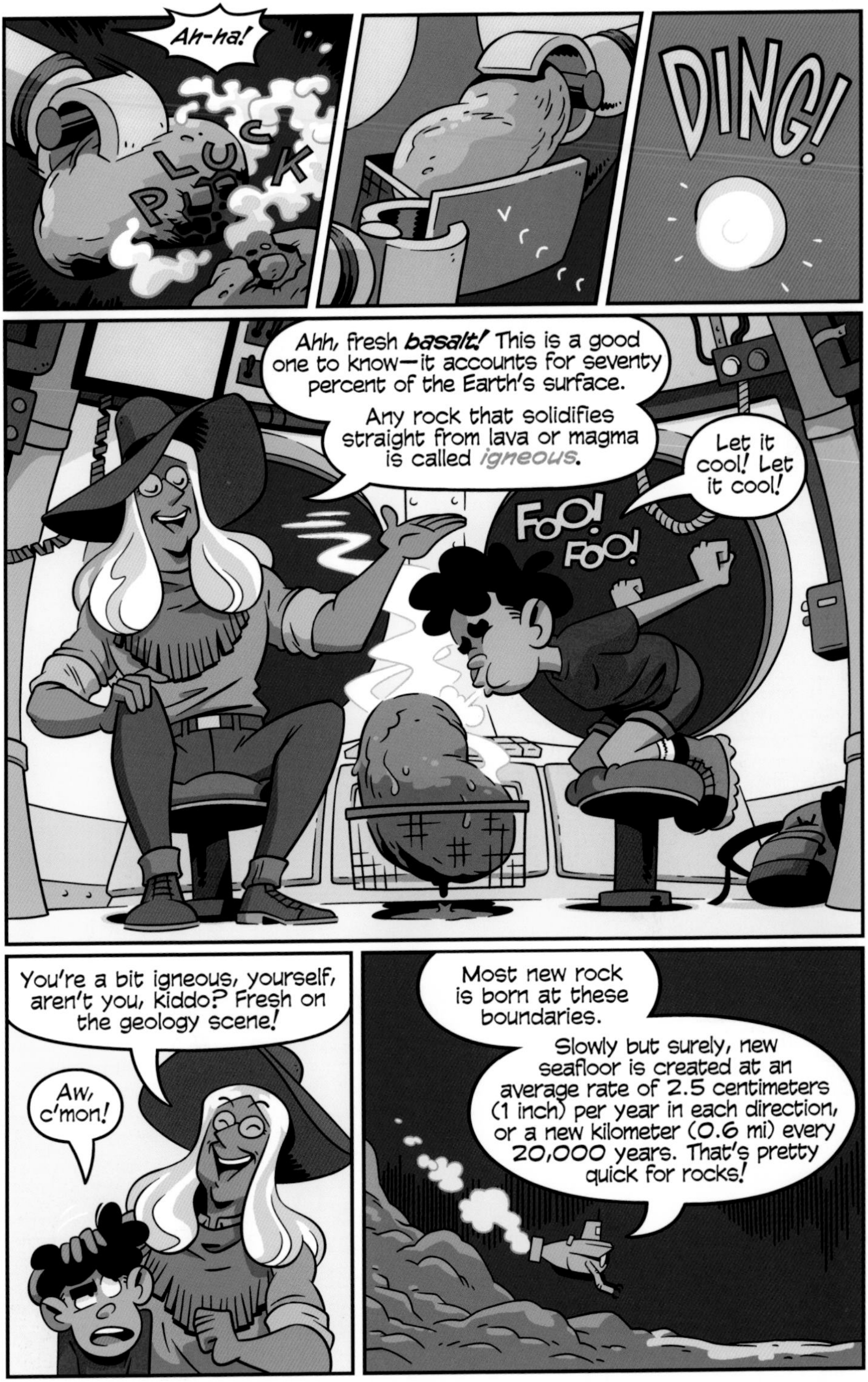
Ah-ha!
PLUCK
DING!
Ahh, fresh basalt! This is a good one to know—it accounts for seventy percent of the Earth's surface.
Any rock that solidifies straight from lava or magma is called igneous.
Let it cool! Let it cool!
FOO! FOO!
You're a bit igneous, yourself, aren't you, kiddo? Fresh on the geology scene!
Aw, c'mon!
Most new rock is born at these boundaries.
Slowly but surely, new seafloor is created at an average rate of 2.5 centimeters (1 inch) per year in each direction, or a new kilometer (0.6 mi) every 20,000 years. That's pretty quick for rocks!

Basalt keeps a diary in the form of tiny *magnetite crystals*. Like the needle of a compass, these point wherever north was when their rocky host cooled.

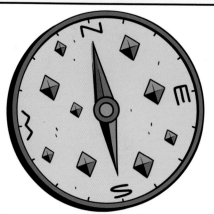

See, the thing about magnetic north is that it isn't always *north*. Once in a while, every 500,000 years or so on average, north... becomes south.

Blame the outer core, that swirling metal sea. It produces Earth's *magnetosphere* with currents so complex that they'll trip and flip that right over.

Then magnetite crystals will be stuck facing the opposite direction!

If you measure the magnetic orientation of seafloor rock, you'll find on either side of a ridge symmetrical stripes that show the rate of spreading. One points "north," the next points "south," the next points "north"...

YA | .78 MYA | NOW | .78 million years ago | .90 MYA | 1.06 MYA | 1.19 MYA | 1.78 MYA | 2 M

If crust is being spat out all the time at divergent boundaries, is Earth getting **bigger?**

Not a chance. To even out that growth, crust is constantly being swallowed at a second plate boundary type: a *convergent boundary*.

When two plates move toward each other, density determines which remains triumphant at the surface and which sinks back to the mantle in defeat.

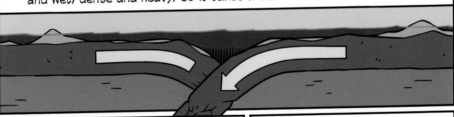

As you'd guess, less dense rock comes out on top. Old seafloor is cold and wet, dense and heavy, so it takes a dive at *subduction zones*.

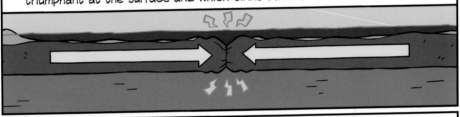

Sinking crust drags more seafloor along behind it, creating the world's great ocean trenches, like the *Mariana Trench* in the Western Pacific Ocean.

You could drop Mount Everest down it and still have over *2 km* (about 1 ¼ mi) to go!

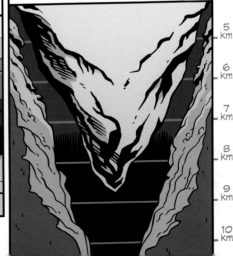

5 km

6 km

7 km

8 km

9 km

10 km

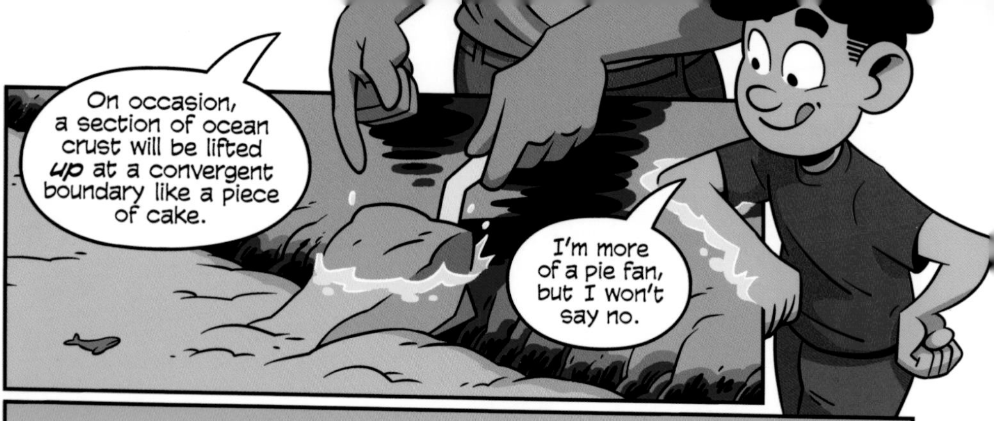
On occasion, a section of ocean crust will be lifted *up* at a convergent boundary like a piece of cake.
I'm more of a pie fan, but I won't say no.

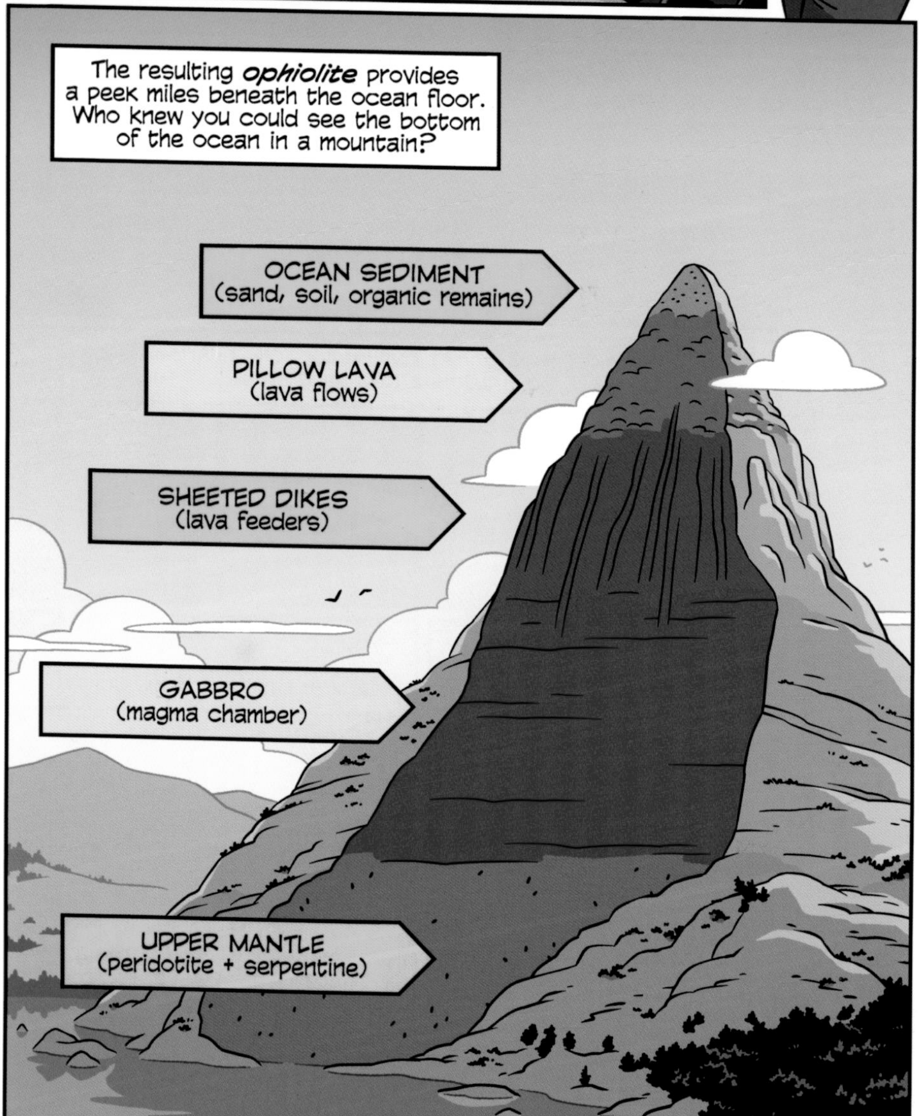
The resulting *ophiolite* provides a peek miles beneath the ocean floor. Who knew you could see the bottom of the ocean in a mountain?
OCEAN SEDIMENT (sand, soil, organic remains)
PILLOW LAVA (lava flows)
SHEETED DIKES (lava feeders)
GABBRO (magma chamber)
UPPER MANTLE (peridotite + serpentine)

As for subducted seafloor, it's subjected to ever greater temperature and pressures. While some of ol' basalt's component minerals can tough it out, others are quick to bail.

Subducted basalt "sweats" out some of its minerals that have a lower melting point at these pressures.

These combine to form new sorts of magma that will cool as new sorts of rocks.

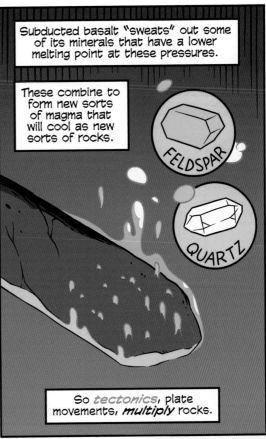

FELDSPAR

QUARTZ

So *tectonics*, plate movements, *multiply* rocks.

Granite is the major rock formed this way. It's a *plutonic* igneous rock, meaning it forms deep underground from magma. It has relatively low density and prefers to float well above the mantle.

So we let some basalt get away, and when it melts out the minerals for granite, we grab *that* as soon as it pops up, *huh?*

It's gonna take a long, *long* time for that granite to make it to the surface.

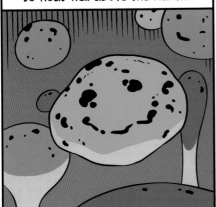

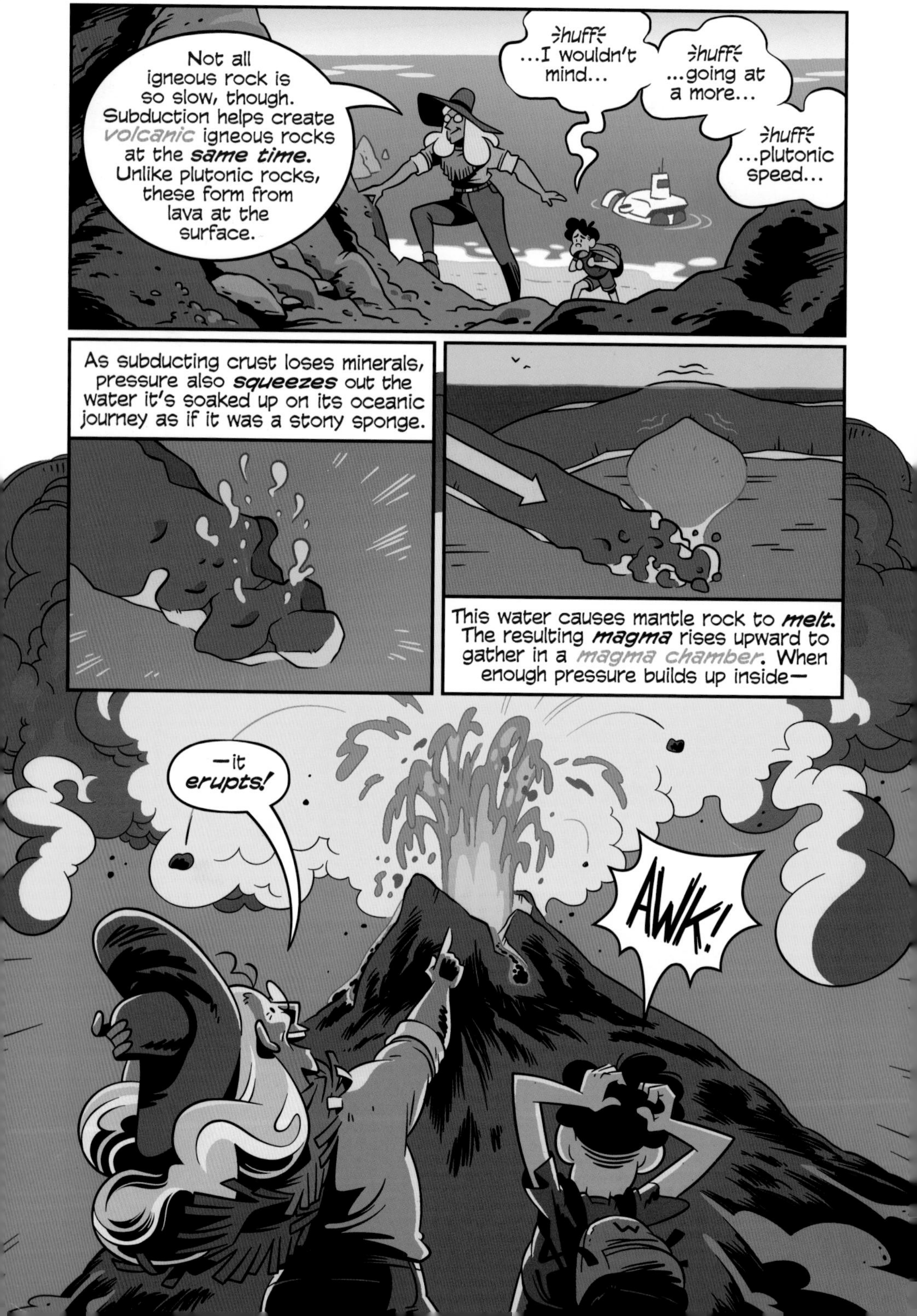
Not all igneous rock is so slow, though. Subduction helps create volcanic igneous rocks at the same time. Unlike plutonic rocks, these form from lava at the surface.
huff ...I wouldn't mind...
huff ...going at a more...
huff ...plutonic speed...
As subducting crust loses minerals, pressure also squeezes out the water it's soaked up on its oceanic journey as if it was a stony sponge.
This water causes mantle rock to melt. The resulting magma rises upward to gather in a magma chamber. When enough pressure builds up inside—
—it erupts!
AWK!

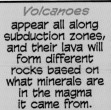

Volcanoes appear all along subduction zones, and their lava will form different rocks based on what minerals are in the magma it came from.

We've already met basalt, the most common volcanic igneous rock.

BLORP

Less teaching, more fleeing!

Obsidian comes from thick, viscous lava full of feldspar and silica. It cools too quickly for large crystals to form and can be shiny as glass.

Boy, you look *tired.*

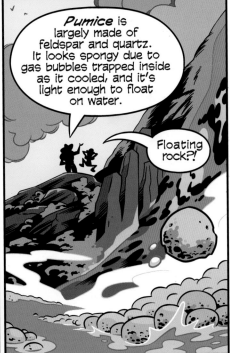

Pumice is largely made of feldspar and quartz. It looks spongy due to gas bubbles trapped inside as it cooled, and it's light enough to float on water.

Floating rock?!

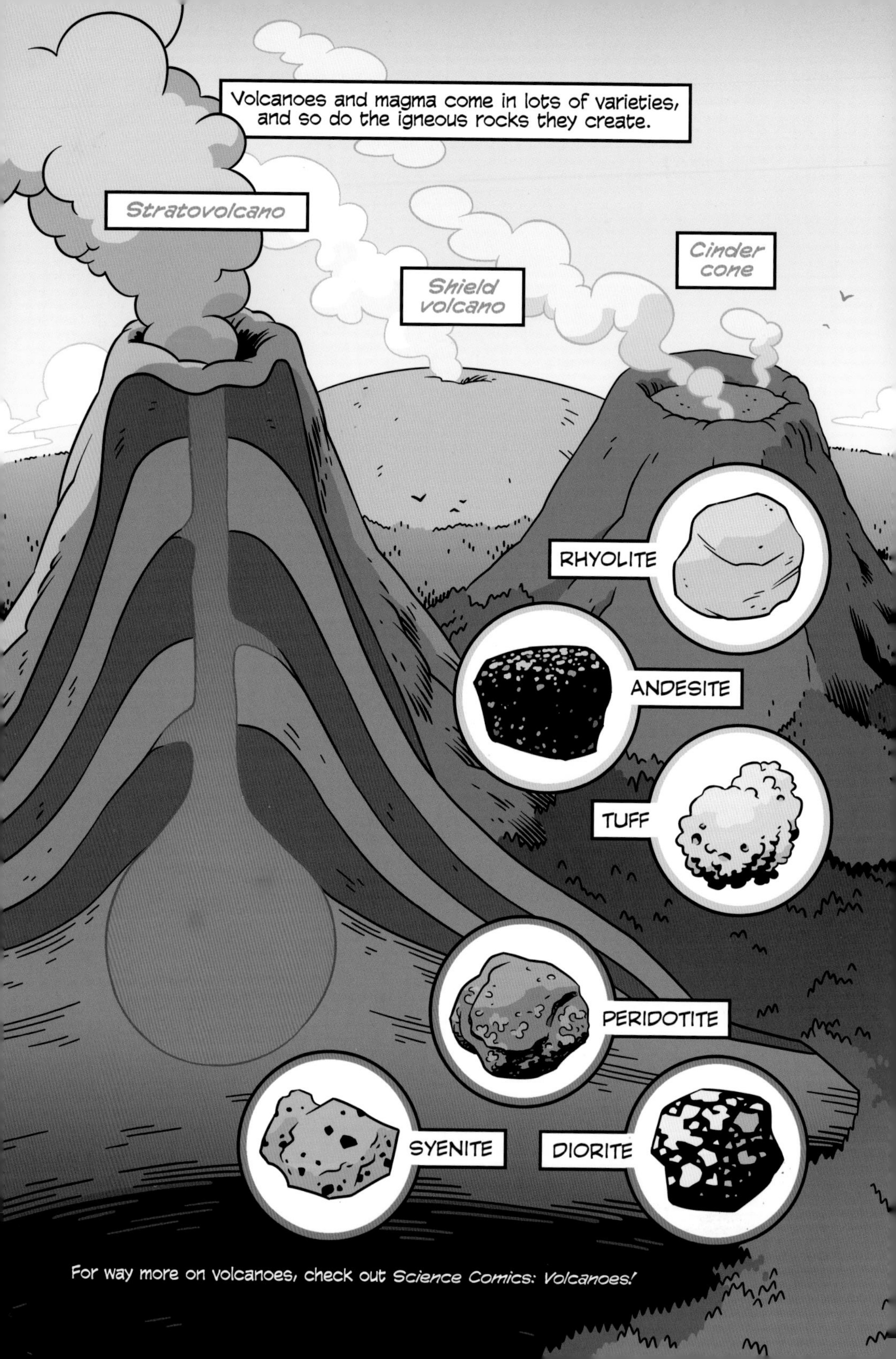
Volcanoes and magma come in lots of varieties, and so do the igneous rocks they create.
Stratovolcano
Shield volcano
Cinder cone
RHYOLITE
ANDESITE
TUFF
PERIDOTITE
SYENITE
DIORITE
For way more on volcanoes, check out *Science Comics: Volcanoes!*

Some volcanoes aren't created anywhere near subduction zones. Look at the Hawaiian Islands, smack in the middle of the Pacific Plate.

Ooh! Can we, please?

Their volcanoes are powered by a *hotspot*, a plume of extra-hot magma from way down at the mantle-core boundary. As the plate moves over the hotspot like a conveyor belt, new volcanoes pop up, which become new islands.

OLDER · · · · · · · · · · · · YOUNGER

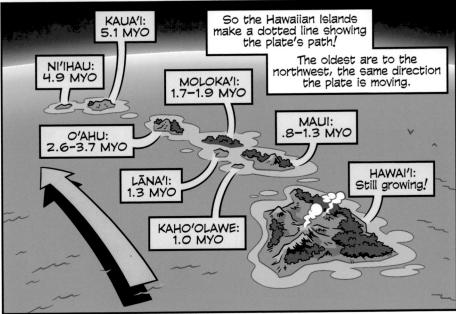

KAUA'I: 5.1 MYO

So the Hawaiian Islands make a dotted line showing the plate's path!

The oldest are to the northwest, the same direction the plate is moving.

NI'IHAU: 4.9 MYO

MOLOKA'I: 1.7–1.9 MYO

MAUI: .8–1.3 MYO

O'AHU: 2.6–3.7 MYO

HAWAI'I: Still growing!

LĀNA'I: 1.3 MYO

KAHO'OLAWE: 1.0 MYO

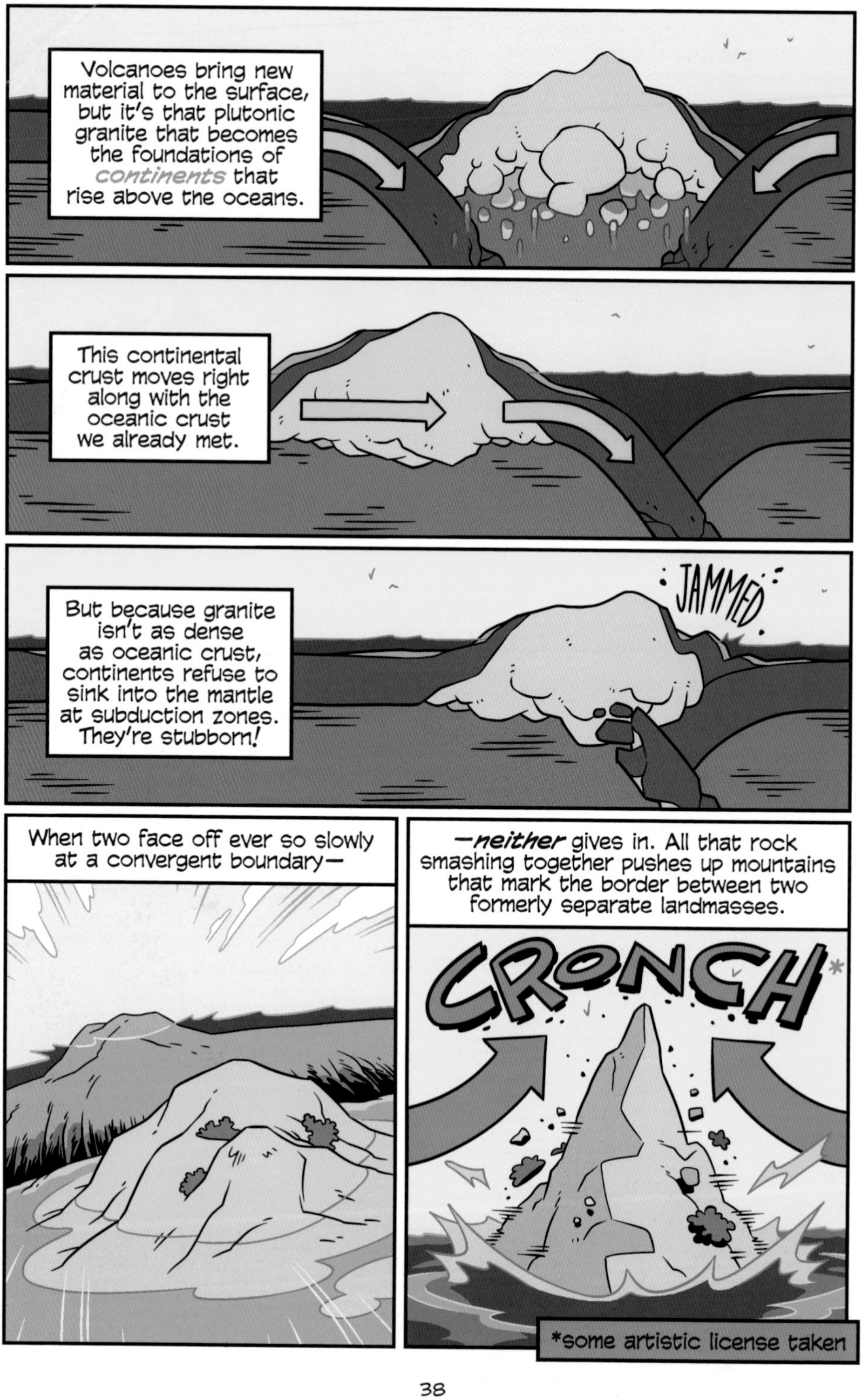
Volcanoes bring new material to the surface, but it's that plutonic granite that becomes the foundations of continents that rise above the oceans.
This continental crust moves right along with the oceanic crust we already met.
But because granite isn't as dense as oceanic crust, continents refuse to sink into the mantle at subduction zones. They're stubborn!
JAMMED
When two face off ever so slowly at a convergent boundary—
—neither gives in. All that rock smashing together pushes up mountains that mark the border between two formerly separate landmasses.
CRONCH*
*some artistic license taken

Small bits of continental crust ride along on plates...

...and much like chondrules gathering to become planetesimals...

...or driftwood catching in a river...

Close one!

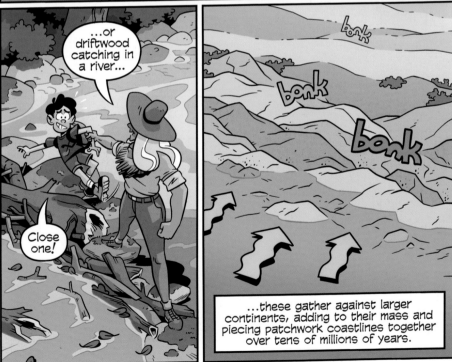

bonk

bonk

bonk

...these gather against larger continents, adding to their mass and piecing patchwork coastlines together over tens of millions of years.

There's still one more type of boundary: *transform boundaries*, where one plate scrapes sideways against another.

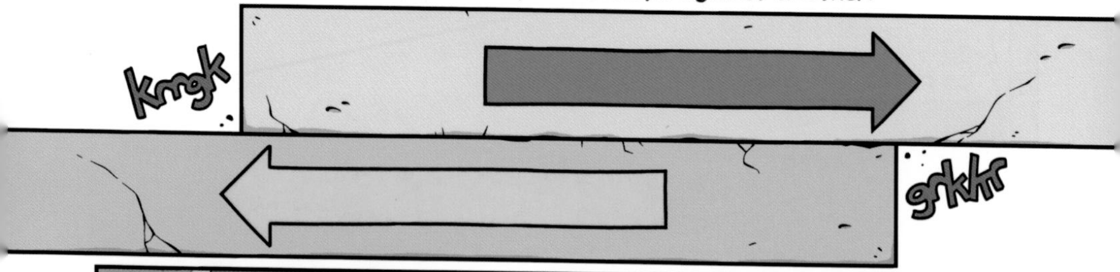

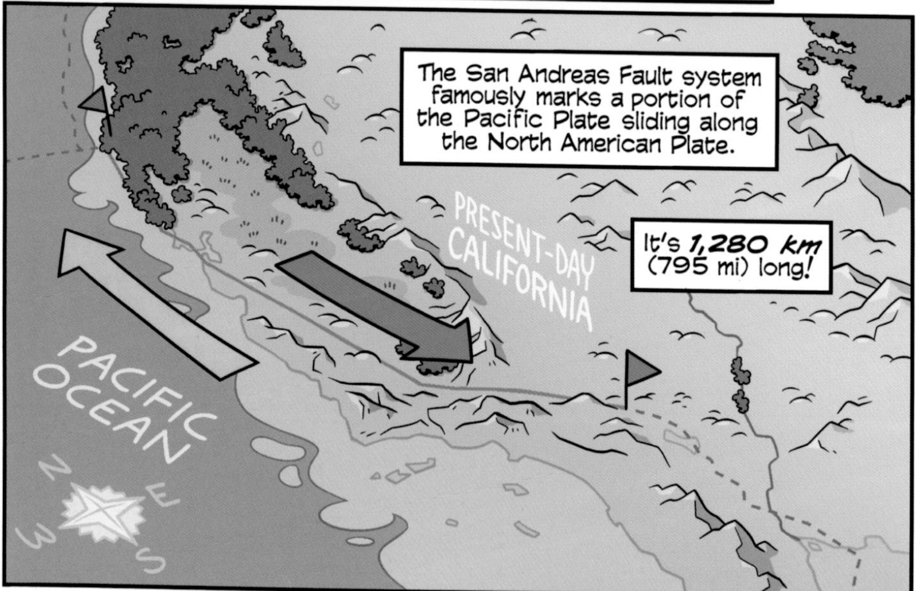

The San Andreas Fault system famously marks a portion of the Pacific Plate sliding along the North American Plate.
PRESENT-DAY CALIFORNIA
It's **1,280 km** (795 mi) long!
PACIFIC OCEAN
N
E
W
S

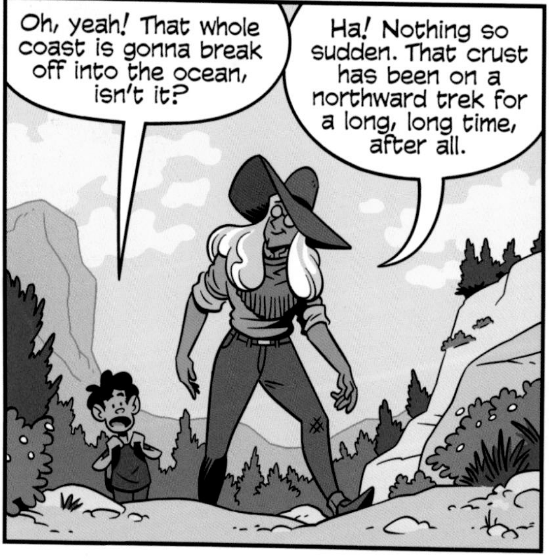

Oh, yeah! That whole coast is gonna break off into the ocean, isn't it?
Ha! Nothing so sudden. That crust has been on a northward trek for a long, long time, after all.

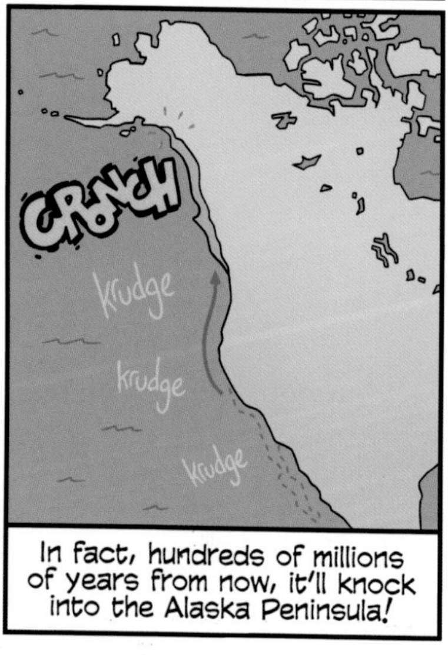

CRUNCH
krudge
krudge
krudge
In fact, hundreds of millions of years from now, it'll knock into the Alaska Peninsula!

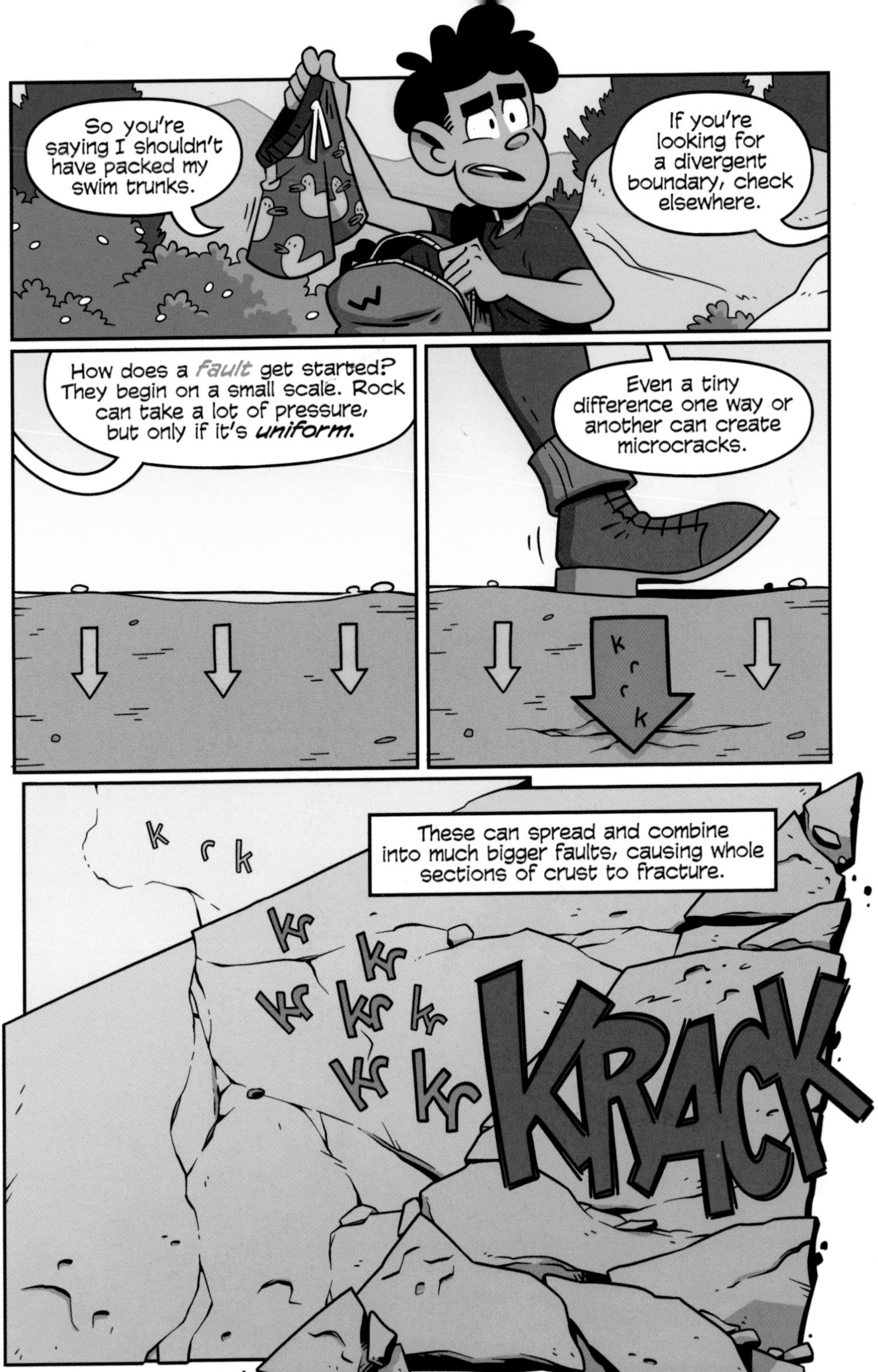
So you're saying I shouldn't have packed my swim trunks.
If you're looking for a divergent boundary, check elsewhere.
How does a *fault* get started? They begin on a small scale. Rock can take a lot of pressure, but only if it's *uniform.*
Even a tiny difference one way or another can create microcracks.
k r c k
k r k
These can spread and combine into much bigger faults, causing whole sections of crust to fracture.
kr kr kr kr kr kr kr
KRACK

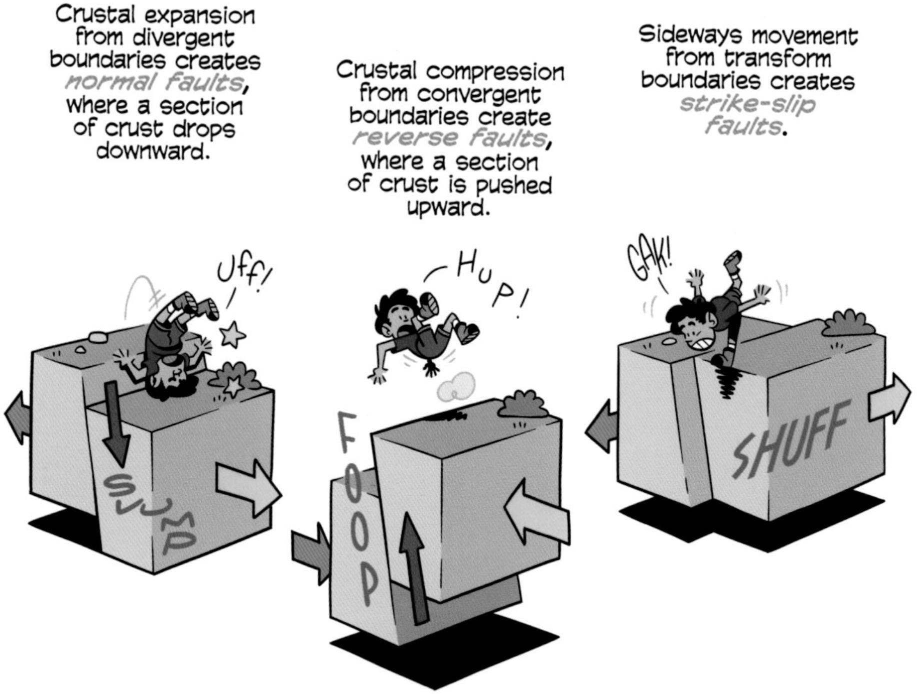
Crustal expansion from divergent boundaries creates normal faults, where a section of crust drops downward.
Uff!
SUMP
Crustal compression from convergent boundaries create reverse faults, where a section of crust is pushed upward.
HUP!
FOOP
Sideways movement from transform boundaries creates strike-slip faults.
GAK!
SHUFF

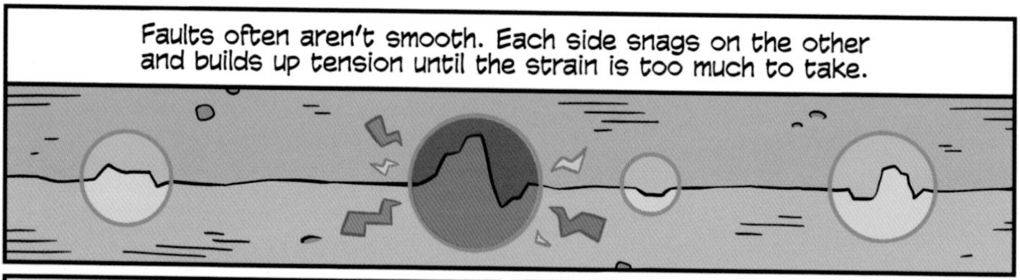
Faults often aren't smooth. Each side snags on the other and builds up tension until the strain is too much to take.

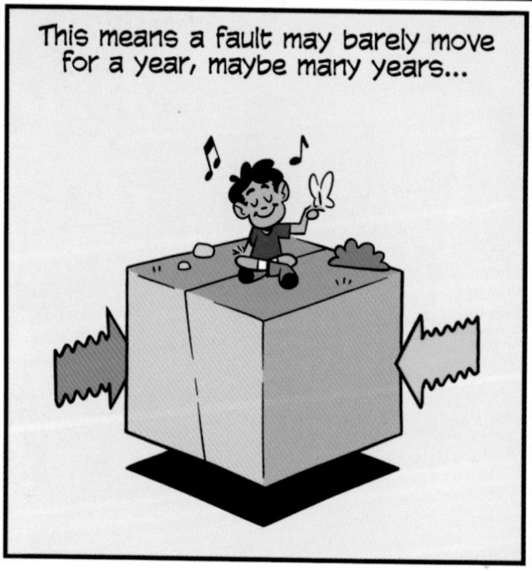
This means a fault may barely move for a year, maybe many years...

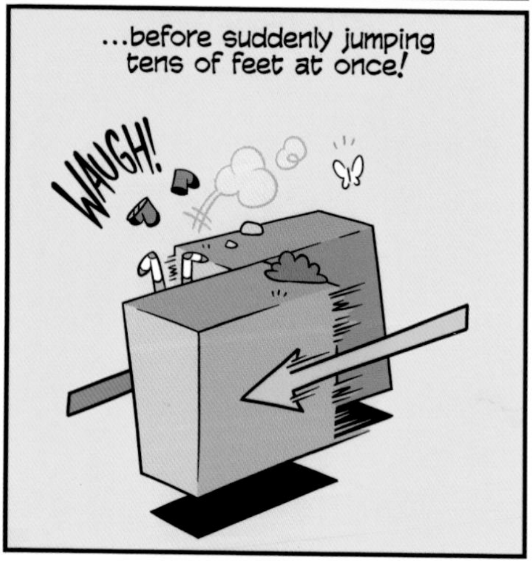
...before suddenly jumping tens of feet at once!
WAUGH!

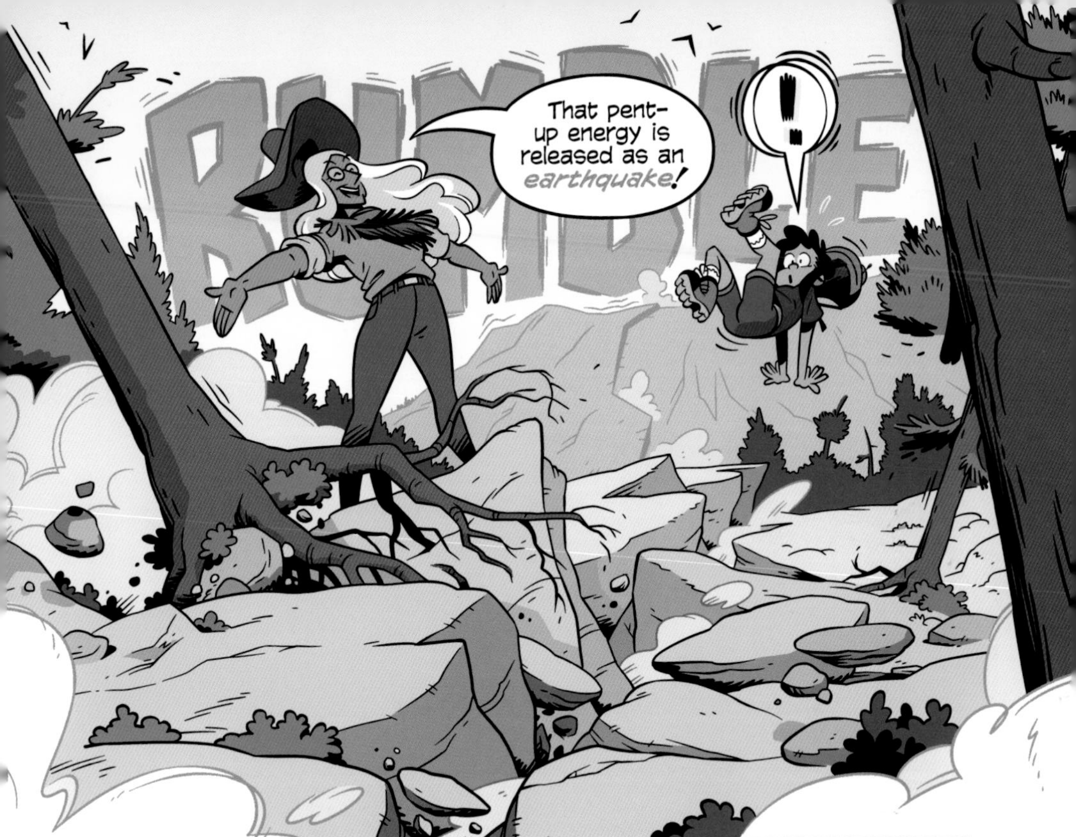
RUMBLE
That pent-up energy is released as an *earthquake!*
!!

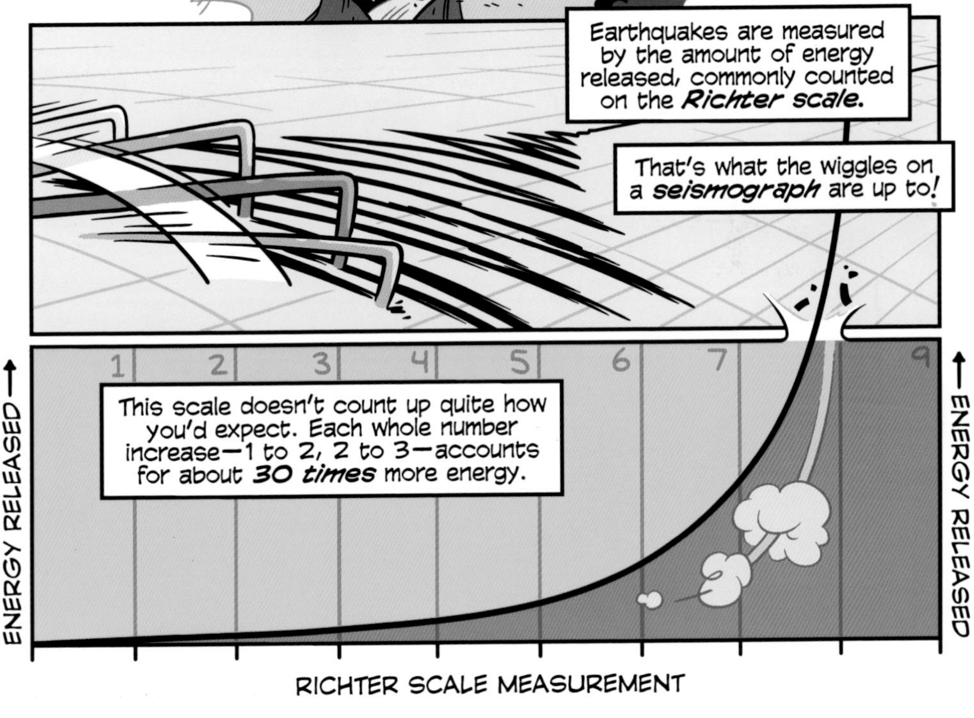
Earthquakes are measured by the amount of energy released, commonly counted on the ***Richter scale.***
That's what the wiggles on a ***seismograph*** are up to!
1
2
3
4
5
6
7
9
This scale doesn't count up quite how you'd expect. Each whole number increase—1 to 2, 2 to 3—accounts for about ***30 times*** more energy.
ENERGY RELEASED
ENERGY RELEASED
RICHTER SCALE MEASUREMENT

While the Richter scale is scientific down to the decimal, the ***Mercalli scale*** is an easier-to-understand 12-step scale measured by humans instead of a gizmo.

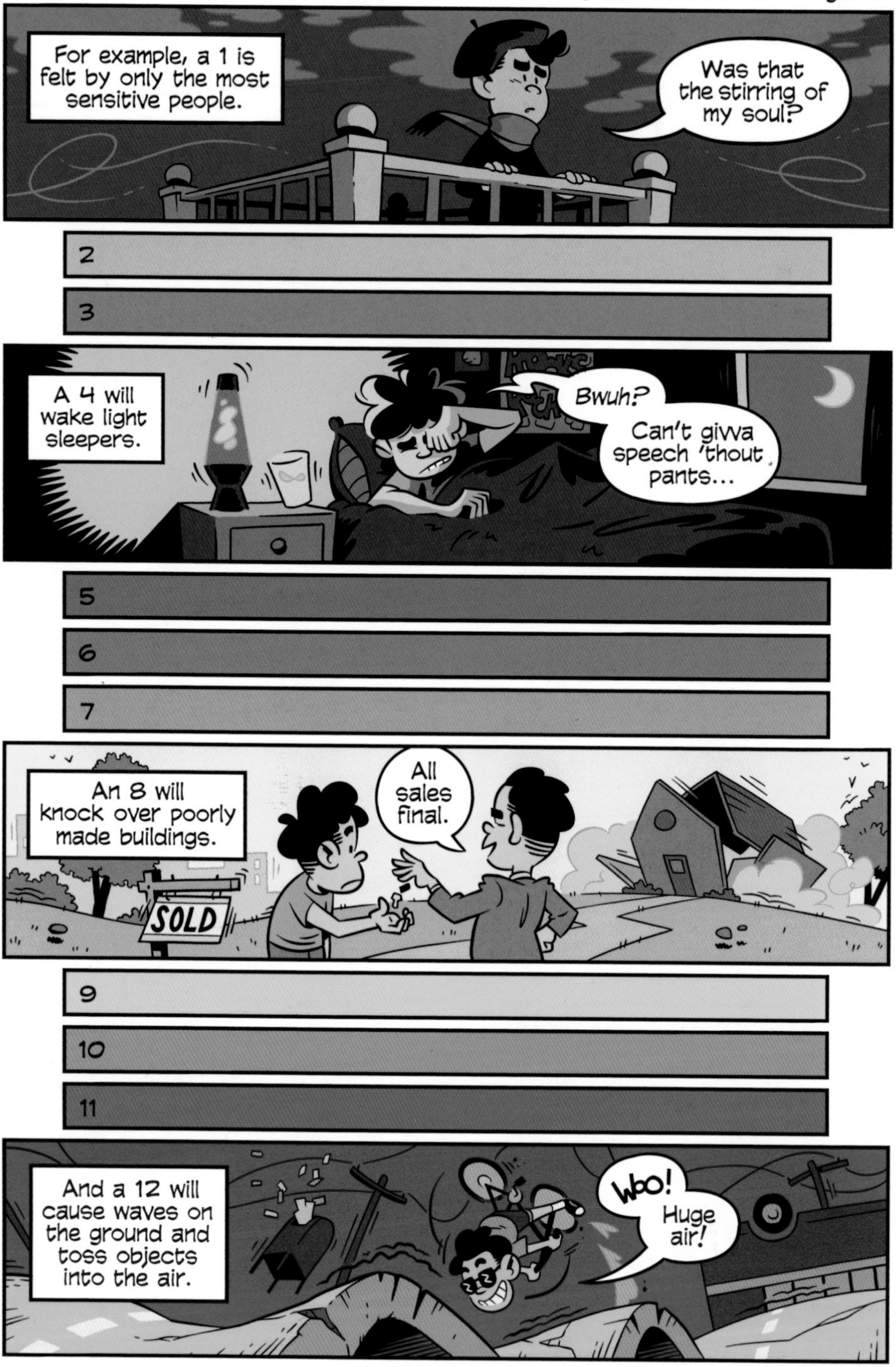

For example, a 1 is felt by only the most sensitive people.
Was that the stirring of my soul?
2
3
A 4 will wake light sleepers.
Bwuh?
Can't givva speech 'thout pants...
5
6
7
An 8 will knock over poorly made buildings.
All sales final.
SOLD
9
10
11
And a 12 will cause waves on the ground and toss objects into the air.
Woo!
Huge air!

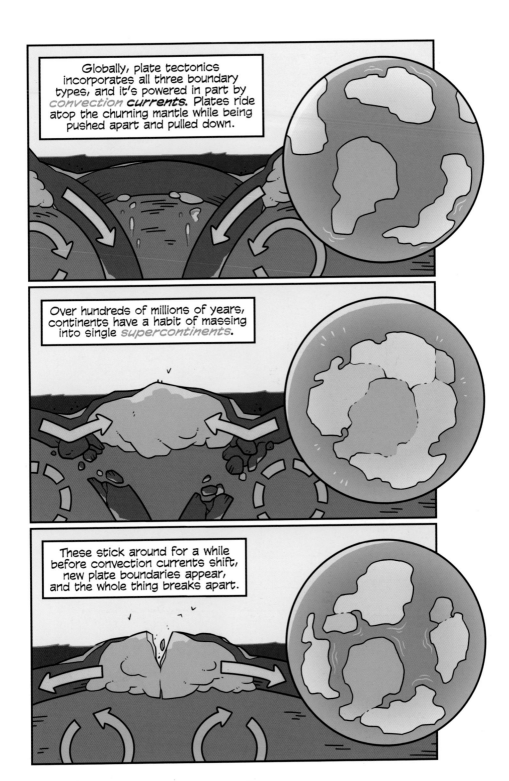

Globally, plate tectonics incorporates all three boundary types, and it's powered in part by *convection* **currents**. Plates ride atop the churning mantle while being pushed apart and pulled down.

Over hundreds of millions of years, continents have a habit of massing into single *supercontinents*.

These stick around for a while before convection currents shift, new plate boundaries appear, and the whole thing breaks apart.

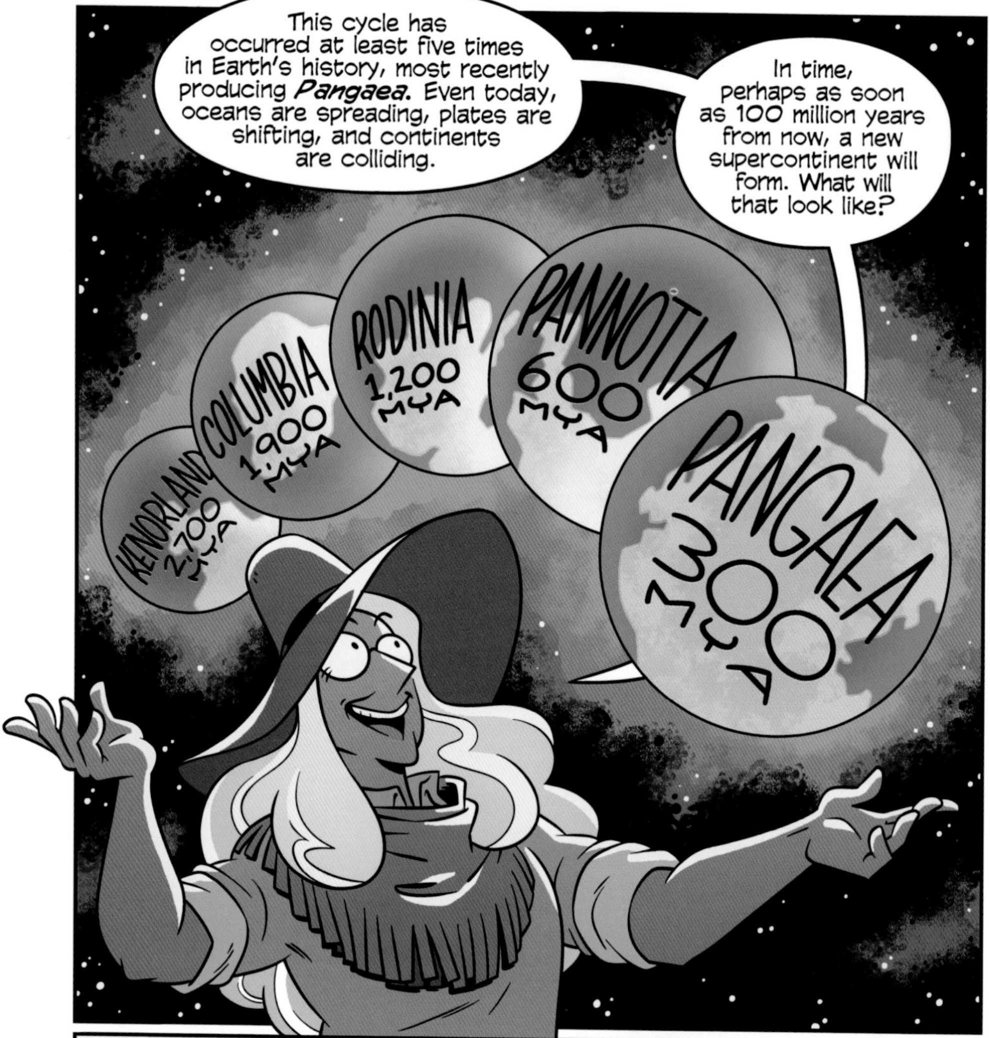
This cycle has occurred at least five times in Earth's history, most recently producing *Pangaea*. Even today, oceans are spreading, plates are shifting, and continents are colliding.
In time, perhaps as soon as 100 million years from now, a new supercontinent will form. What will that look like?
KENORLAND 2,700 MYA
COLUMBIA 1,900 MYA
RODINIA 1,200 MYA
PANNOTIA 600 MYA
PANGAEA 300 MYA

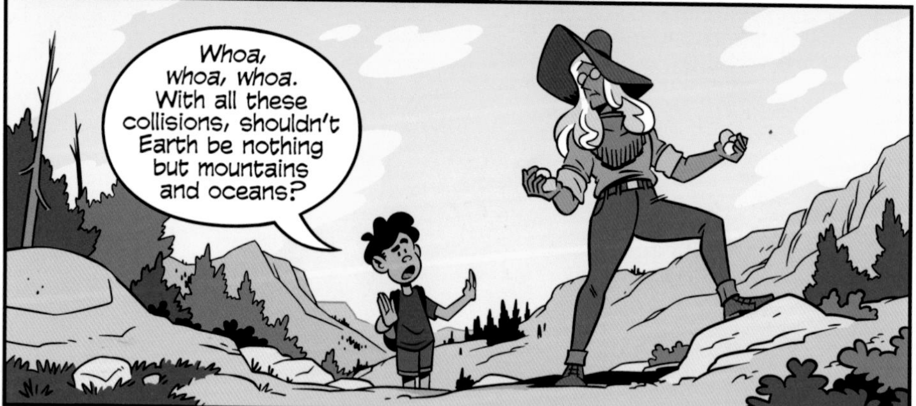
Whoa, whoa, whoa. With all these collisions, shouldn't Earth be nothing but mountains and oceans?

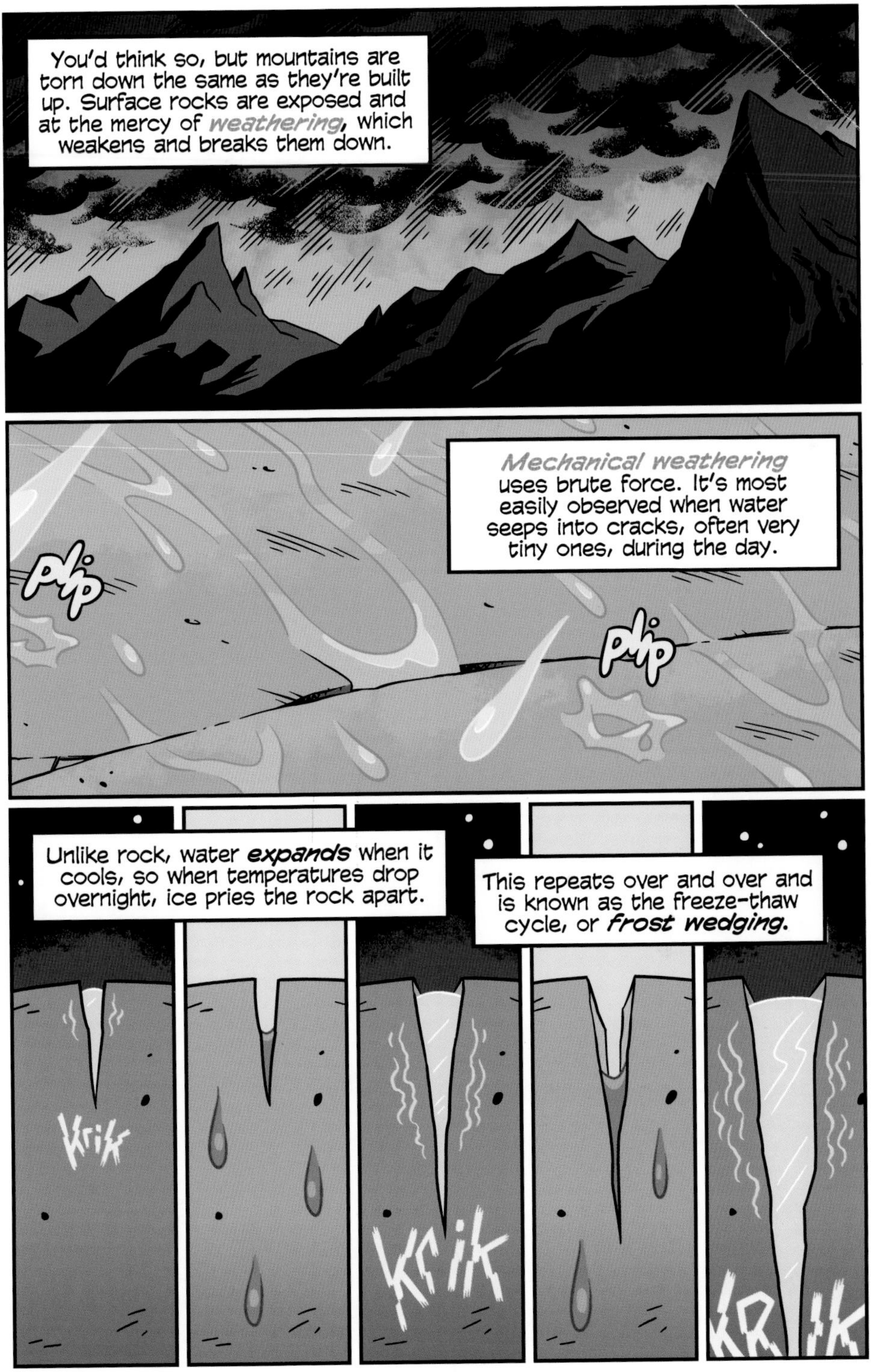
You'd think so, but mountains are torn down the same as they're built up. Surface rocks are exposed and at the mercy of weathering, which weakens and breaks them down.
Mechanical weathering uses brute force. It's most easily observed when water seeps into cracks, often very tiny ones, during the day.
plip
plip
Unlike rock, water expands when it cools, so when temperatures drop overnight, ice pries the rock apart.
This repeats over and over and is known as the freeze-thaw cycle, or frost wedging.
krik
krik
KRIK

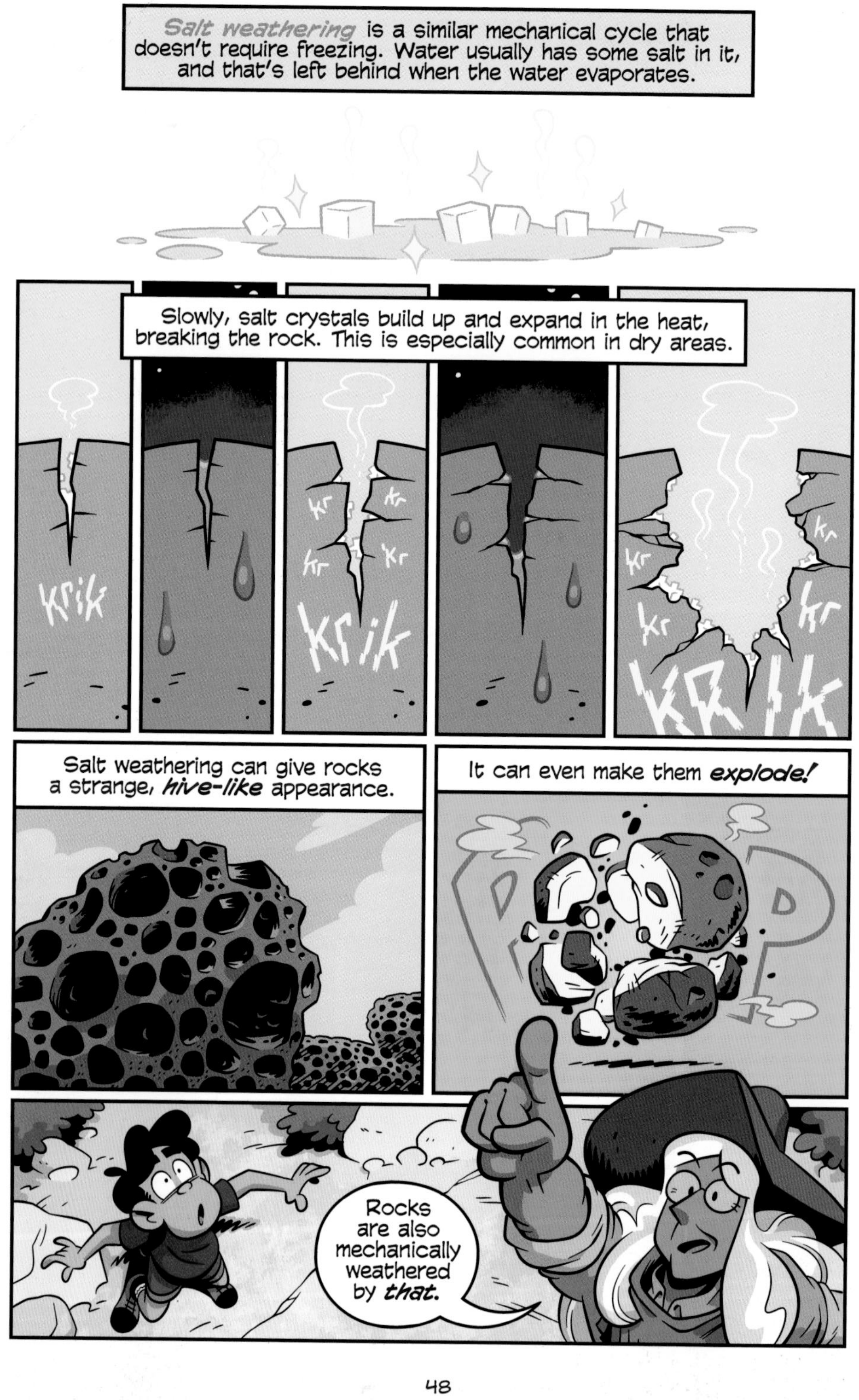
Salt weathering is a similar mechanical cycle that doesn't require freezing. Water usually has some salt in it, and that's left behind when the water evaporates.
Slowly, salt crystals build up and expand in the heat, breaking the rock. This is especially common in dry areas.
krik
kr kr
kr kr
krik
kr kr
kr kr
KRIK
Salt weathering can give rocks a strange, *hive-like* appearance.
It can even make them *explode!*
Rocks are also mechanically weathered by *that.*

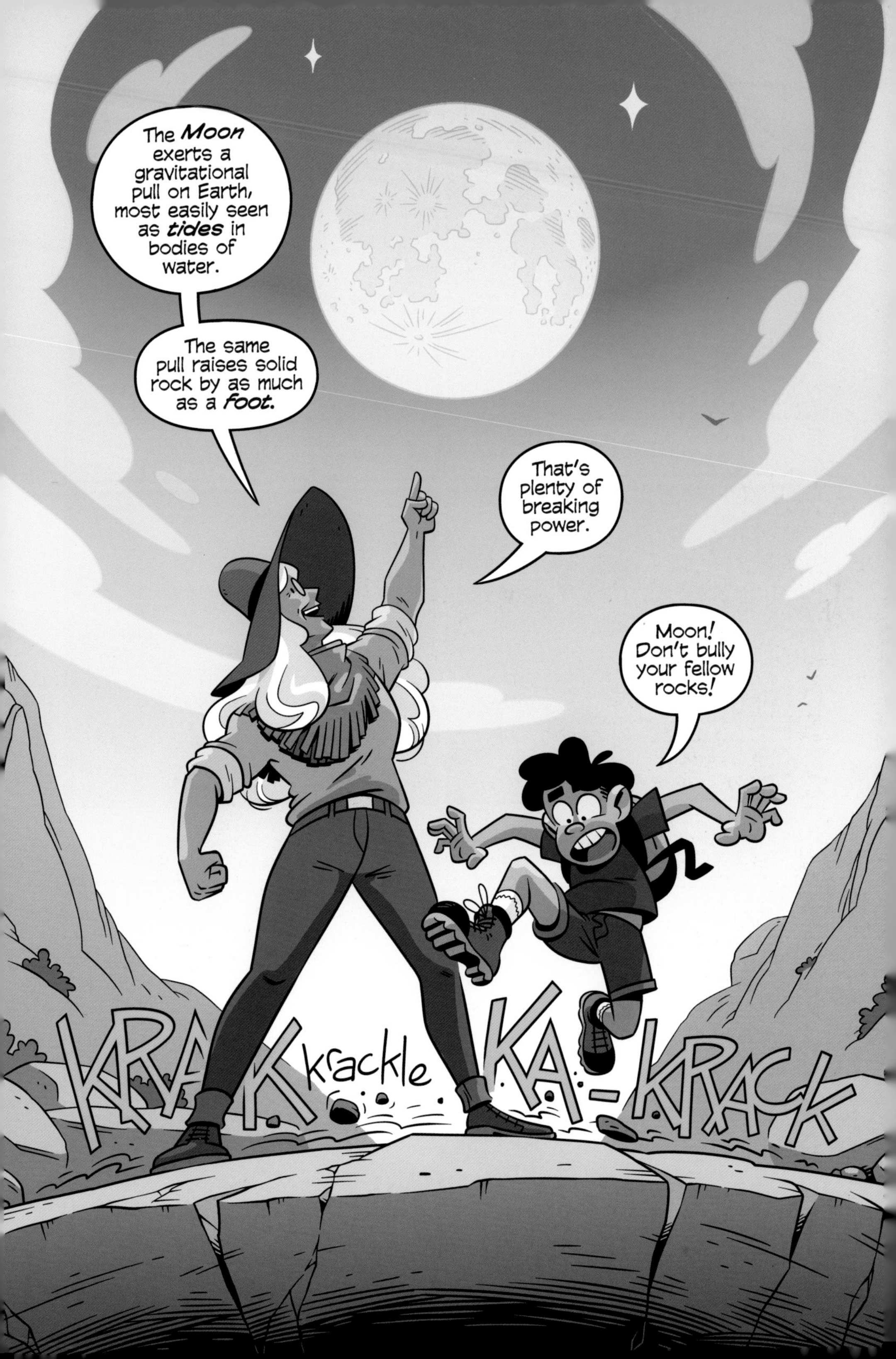
The *Moon* exerts a gravitational pull on Earth, most easily seen as *tides* in bodies of water.
The same pull raises solid rock by as much as a *foot.*
That's plenty of breaking power.
Moon! Don't bully your fellow rocks!
KRAK
krackle
KA-KRACK

Chemical weathering is subtler, but it breaks down rock all the same. Reactions with everyday things like rainwater and oxygen can dissolve mineral components or transform them into weaker ones.

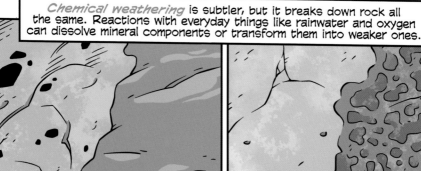

Common feldspar is turned to clay by acid rain.

Iron-bearing rock will rust when exposed to oxygen in the air.

BURP

Living things are responsible for *biological weathering*. Some algae and bacteria *eat* rocks.

Plants will take root in small cracks and turn them into *big* cracks as the roots grow.

Weathering weakens rocks but leaves them in place.

Erosion is less gentle. It not only wears away and breaks up rocks but scatters the pieces all over.

Pleasant breeze, huh?

Yeah.

Yeah, this is nice.

ACK!

Ow! Something's in my eye!

Probably a little rock particle.

Well, it's the worst!

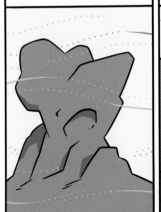

Imagine how you'd feel after thousands or millions of years of that kind of treatment.

You might not think wind could beat rock, but when it carries abrasive particles, the impacts add up.

pok

pok

pok

Plus, when a piece of rock gets worn off, it's just added to the situation.

POk

Even pebbles too heavy to get fully airborne are blown along the ground, bouncing into each other and chipping off pieces small enough to lift off.
klonk
klonk
CHIP
woosh
Millennia of abrasion can result in towering pillars, improbable arches, and polished waves. Look for these in dry areas where ample loose grit makes wind erosion especially effective.
Good grief!

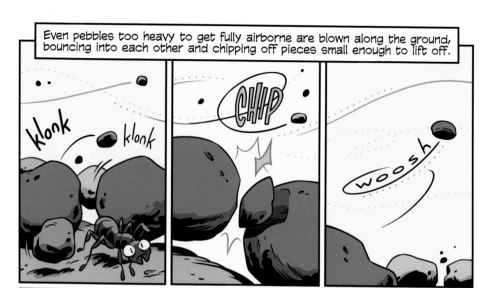

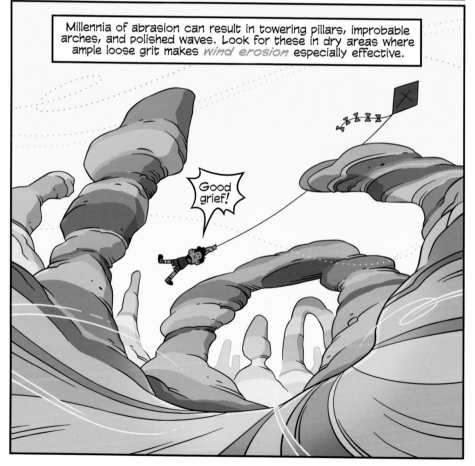

Hold still. I'll wash it out.

≋whimper≋ Oh, water, *you'd* never hurt me.

Mmm, that's another powerful erosive agent.

STOP ERODING ME!

Oh, please. You think I've got time for that?

I *think* it's gonna—

plink

—rain?

Thanks for warning me.

Now, how about that? Water moved you even more than wind.

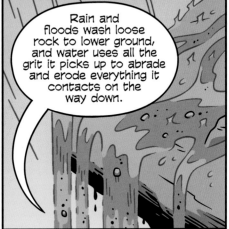

Rain and floods wash loose rock to lower ground, and water uses all the grit it picks up to abrade and erode everything it contacts on the way down.

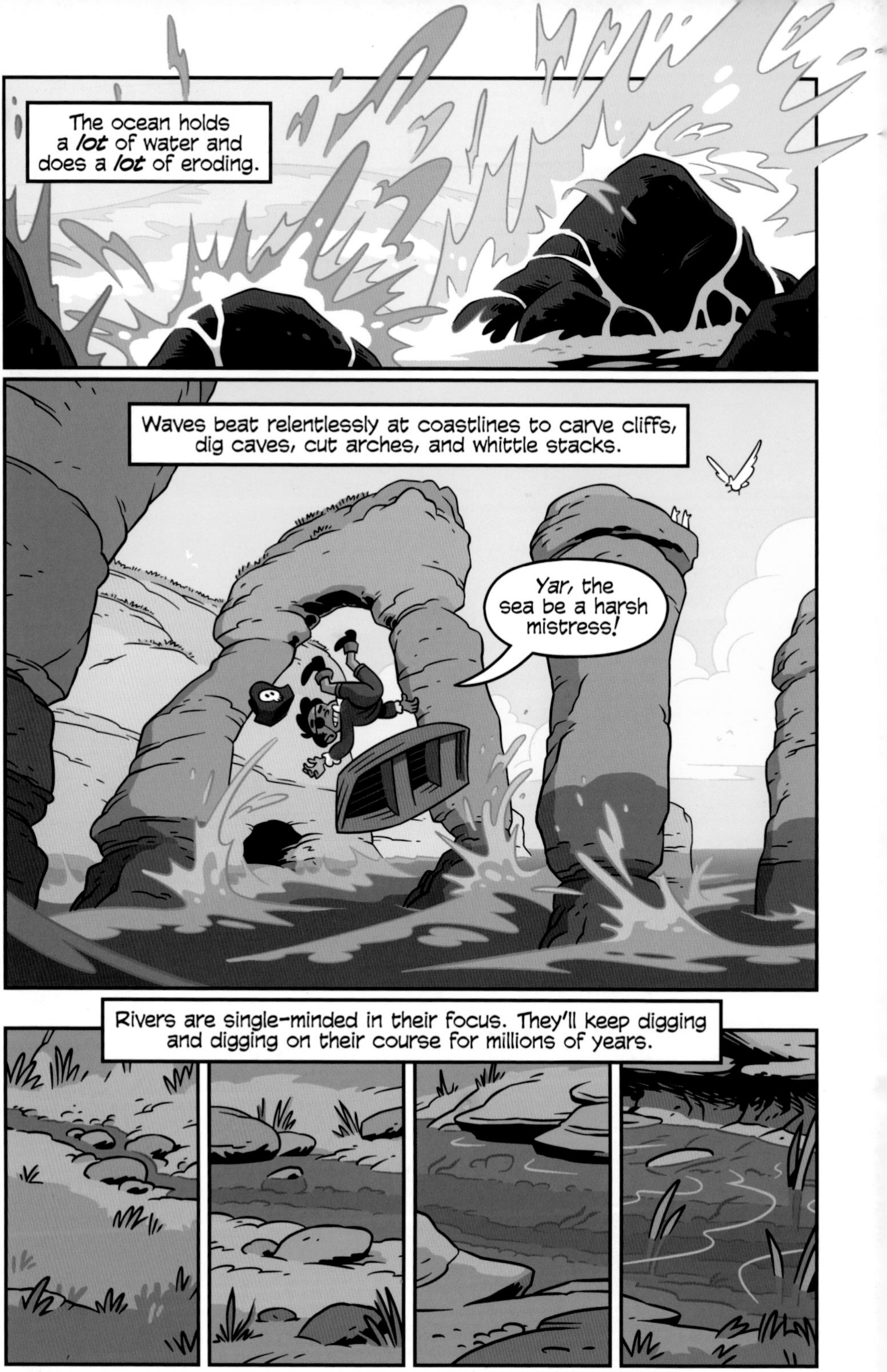
The ocean holds a *lot* of water and does a *lot* of eroding.
Waves beat relentlessly at coastlines to carve cliffs, dig caves, cut arches, and whittle stacks.
Yar, the sea be a harsh mistress!
Rivers are single-minded in their focus. They'll keep digging and digging on their course for millions of years.

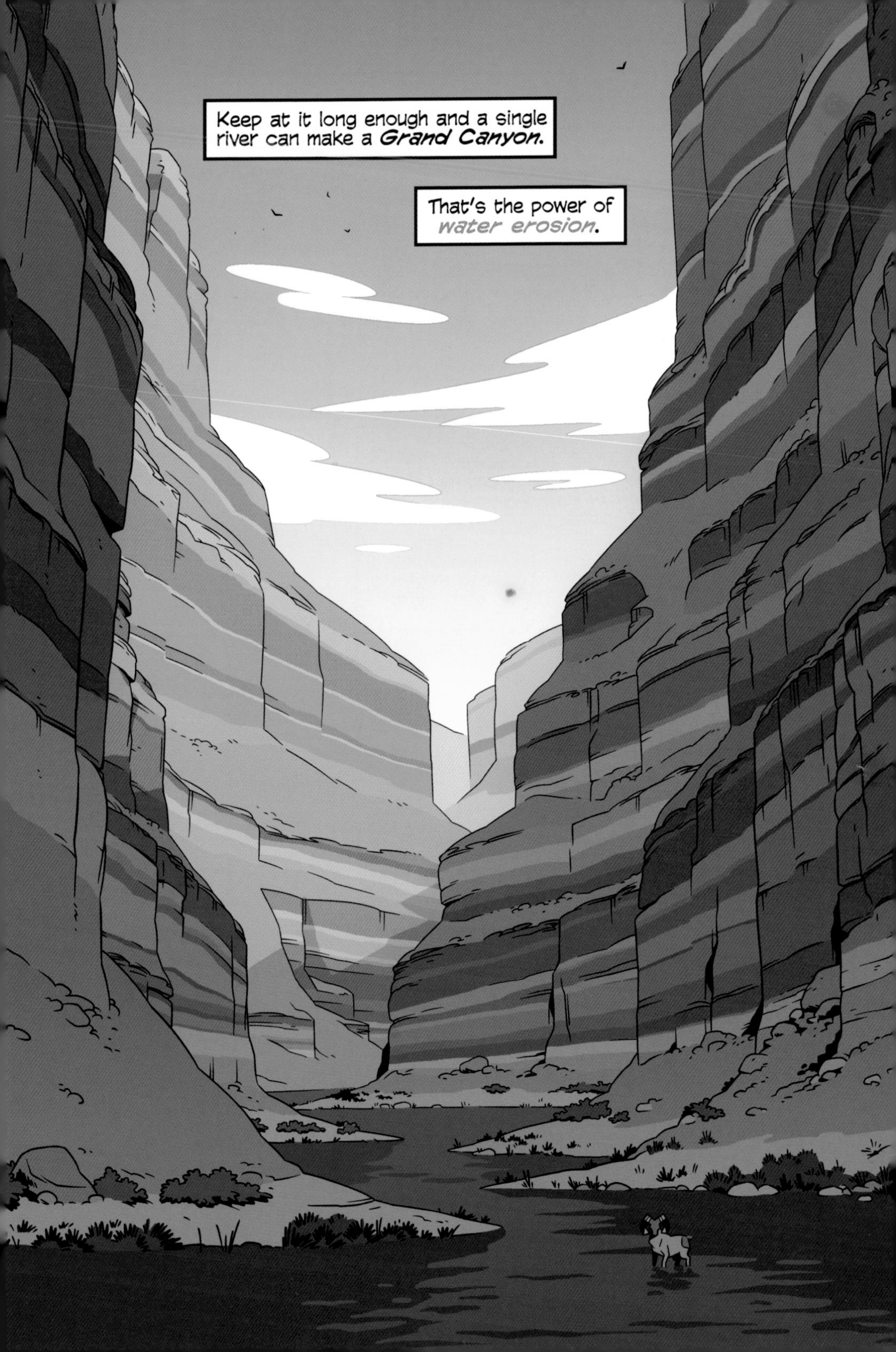
Keep at it long enough and a single river can make a *Grand Canyon*.
That's the power of *water erosion*.

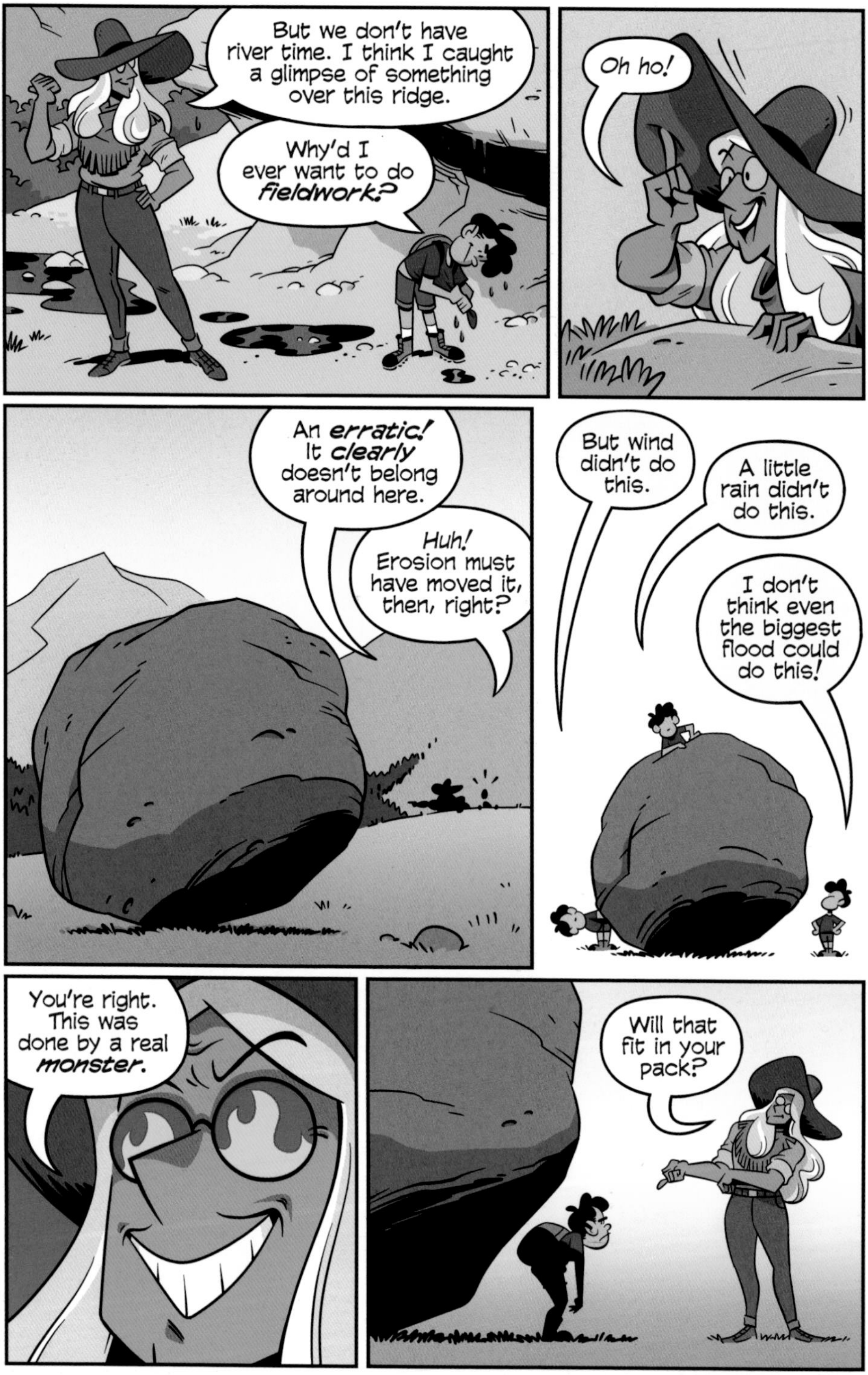
But we don't have river time. I think I caught a glimpse of something over this ridge.
Why'd I ever want to do *fieldwork?*
Oh ho!
An *erratic!* It *clearly* doesn't belong around here.
Huh! Erosion must have moved it, then, right?
But wind didn't do this.
A little rain didn't do this.
I don't think even the biggest flood could do this*!*
You're right. This was done by a real *monster*.
Will that fit in your pack?

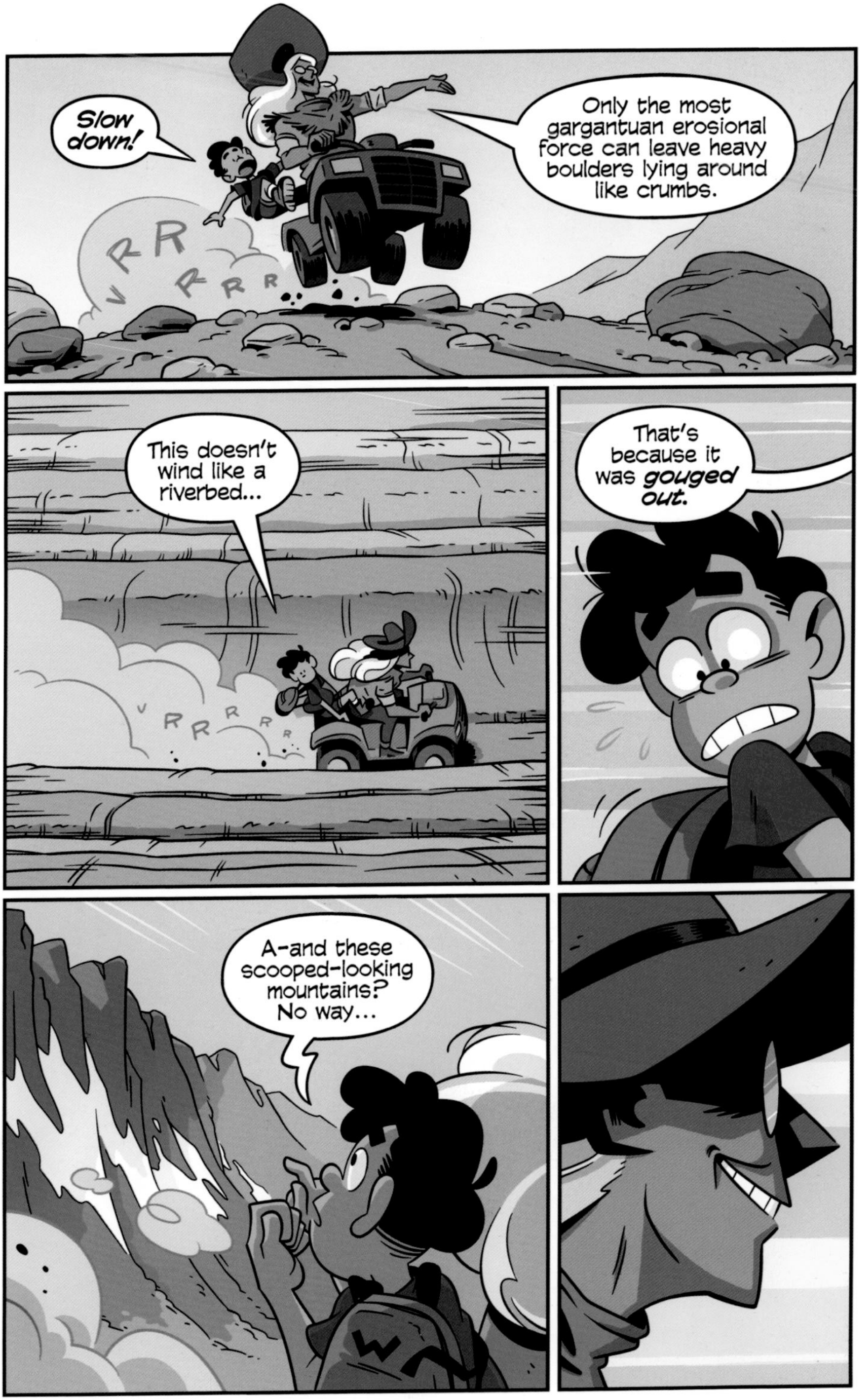
Slow down!
Only the most gargantuan erosional force can leave heavy boulders lying around like crumbs.
RR RRRR
This doesn't wind like a riverbed...
VRRRRR
That's because it was gouged out.
A-and these scooped-looking mountains? No way...

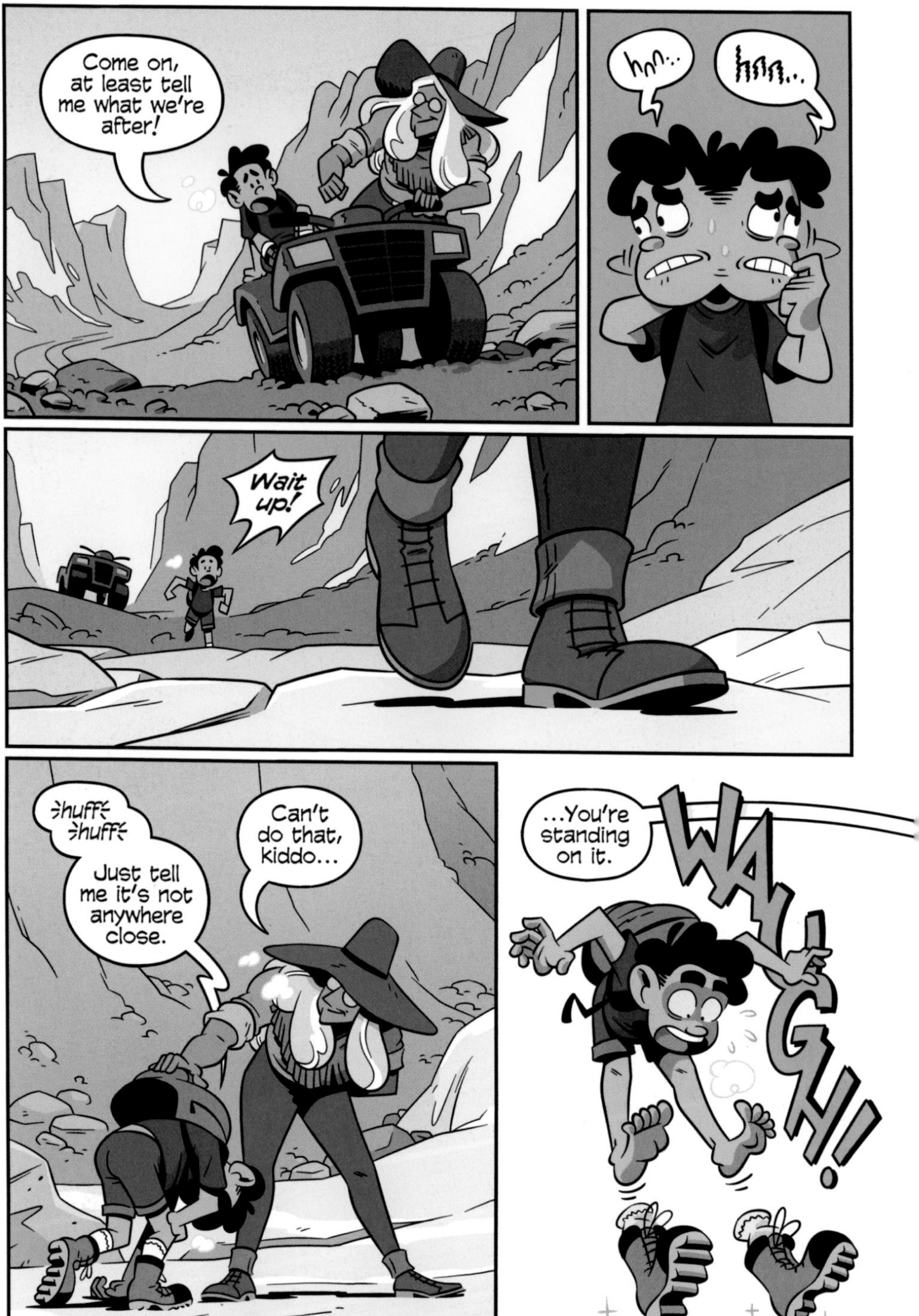
Come on, at least tell me what we're after!
hnn...
hnn...
Wait up!
huff huff
Just tell me it's not anywhere close.
Can't do that, kiddo...
...You're standing on it.
WAUGH!!

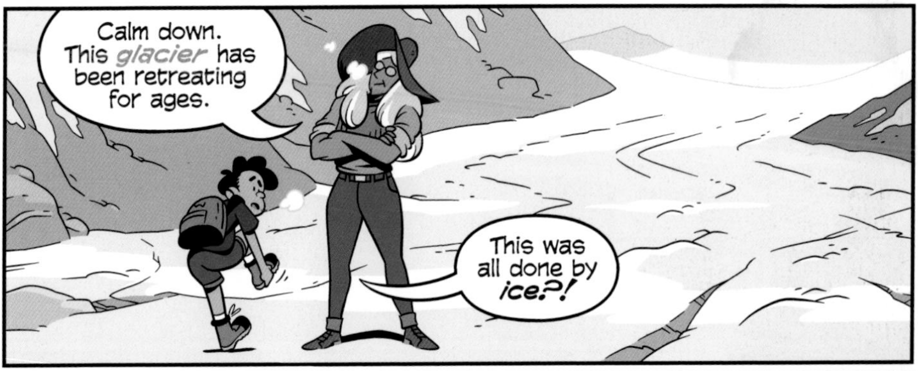
Calm down. This glacier has been retreating for ages.
This was all done by ice?!

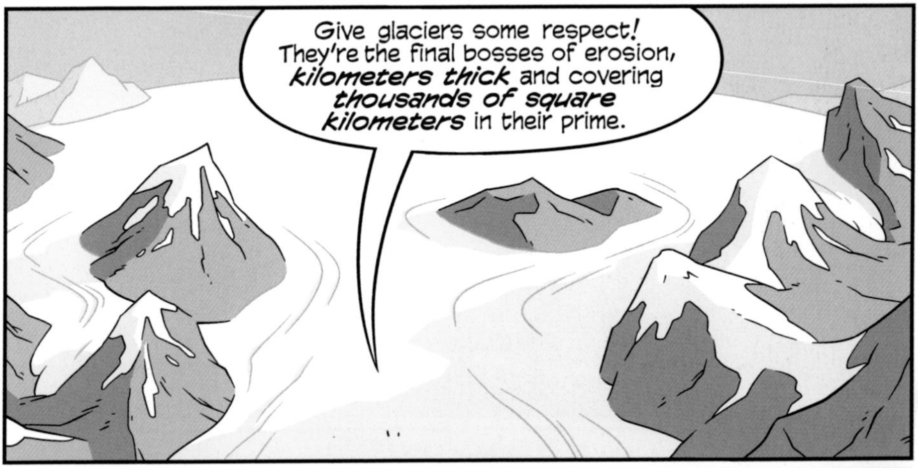
Give glaciers some respect! They're the final bosses of erosion, kilometers thick and covering thousands of square kilometers in their prime.

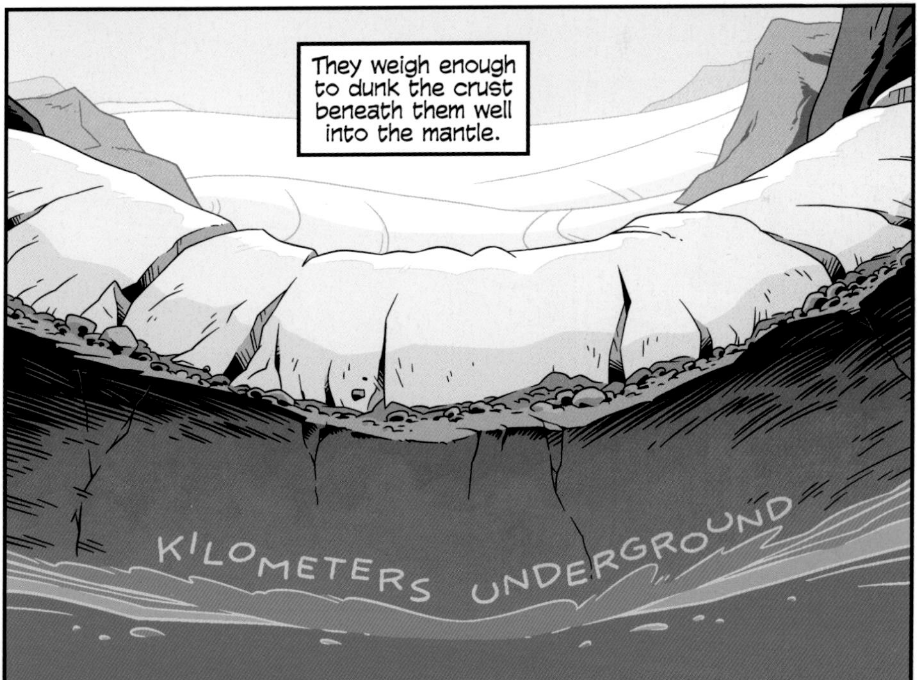
They weigh enough to dunk the crust beneath them well into the mantle.
KILOMETERS UNDERGROUND

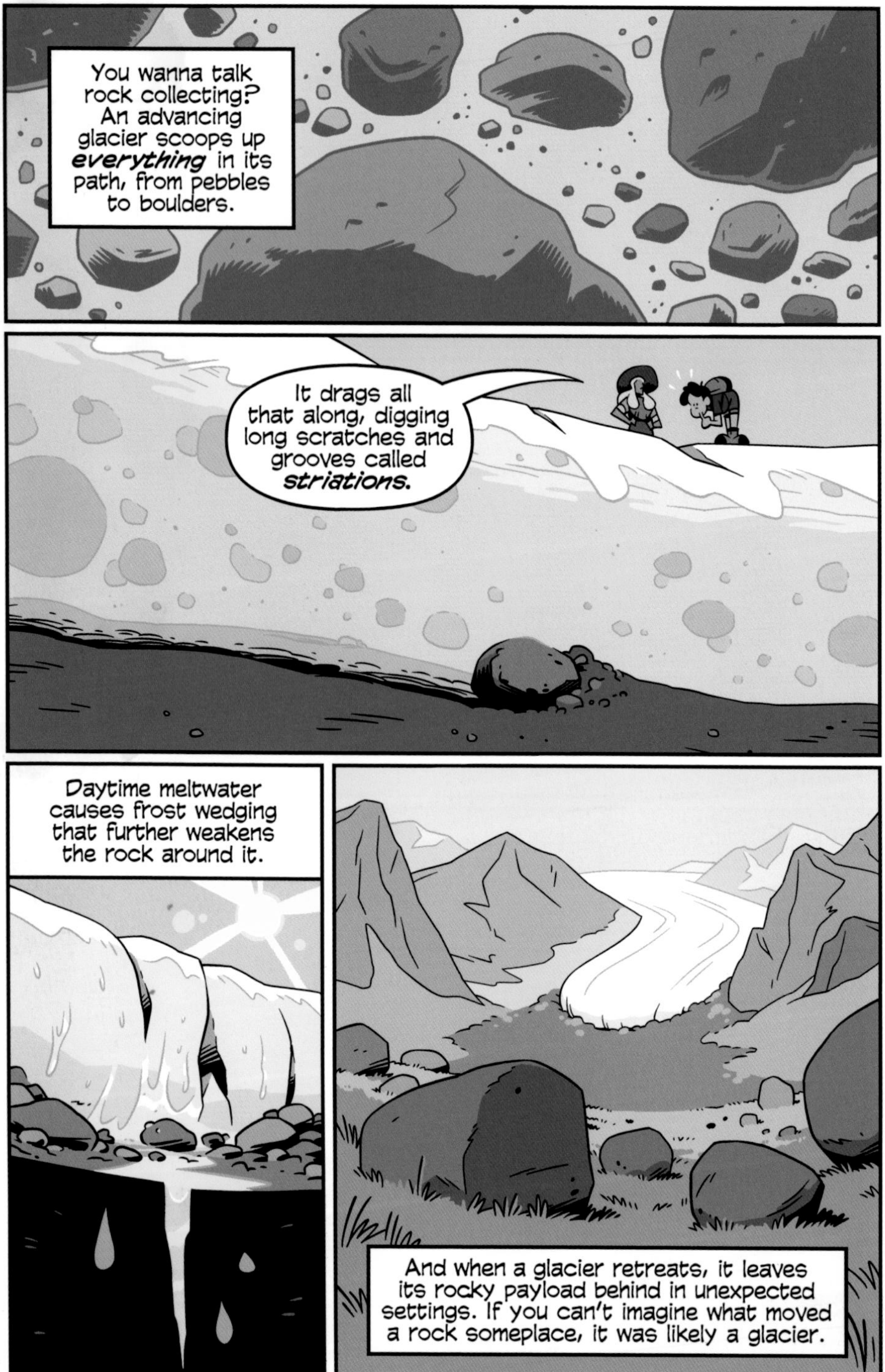
You wanna talk rock collecting? An advancing glacier scoops up *everything* in its path, from pebbles to boulders.
It drags all that along, digging long scratches and grooves called *striations.*
Daytime meltwater causes frost wedging that further weakens the rock around it.
And when a glacier retreats, it leaves its rocky payload behind in unexpected settings. If you can't imagine what moved a rock someplace, it was likely a glacier.

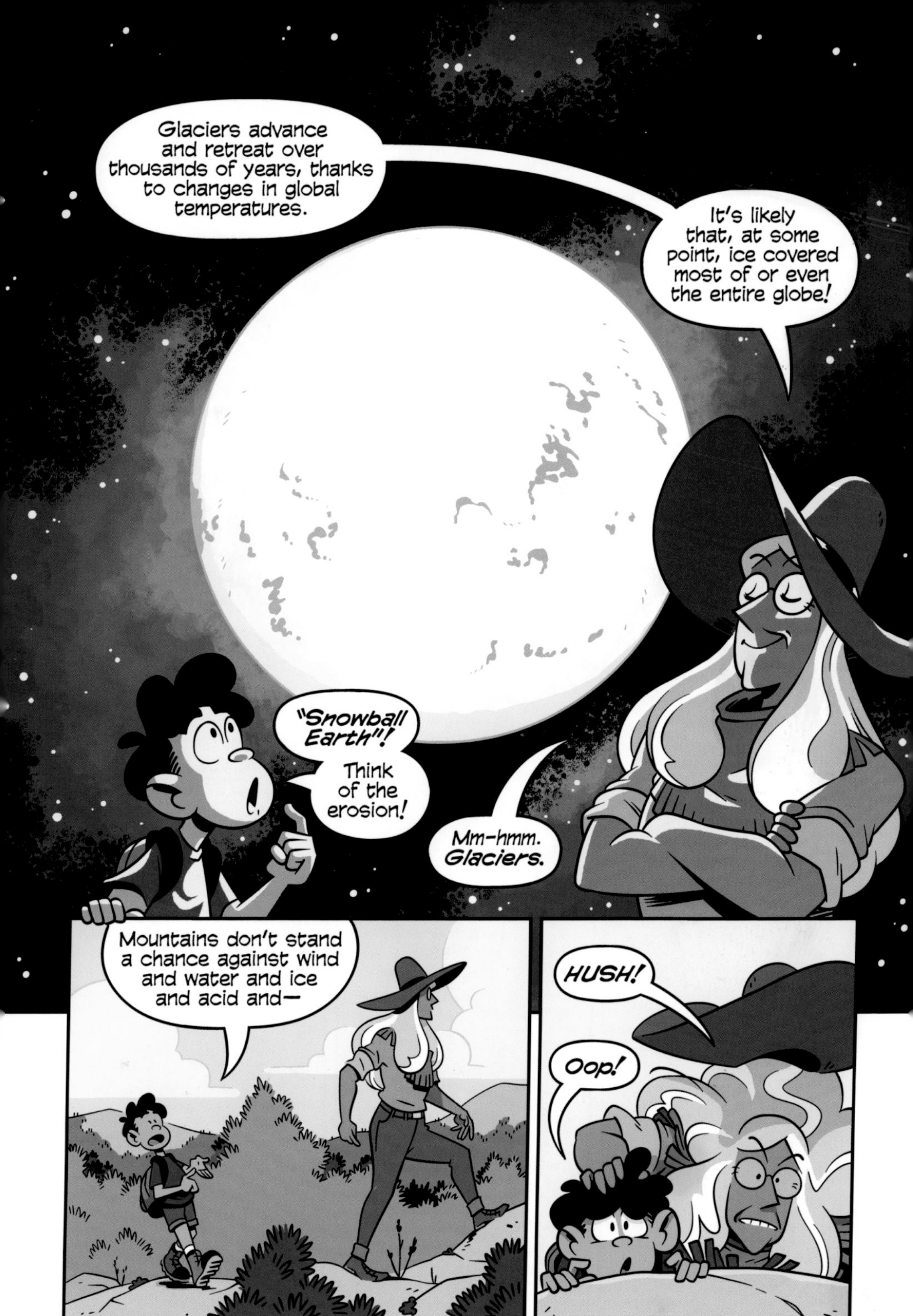

Glaciers advance and retreat over thousands of years, thanks to changes in global temperatures.
It's likely that, at some point, ice covered most of or even the entire globe!
"Snowball Earth"!
Think of the erosion!
Mm-hmm. Glaciers.
Mountains don't stand a chance against wind and water and ice and acid and—
HUSH!
Oop!

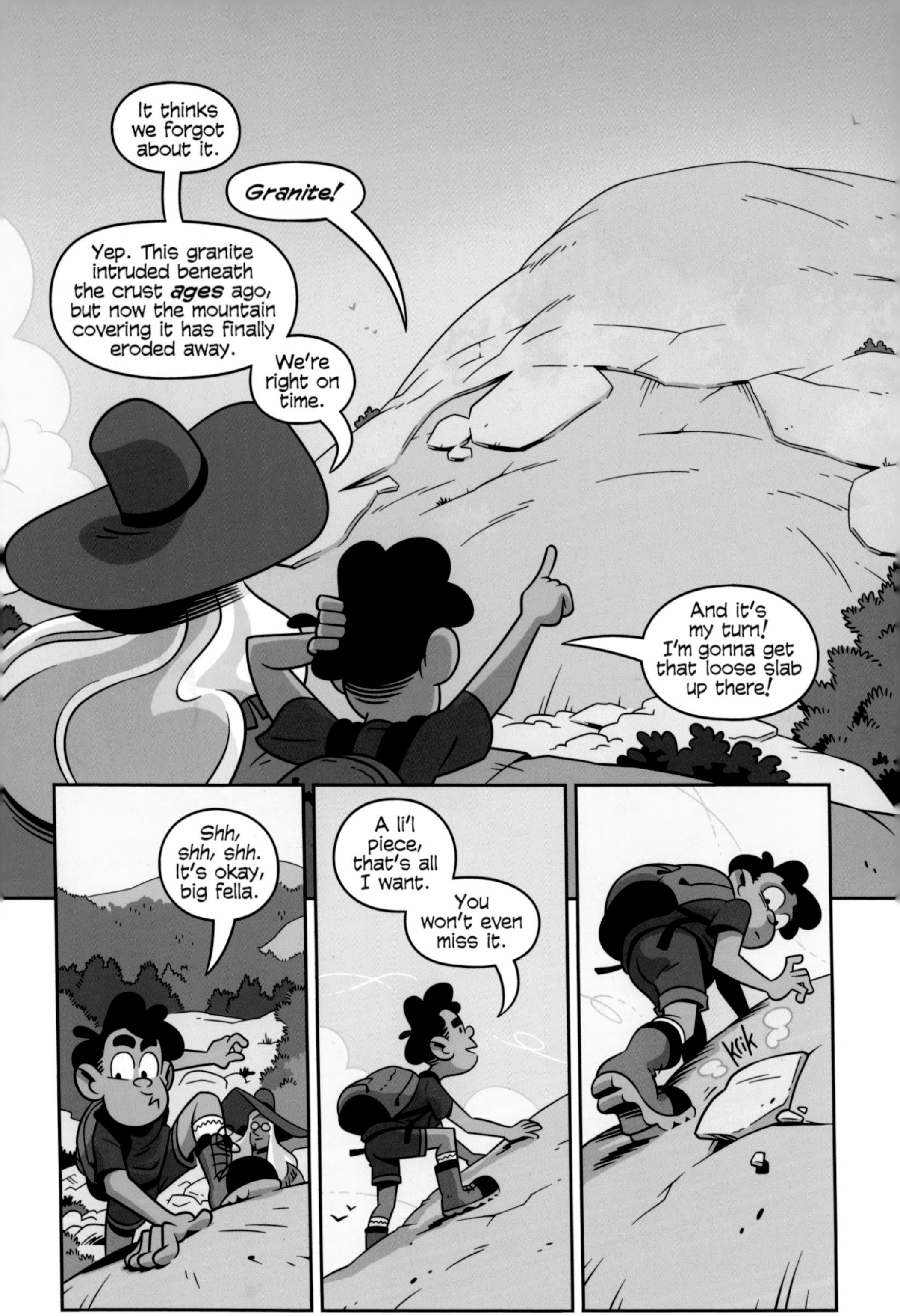
It thinks we forgot about it.
Granite!
Yep. This granite intruded beneath the crust ages ago, but now the mountain covering it has finally eroded away.
We're right on time.
And it's my turn! I'm gonna get that loose slab up there!
Shh, shh, shh. It's okay, big fella.
A li'l piece, that's all I want.
You won't even miss it.
krik

Sedona?

Sedona.

krik

krik

krik

That's just some *exfoliation.*

It's a kind of mechanical weathering where rock is finally allowed to expand after having been buried.

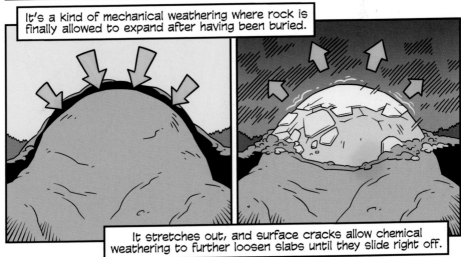

It stretches out, and surface cracks allow chemical weathering to further loosen slabs until they slide right off.

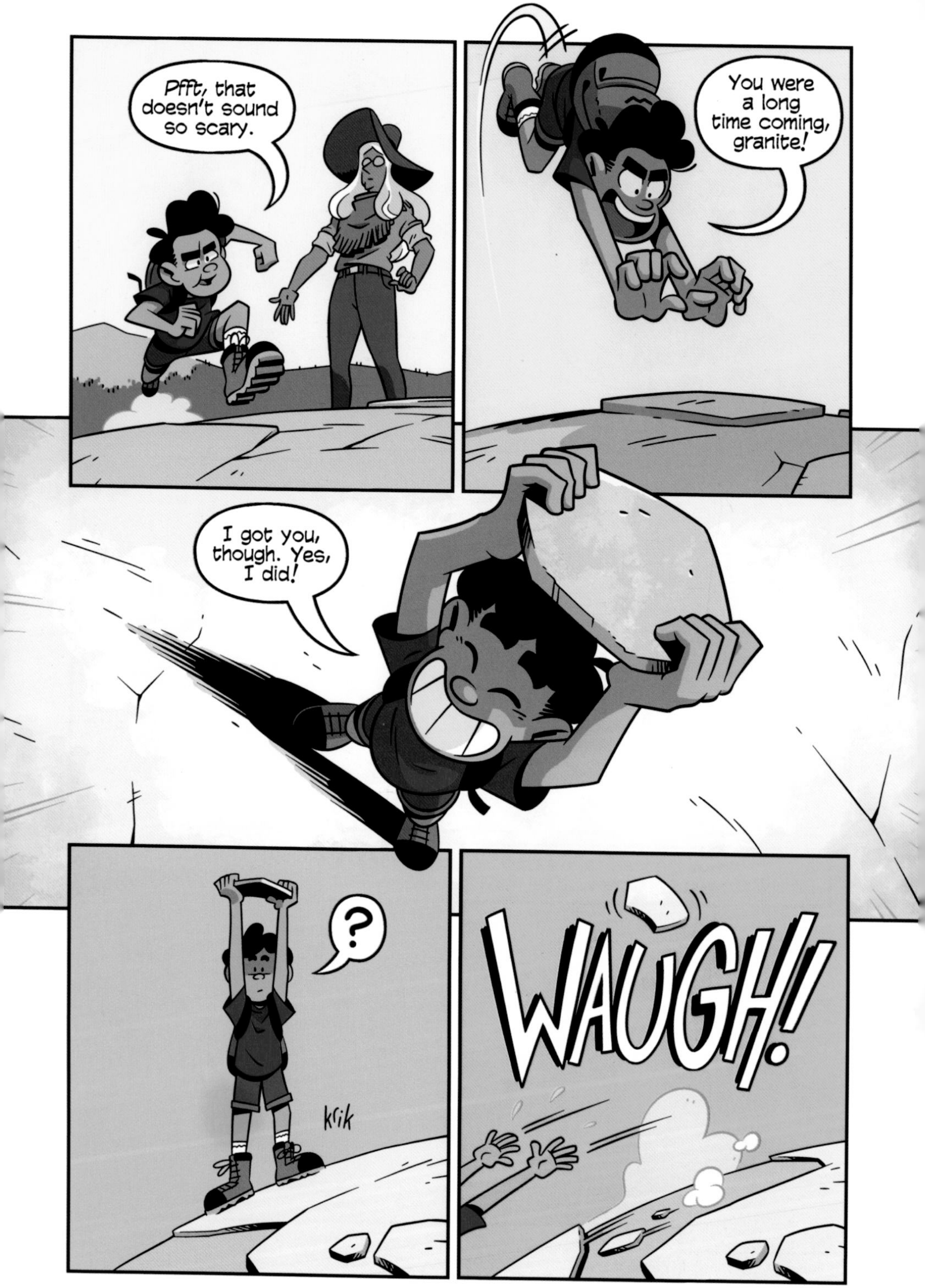
Pfft, that doesn't sound so scary.
You were a long time coming, granite!
I got you, though. Yes, I did!
?
krik
WAUGH!

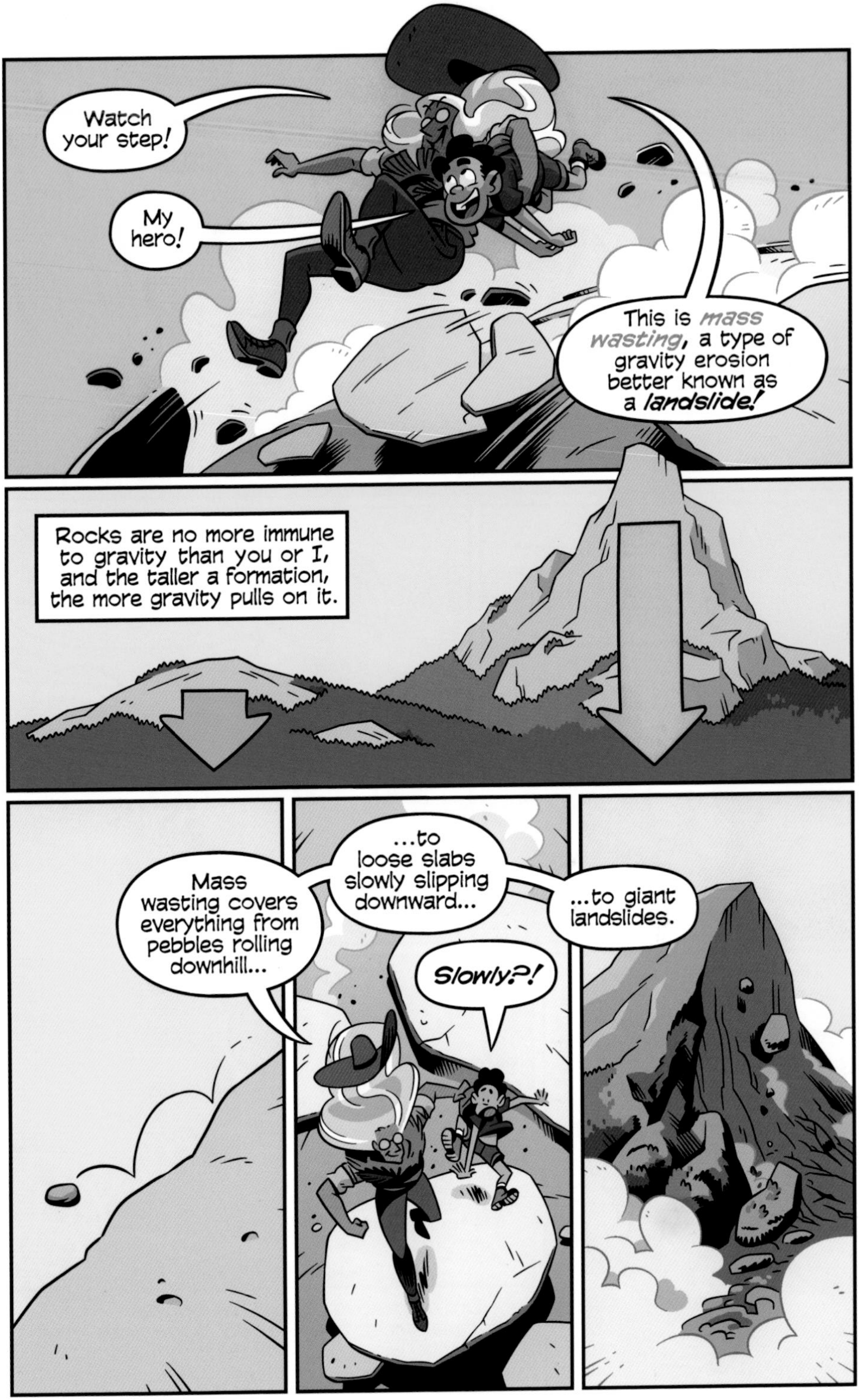
Watch your step!
My hero!
This is *mass wasting*, a type of gravity erosion better known as a *landslide!*
Rocks are no more immune to gravity than you or I, and the taller a formation, the more gravity pulls on it.
Mass wasting covers everything from pebbles rolling downhill...
...to loose slabs slowly slipping downward...
Slowly?!
...to giant landslides.

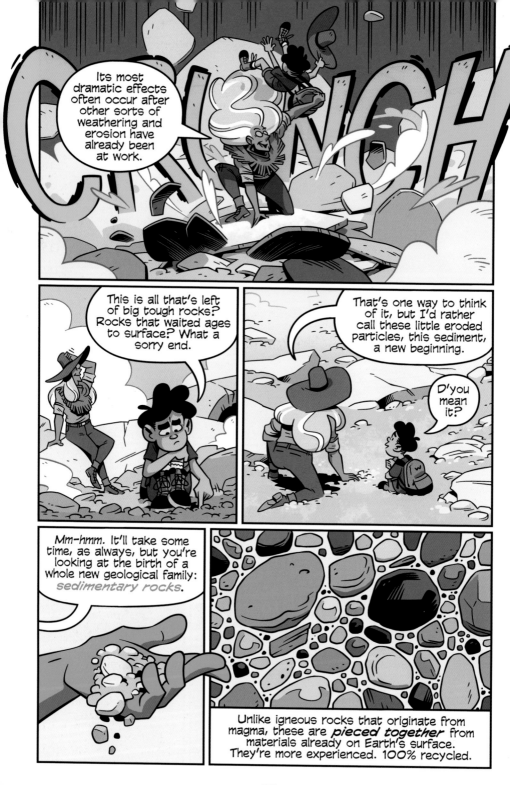

Its most dramatic effects often occur after other sorts of weathering and erosion have already been at work.

This is all that's left of big tough rocks? Rocks that waited ages to surface? What a sorry end.

That's one way to think of it, but I'd rather call these little eroded particles, this sediment, a new beginning.

D'you mean it?

Mm-hmm. It'll take some time, as always, but you're looking at the birth of a whole new geological family: *sedimentary rocks.*

Unlike igneous rocks that originate from magma, these are *pieced together* from materials already on Earth's surface. They're more experienced. 100% recycled.

Clastic sedimentary rocks form when remains of existing rock are pressed or stuck together. Built up in layers over many, many years, they're full of clues to both what they came from and how they got to where they are.

Any sedimentary rock's mineral makeup is determined entirely by what its sources were made of. We've seen all these materials in igneous rocks, so they show up in those rocks' descendants as well.

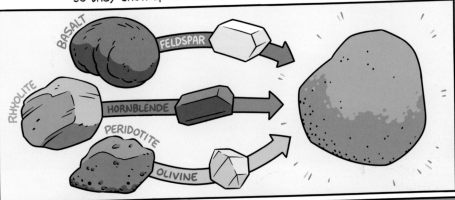

BASALT — FELDSPAR

RHYOLITE — HORNBLENDE

PERIDOTITE — OLIVINE

Quartz's durability makes it by far the most common sedimentary mineral. When others weather away, it remains. That means a rock made mainly of quartz grains is likely older than one that still holds lots of other minerals.

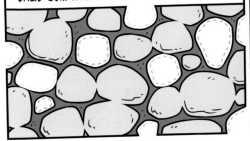

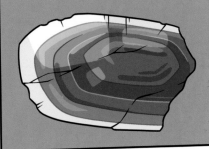

One mineral puts even quartz to shame. Rare sedimentary rocks hold *zircon* crystals 4.4 billion years old, nearly as old as Earth!

Water and wind deposit grains based on size and weight. In a fast-moving river, only larger grains will be deposited.

Slower water deposits smaller grains.

Still water allows the very finest sediment to settle.

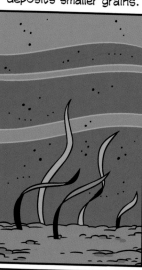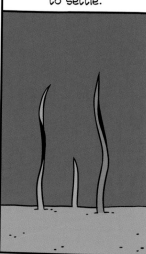

Layers build up, burying and compressing the lowest, and minerals in the spaces between grains cement everything together to become a collective rock.

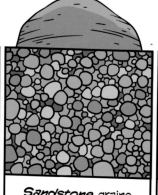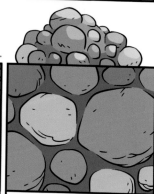

Mudstone is made of clay particles too small to pick apart with the naked eye.

Sandstone grains are bigger, up to 2 mm across.

Conglomerates are made of even larger rounded pieces.

Remember that our old friends glaciers aren't picky about what they grab.

This mess can become *tillite*, a sedimentary rock found throughout a glacier's range.

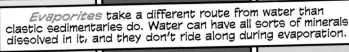

Evaporites take a different route from water than clastic sedimentaries do. Water can have all sorts of minerals dissolved in it, and they don't ride along during evaporation.

Mineral deposits are left behind to become *gypsum, calcite, halite,* and more. You might know halite by its more common name: *rock salt.*

GYPSUM CALCITE HALITE

Mmm, that's tasty rock!

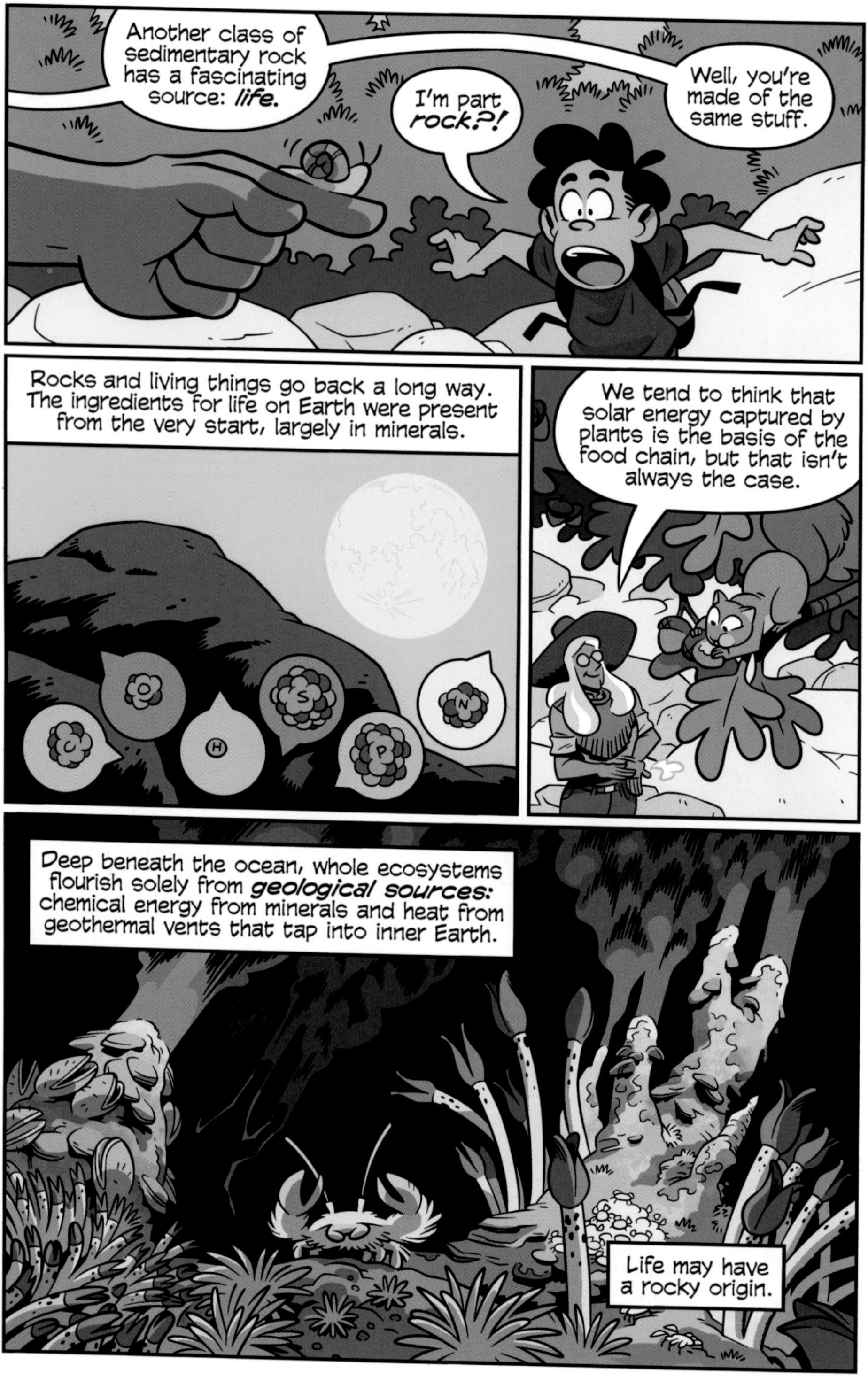

Another class of sedimentary rock has a fascinating source: *life.*
I'm part *rock?!*
Well, you're made of the same stuff.
Rocks and living things go back a long way. The ingredients for life on Earth were present from the very start, largely in minerals.
O
S
N
C
H
P
We tend to think that solar energy captured by plants is the basis of the food chain, but that isn't always the case.
Deep beneath the ocean, whole ecosystems flourish solely from *geological sources:* chemical energy from minerals and heat from geothermal vents that tap into inner Earth.
Life may have a rocky origin.

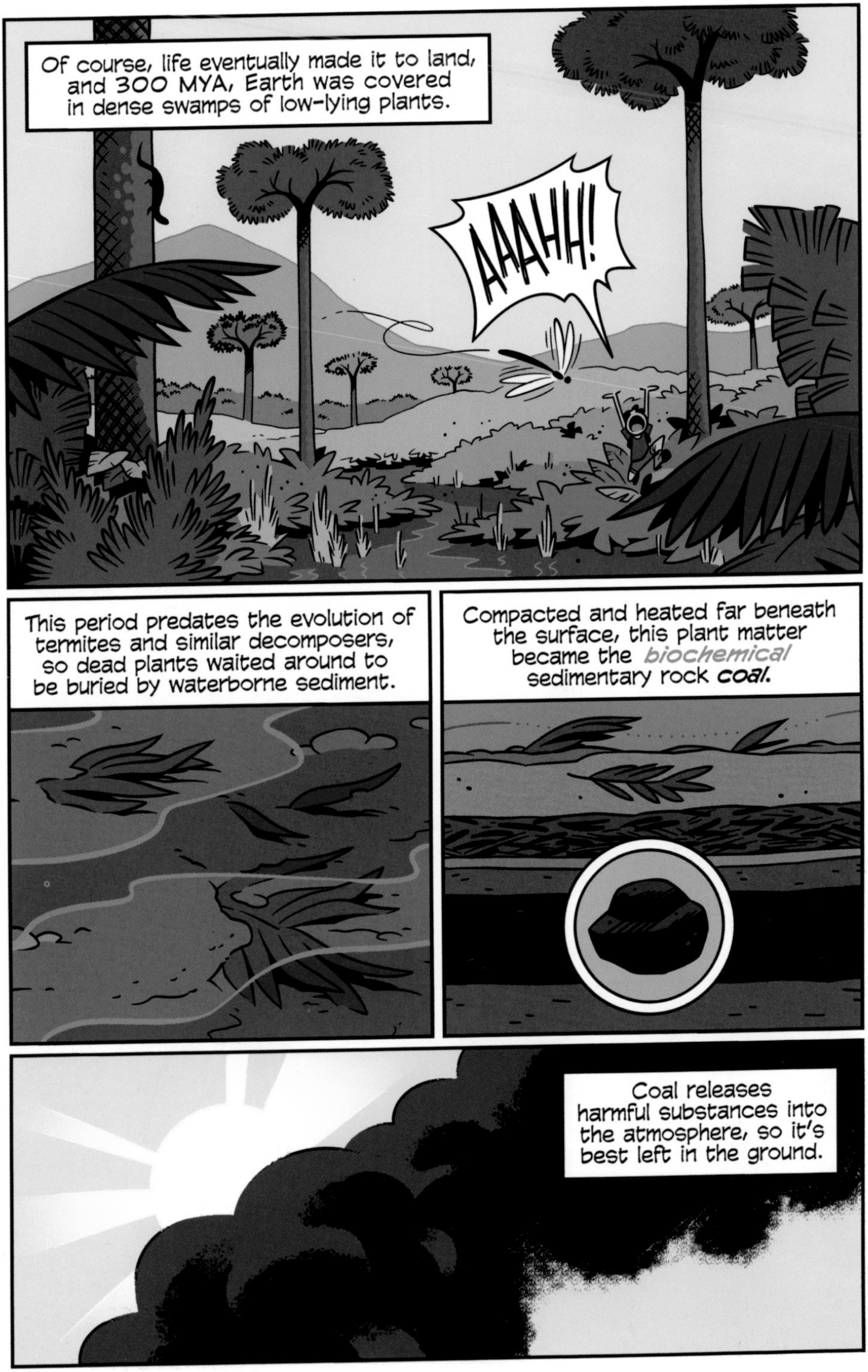
Of course, life eventually made it to land, and 300 MYA, Earth was covered in dense swamps of low-lying plants.
AAAHH!
This period predates the evolution of termites and similar decomposers, so dead plants waited around to be buried by waterborne sediment.
Compacted and heated far beneath the surface, this plant matter became the biochemical sedimentary rock coal.
Coal releases harmful substances into the atmosphere, so it's best left in the ground.

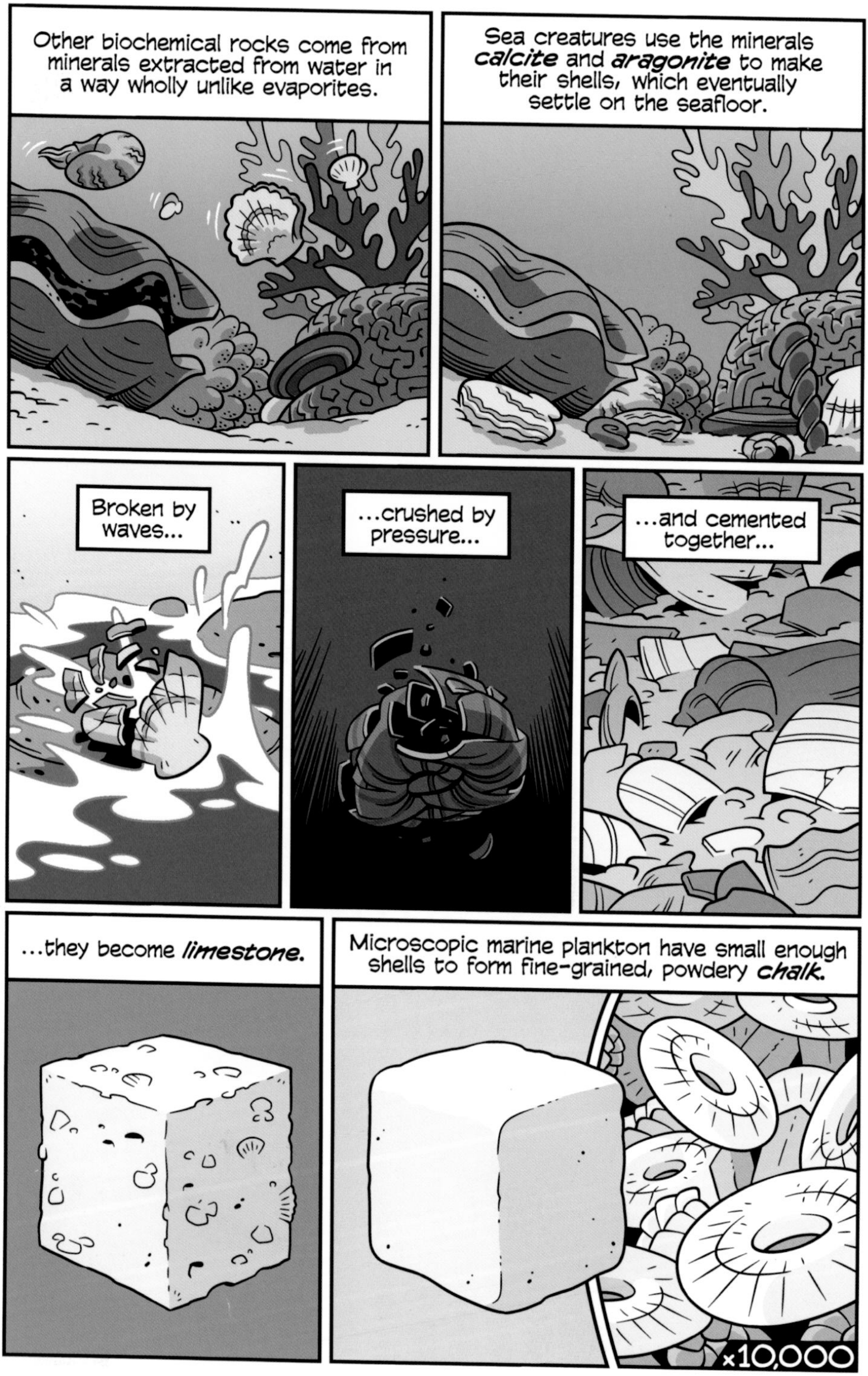
Other biochemical rocks come from minerals extracted from water in a way wholly unlike evaporites.
Sea creatures use the minerals *calcite* and *aragonite* to make their shells, which eventually settle on the seafloor.
Broken by waves...
...crushed by pressure...
...and cemented together...
...they become *limestone.*
Microscopic marine plankton have small enough shells to form fine-grained, powdery *chalk.*
×10,000

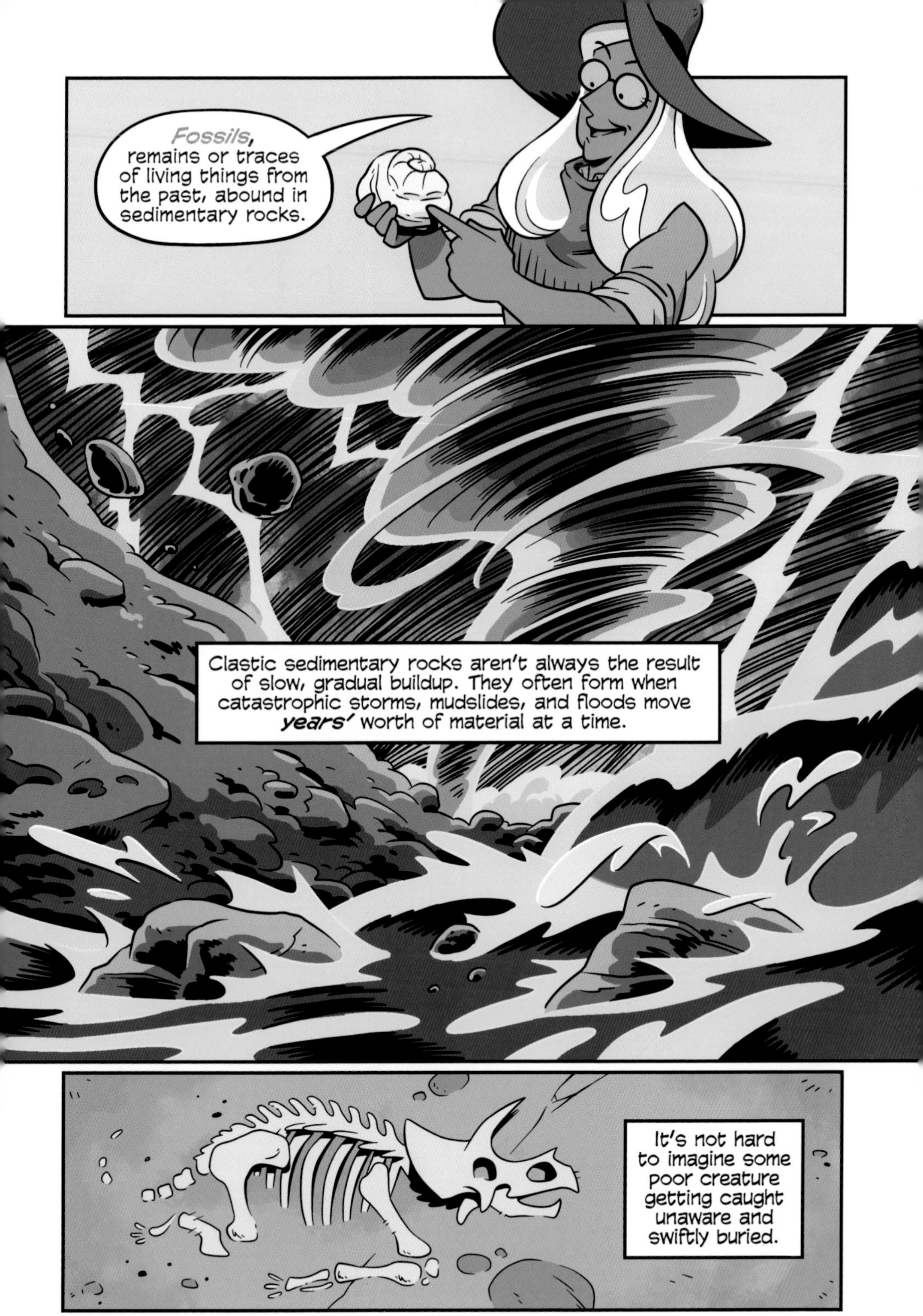
Fossils, remains or traces of living things from the past, abound in sedimentary rocks.
Clastic sedimentary rocks aren't always the result of slow, gradual buildup. They often form when catastrophic storms, mudslides, and floods move *years'* worth of material at a time.
It's not hard to imagine some poor creature getting caught unaware and swiftly buried.

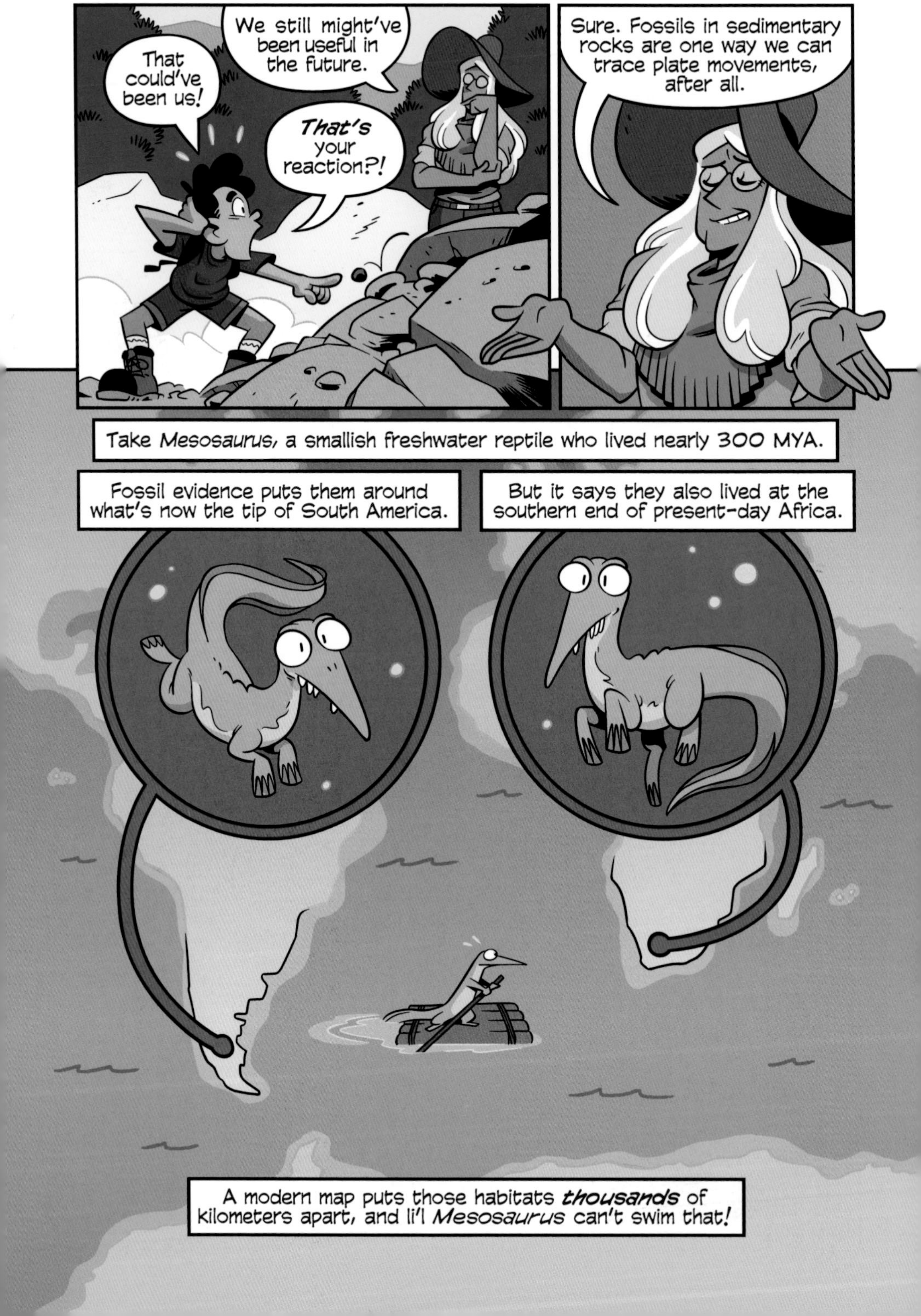
That could've been us!
We still might've been useful in the future.
That's your reaction?!
Sure. Fossils in sedimentary rocks are one way we can trace plate movements, after all.
Take Mesosaurus, a smallish freshwater reptile who lived nearly 300 MYA.
Fossil evidence puts them around what's now the tip of South America.
But it says they also lived at the southern end of present-day Africa.
A modern map puts those habitats thousands of kilometers apart, and li'l Mesosaurus can't swim that!

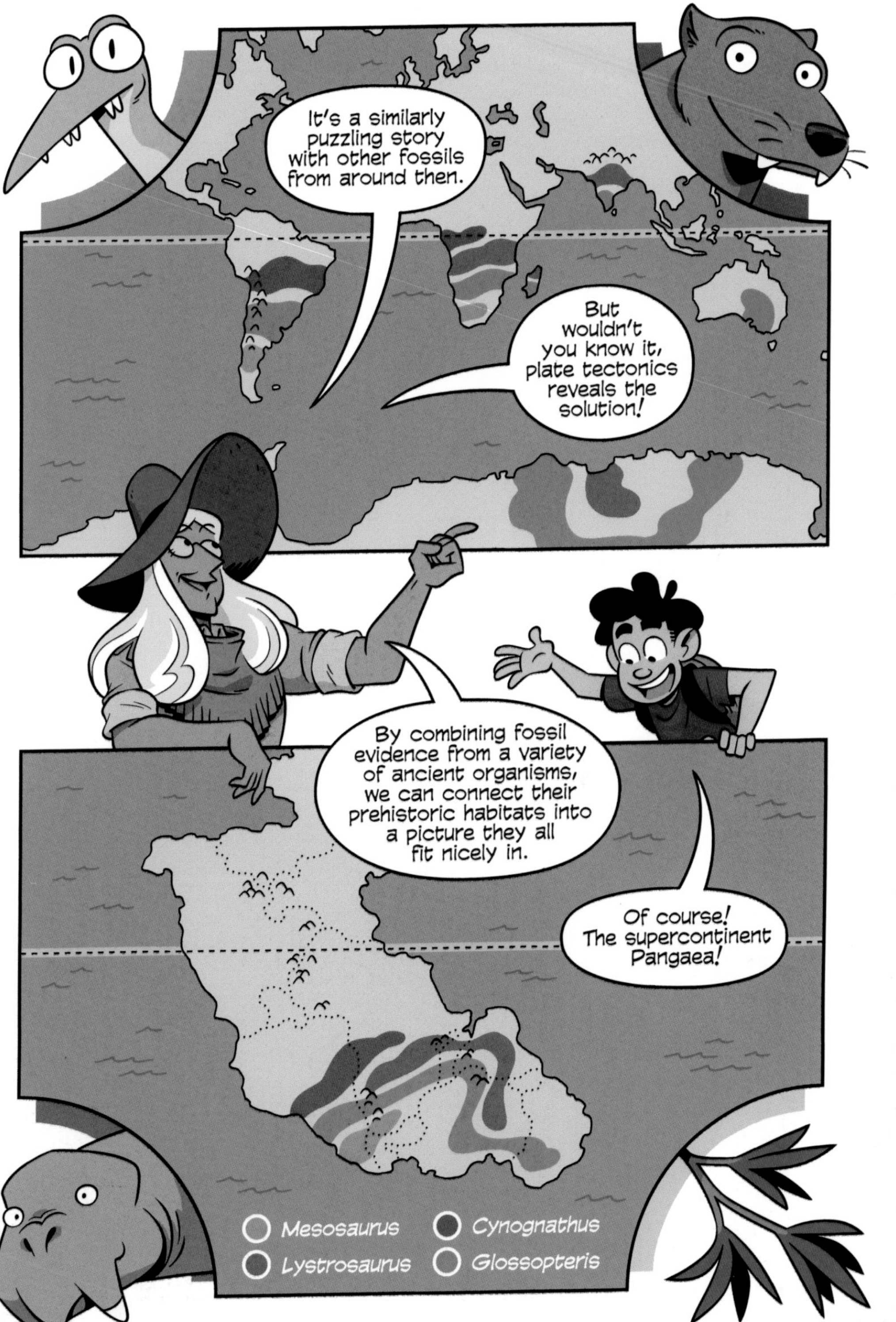
It's a similarly puzzling story with other fossils from around then.
But wouldn't you know it, plate tectonics reveals the solution!
By combining fossil evidence from a variety of ancient organisms, we can connect their prehistoric habitats into a picture they all fit nicely in.
Of course! The supercontinent Pangaea!
Mesosaurus
Cynognathus
Lystrosaurus
Glossopteris

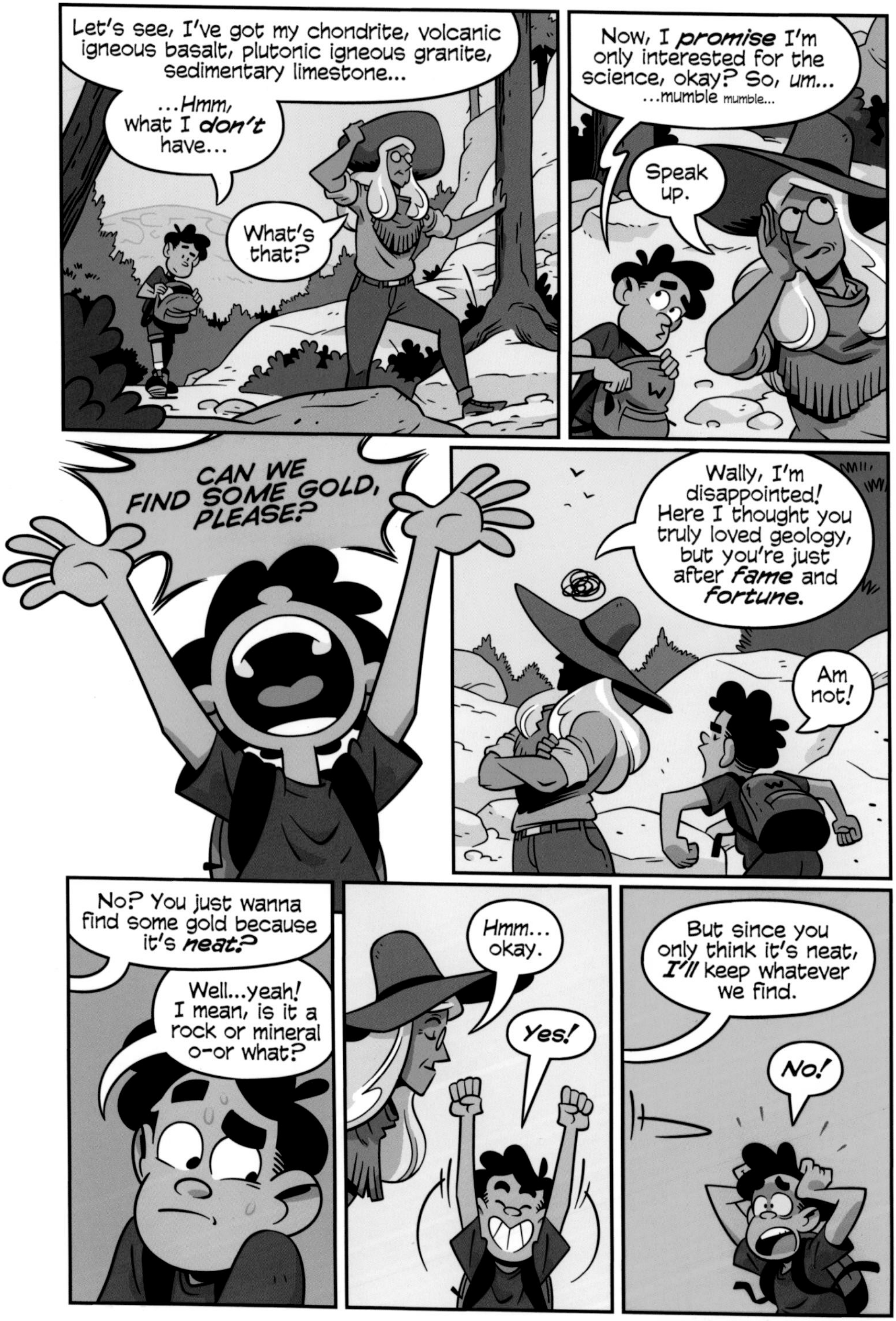
Let's see, I've got my chondrite, volcanic igneous basalt, plutonic igneous granite, sedimentary limestone...
...Hmm, what I *don't* have...
What's that?
Now, I *promise* I'm only interested for the science, okay? So, *um*...
...mumble mumble...
Speak up.
CAN WE FIND SOME GOLD, PLEASE?
Wally, I'm disappointed! Here I thought you truly loved geology, but you're just after *fame* and *fortune*.
Am not!
No? You just wanna find some gold because it's *neat?*
Well...yeah! I mean, is it a rock or mineral o-or what?
Hmm... okay.
Yes!
But since you only think it's neat, *I'll* keep whatever we find.
No!

Gold, silver, copper, zinc...these aren't true minerals because they're single, pure elements. Atoms of each are scattered throughout the crust, but they need help to concentrate.

Enter water. Heat from the mantle causes it to circulate through pores and cracks in the crust. As this super-hot fluid percolates, it picks up atoms of rare elements.

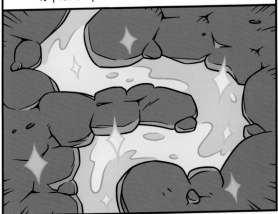

When the water cools and interacts with rock farther up, its newly concentrated contents are released.

Release enough, and you've got a *vein*.

Oh, boy! You said *fifty-fifty*, right?

Of course, other minerals form veins as well.

CLANG

PYRITE (fool's gold)

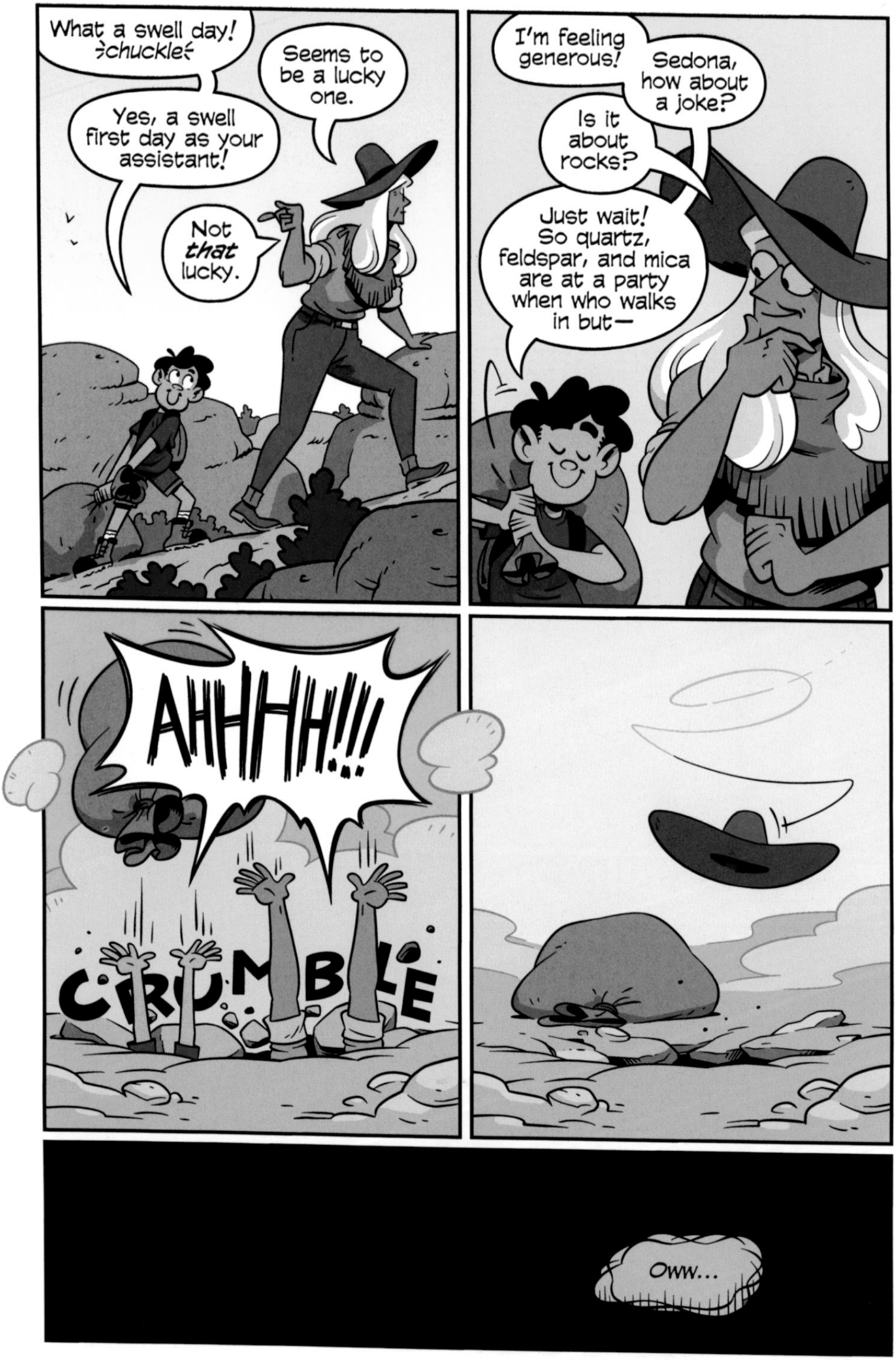
What a swell day! ≯chuckle≮
Yes, a swell first day as your assistant!
Seems to be a lucky one.
Not *that* lucky.
I'm feeling generous!
Sedona, how about a joke?
Is it about rocks?
Just wait! So quartz, feldspar, and mica are at a party when who walks in but—
AHHHH!!!
CRUMBLE
Oww...

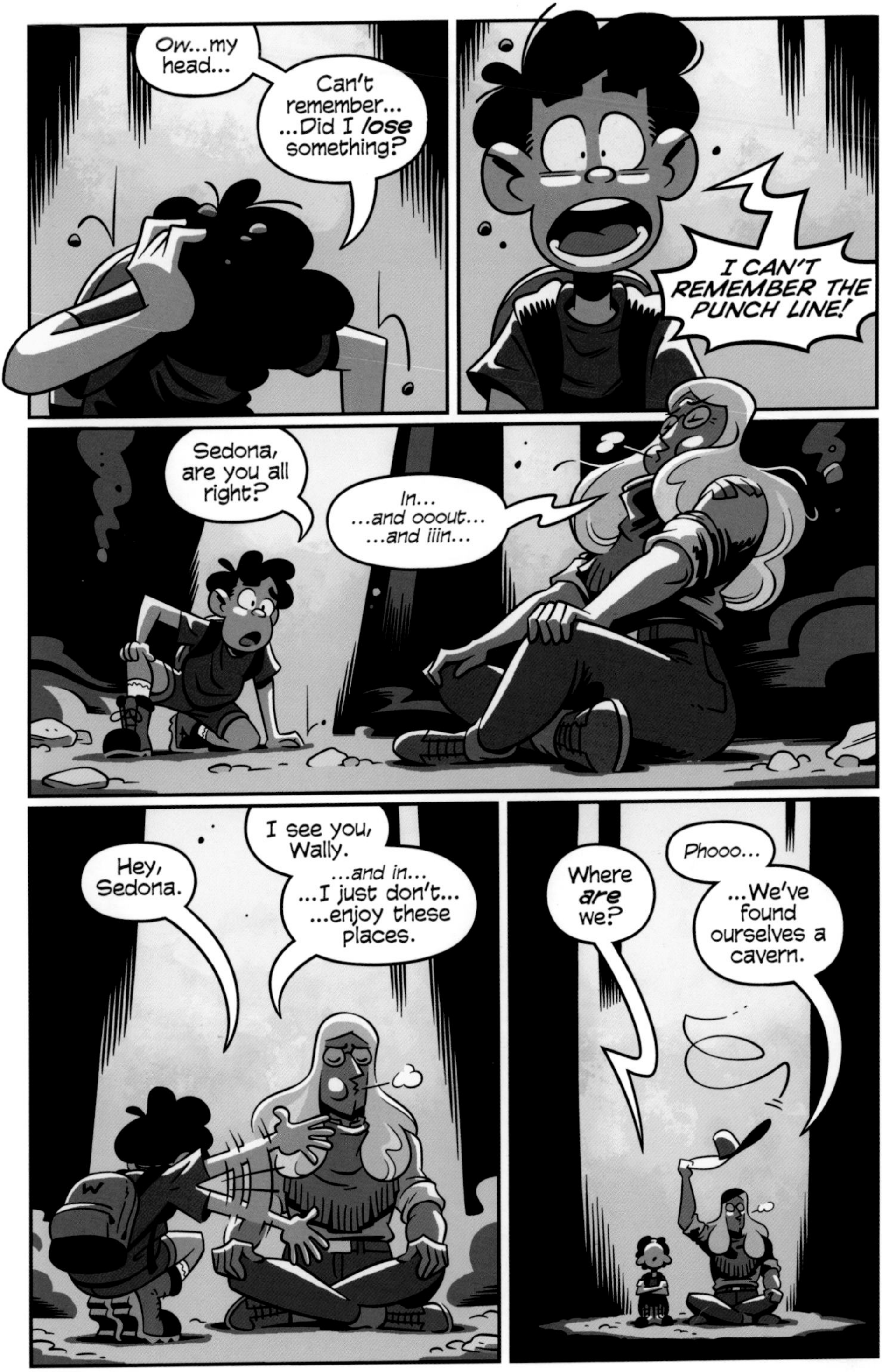
Ow...my head...
Can't remember... ...Did I *lose* something?
I CAN'T REMEMBER THE PUNCH LINE!
Sedona, are you all right?
In... ...and ooout... ...and iiin...
Hey, Sedona.
I see you, Wally.
...and in... ...I just don't... ...enjoy these places.
Where *are* we?
Phooo...
...We've found ourselves a cavern.

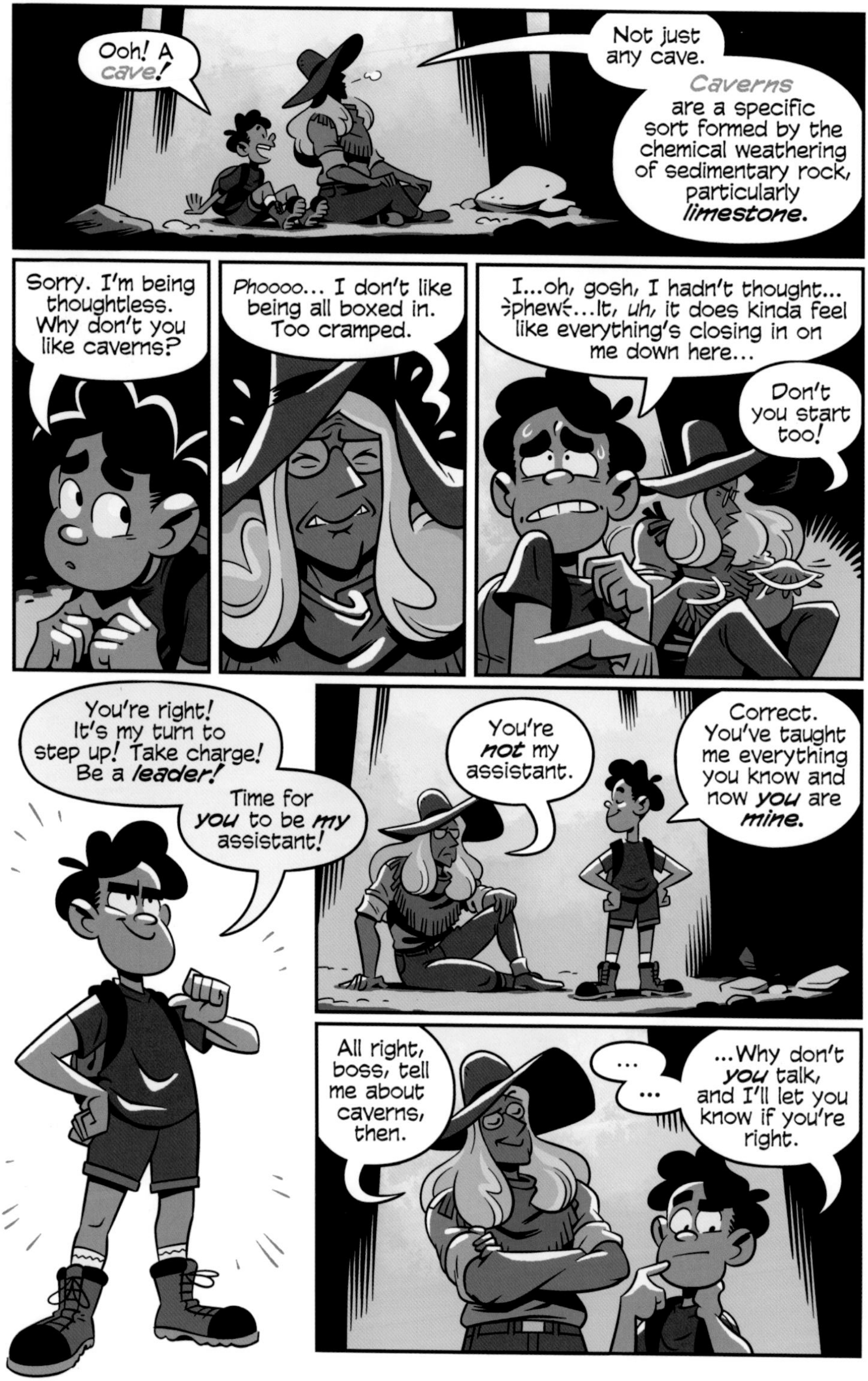
Ooh! A cave!
Not just any cave.
Caverns are a specific sort formed by the chemical weathering of sedimentary rock, particularly limestone.
Sorry. I'm being thoughtless. Why don't you like caverns?
Phoooo... I don't like being all boxed in. Too cramped.
I...oh, gosh, I hadn't thought... phew...It, uh, it does kinda feel like everything's closing in on me down here...
Don't you start too!
You're right! It's my turn to step up! Take charge! Be a leader!
Time for you to be my assistant!
You're not my assistant.
Correct. You've taught me everything you know and now you are mine.
All right, boss, tell me about caverns, then.
...
...
...Why don't you talk, and I'll let you know if you're right.

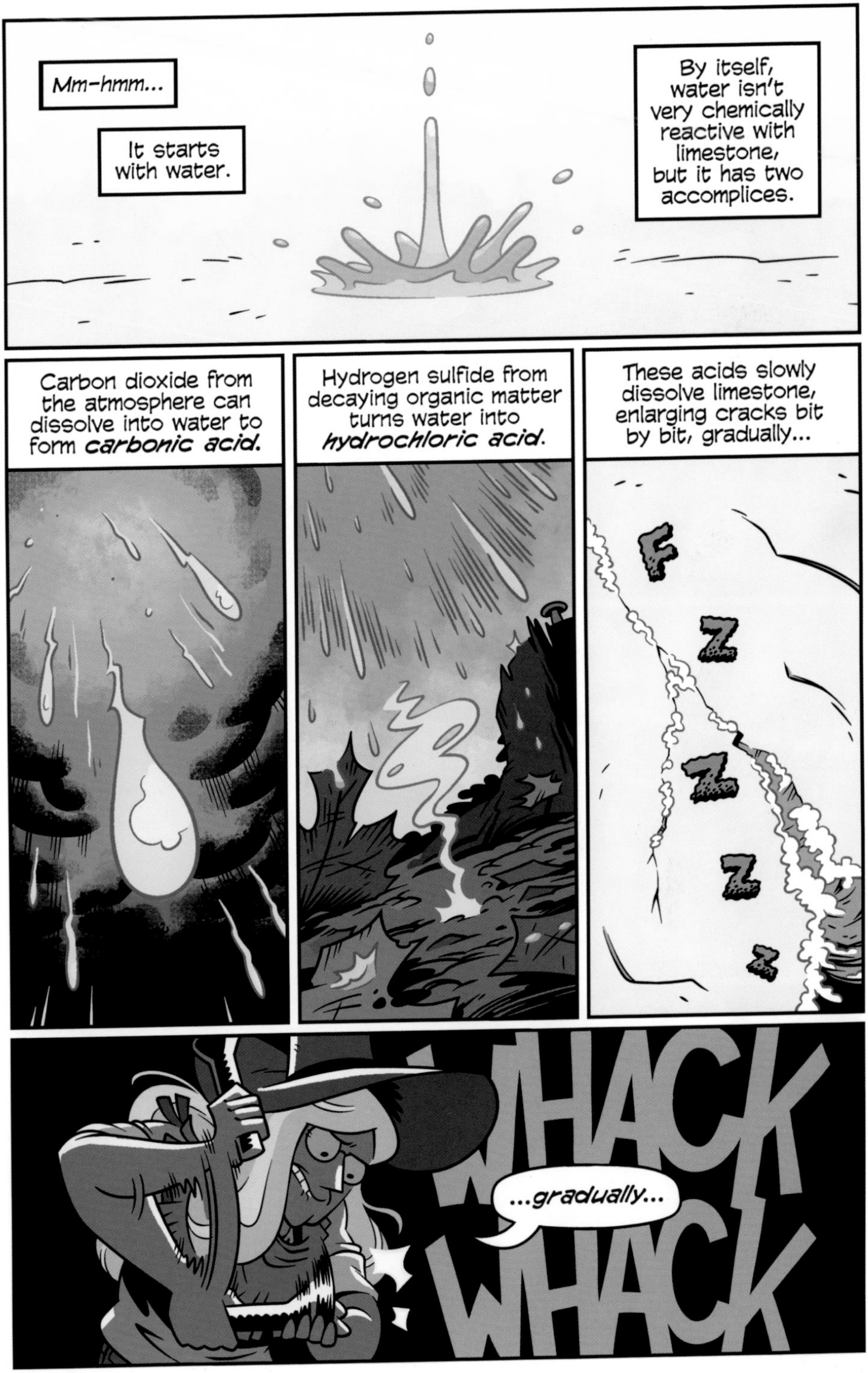
Mm-hmm...
It starts with water.
By itself, water isn't very chemically reactive with limestone, but it has two accomplices.
Carbon dioxide from the atmosphere can dissolve into water to form **carbonic acid**.
Hydrogen sulfide from decaying organic matter turns water into **hydrochloric acid**.
These acids slowly dissolve limestone, enlarging cracks bit by bit, gradually...
F
Z
Z
Z
Z
WHACK
...gradually...
WHACK

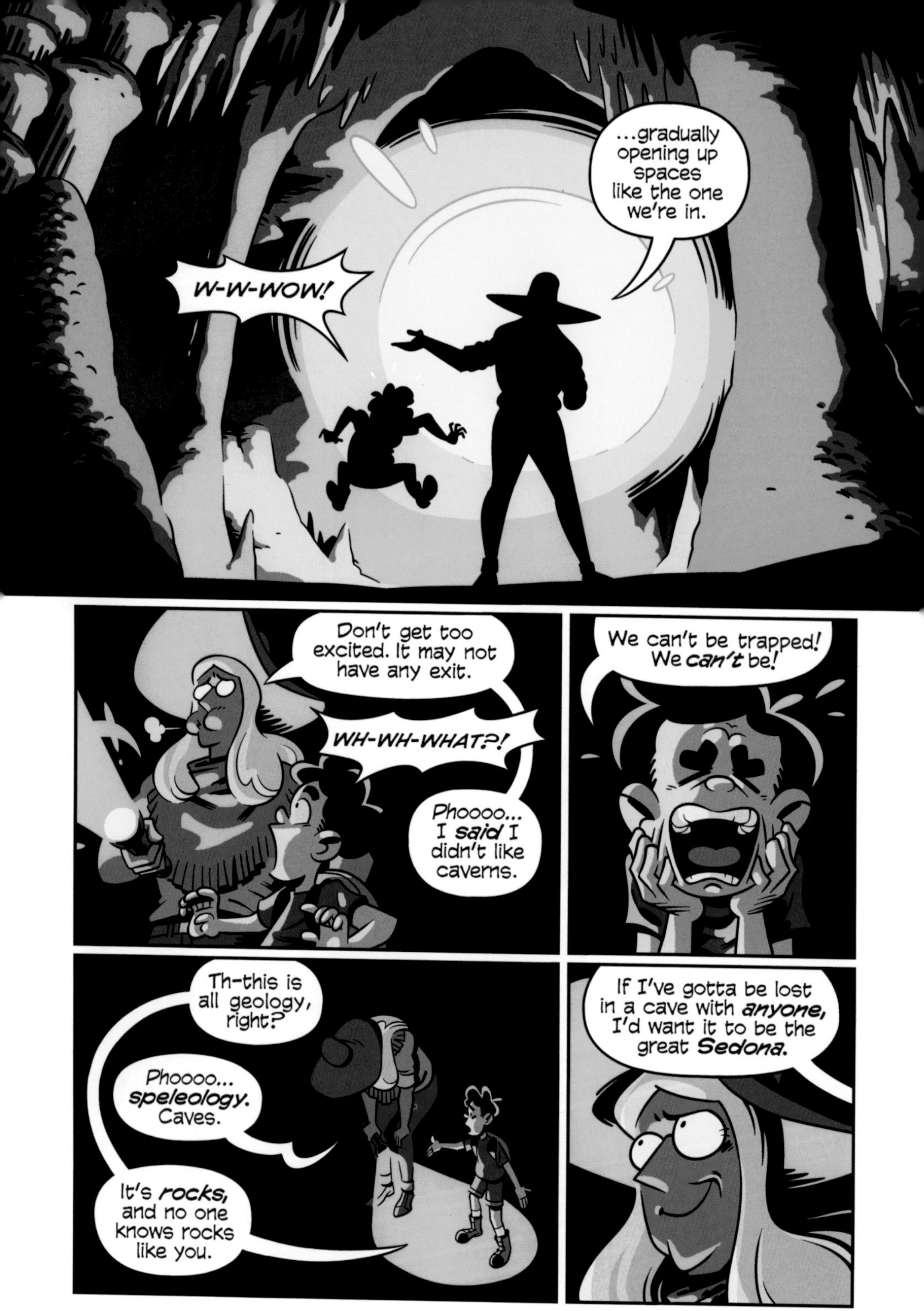
...gradually opening up spaces like the one we're in.
W-W-WOW!
Don't get too excited. It may not have any exit.
WH-WH-WHAT?!
Phoooo... I *said* I didn't like caverns.
We can't be trapped! We *can't* be!
Th-this is all geology, right?
Phoooo... *speleology.* Caves.
It's *rocks,* and no one knows rocks like you.
If I've gotta be lost in a cave with *anyone,* I'd want it to be the great *Sedona.*

Hmph! Come on, let's see what we see.

Phew...

Lookit! Why does rock dissolve into shapes like this?

Ah, *speleothems*, cave formations, come *after* the cave body.

Dissolved limestone doesn't just disappear into water—its parts are still there.

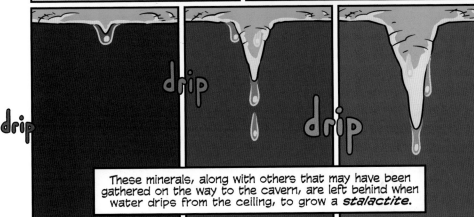

drip

drip

drip

These minerals, along with others that may have been gathered on the way to the cavern, are left behind when water drips from the ceiling, to grow a *stalactite*.

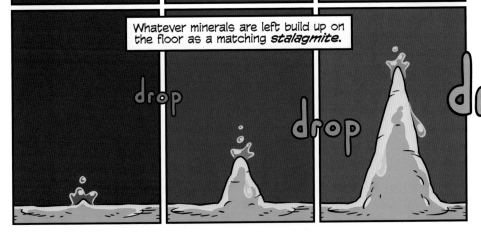

Whatever minerals are left build up on the floor as a matching *stalagmite*.

drop

drop

dro

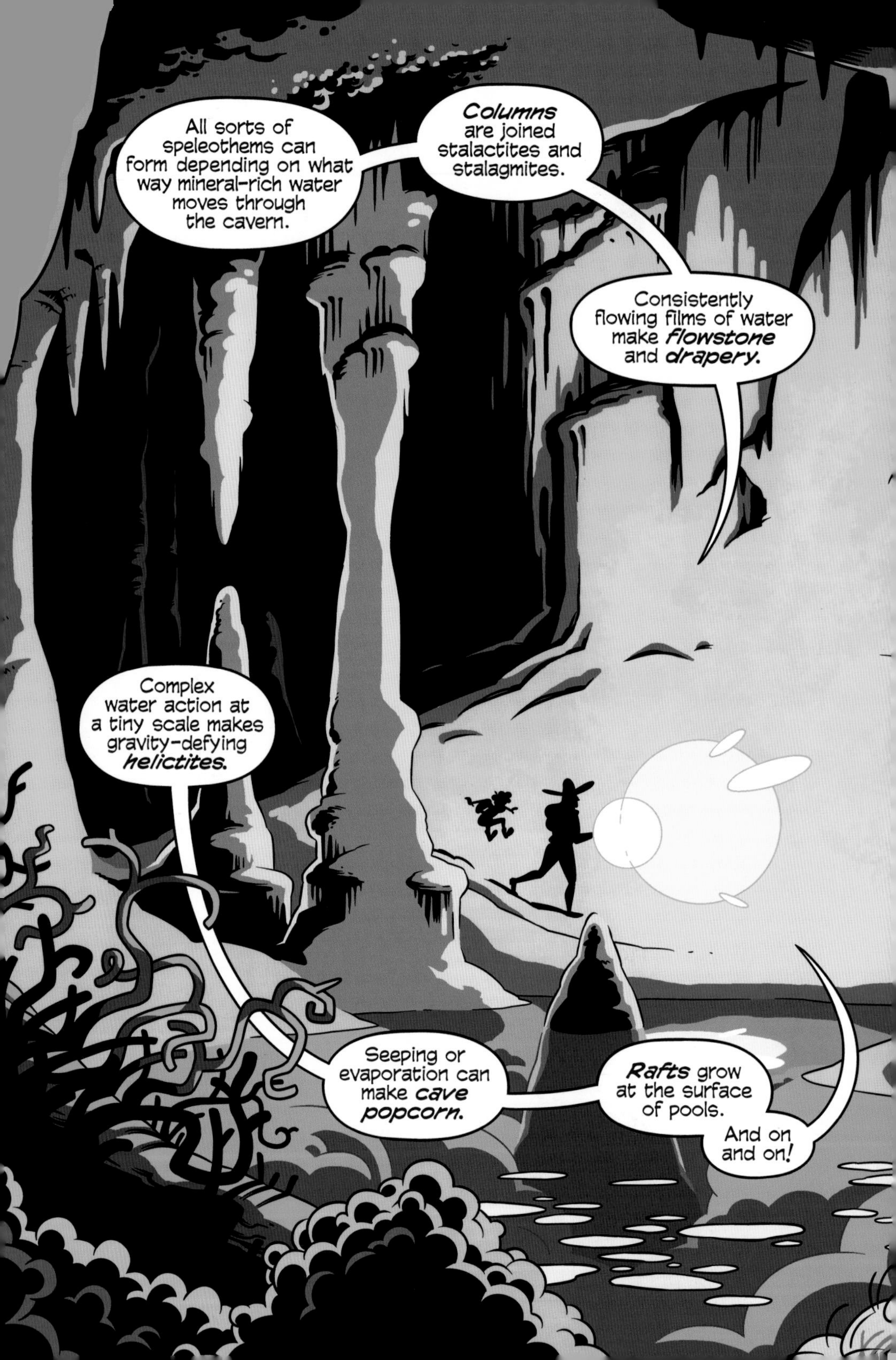
All sorts of speleothems can form depending on what way mineral-rich water moves through the cavern.
Columns are joined stalactites and stalagmites.
Consistently flowing films of water make ***flowstone*** and ***drapery.***
Complex water action at a tiny scale makes gravity-defying ***helictites.***
Seeping or evaporation can make ***cave popcorn.***
Rafts grow at the surface of pools.
And on and on!

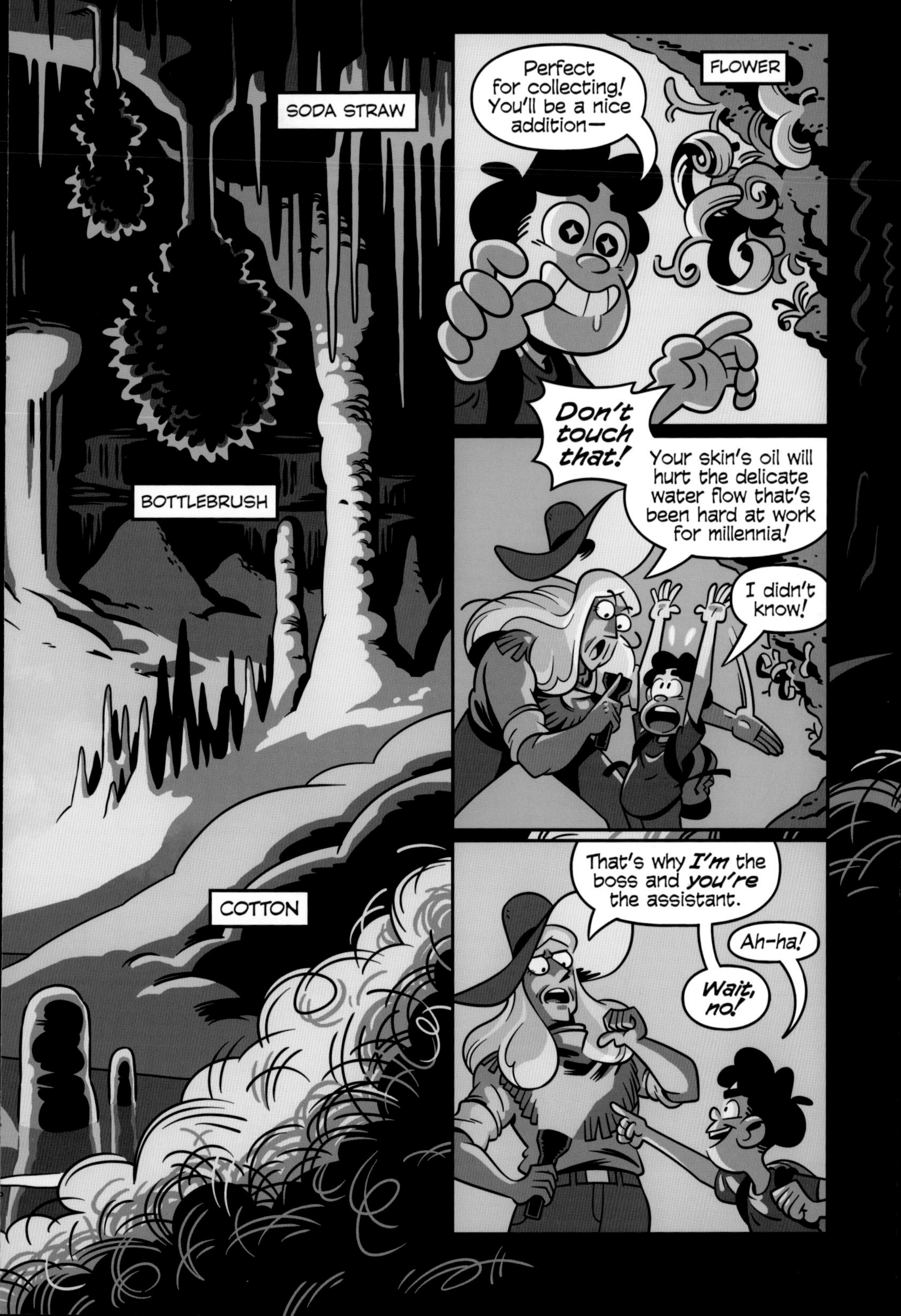
SODA STRAW
BOTTLEBRUSH
COTTON
FLOWER
Perfect for collecting! You'll be a nice addition—
Don't touch that!
Your skin's oil will hurt the delicate water flow that's been hard at work for millennia!
I didn't know!
That's why I'm the boss and you're the assistant.
Ah-ha!
Wait, no!

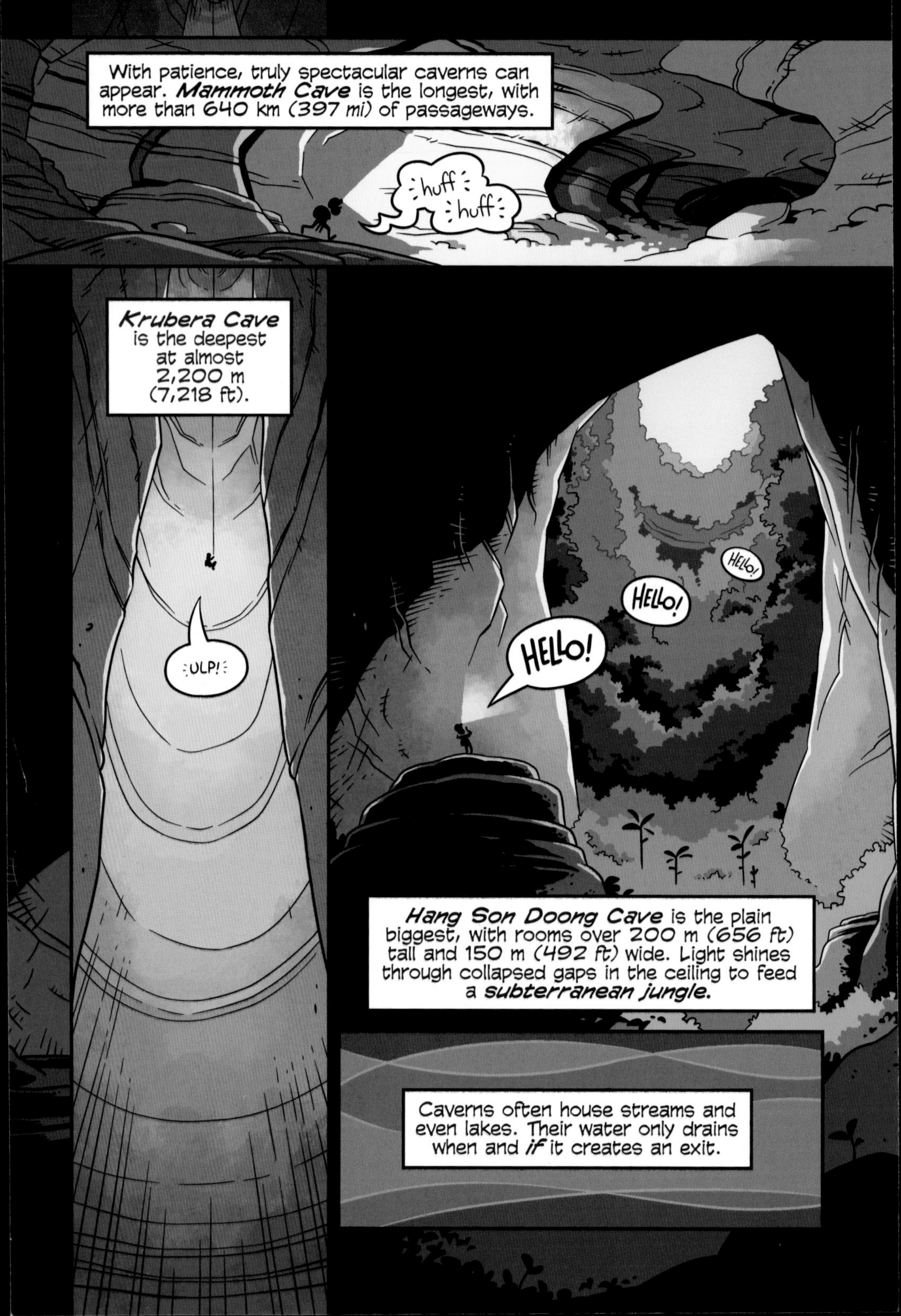

With patience, truly spectacular caverns can appear. *Mammoth Cave* is the longest, with more than 640 km (397 mi) of passageways.
huff huff
Krubera Cave is the deepest at almost 2,200 m (7,218 ft).
ULP!
HELLO!
HELLO!
HELLO!
Hang Son Doong Cave is the plain biggest, with rooms over 200 m (656 ft) tall and 150 m (492 ft) wide. Light shines through collapsed gaps in the ceiling to feed a *subterranean jungle.*
Caverns often house streams and even lakes. Their water only drains when and *if* it creates an exit.

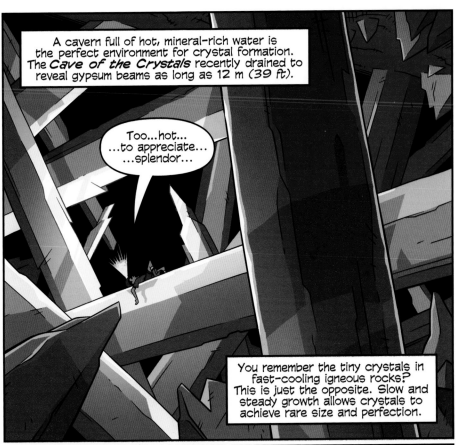

A cavern full of hot, mineral-rich water is the perfect environment for crystal formation. The *Cave of the Crystals* recently drained to reveal gypsum beams as long as 12 m (*39 ft*).

Too...hot...
...to appreciate...
...splendor...

You remember the tiny crystals in fast-cooling igneous rocks? This is just the opposite. Slow and steady growth allows crystals to achieve rare size and perfection.

A mineral's crystal shape is determined by its chemical structure. For instance, microscopic beryl molecules are simple hexagons.

Large beryl crystals keep that hexagonal shape. Get ready, crystals can look pretty weird...

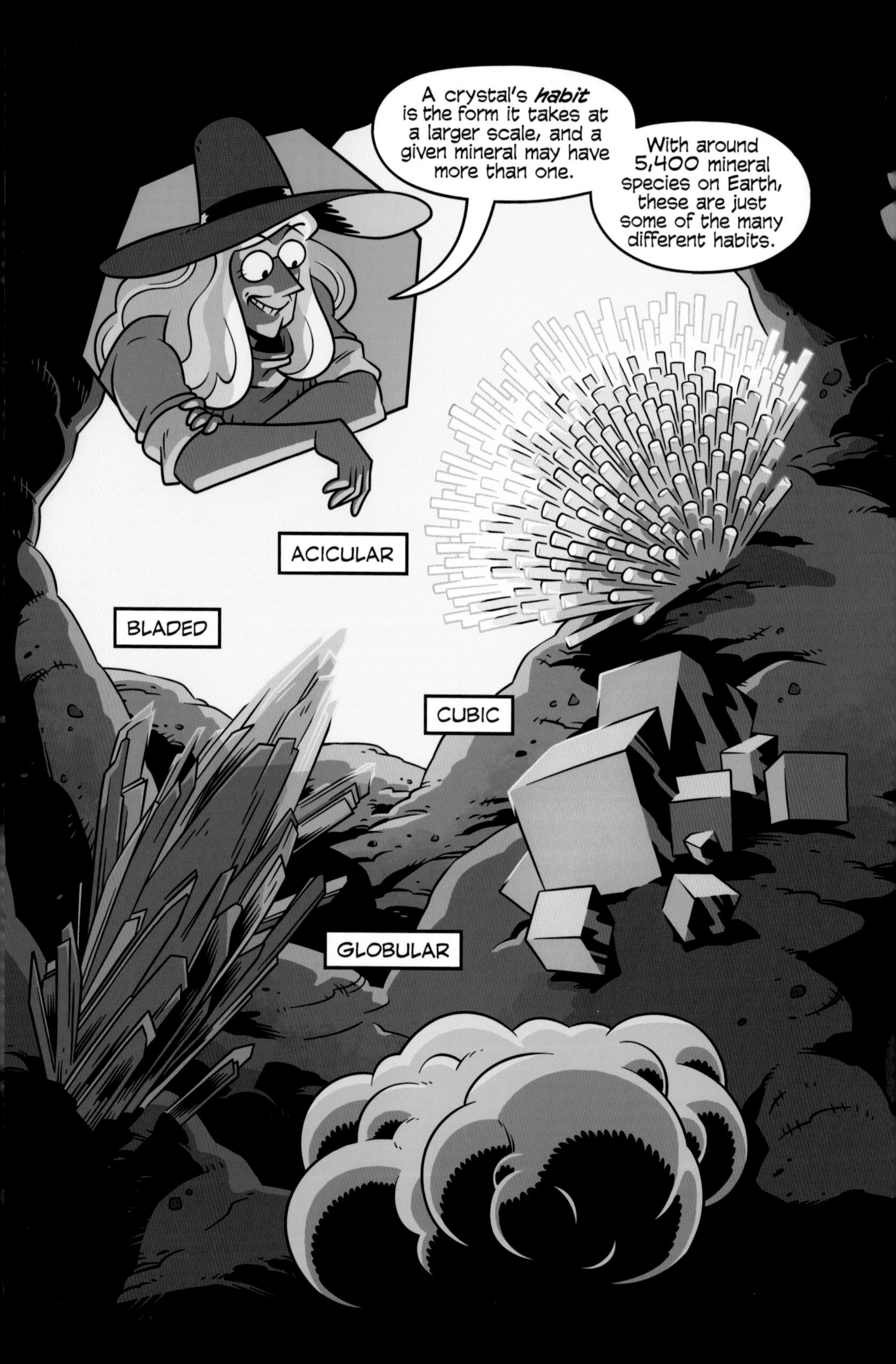

A crystal's *habit* is the form it takes at a larger scale, and a given mineral may have more than one.
With around 5,400 mineral species on Earth, these are just some of the many different habits.
ACICULAR
BLADED
CUBIC
GLOBULAR

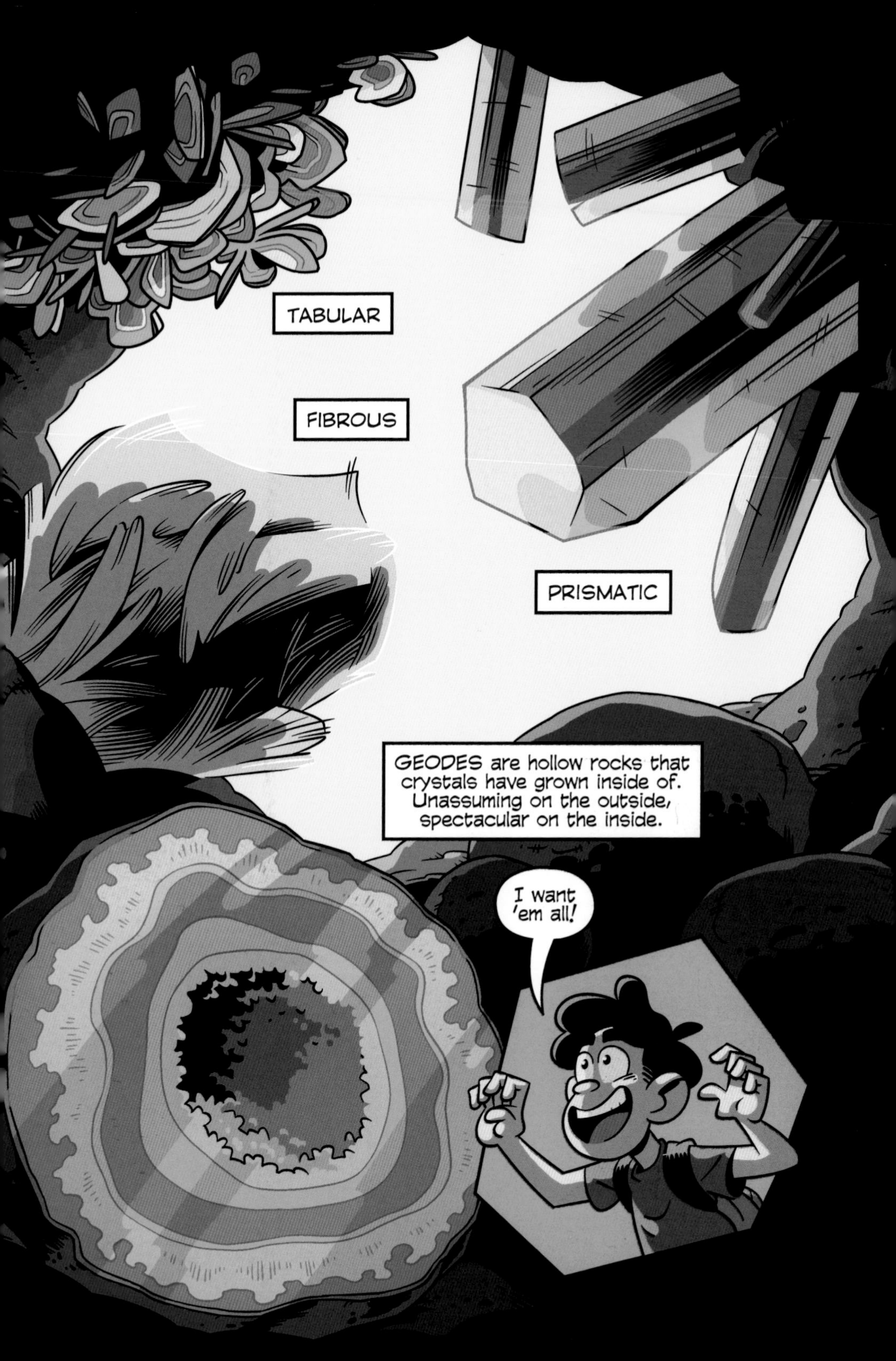
TABULAR
FIBROUS
PRISMATIC
GEODES are hollow rocks that crystals have grown inside of. Unassuming on the outside, spectacular on the inside.
I want 'em all!

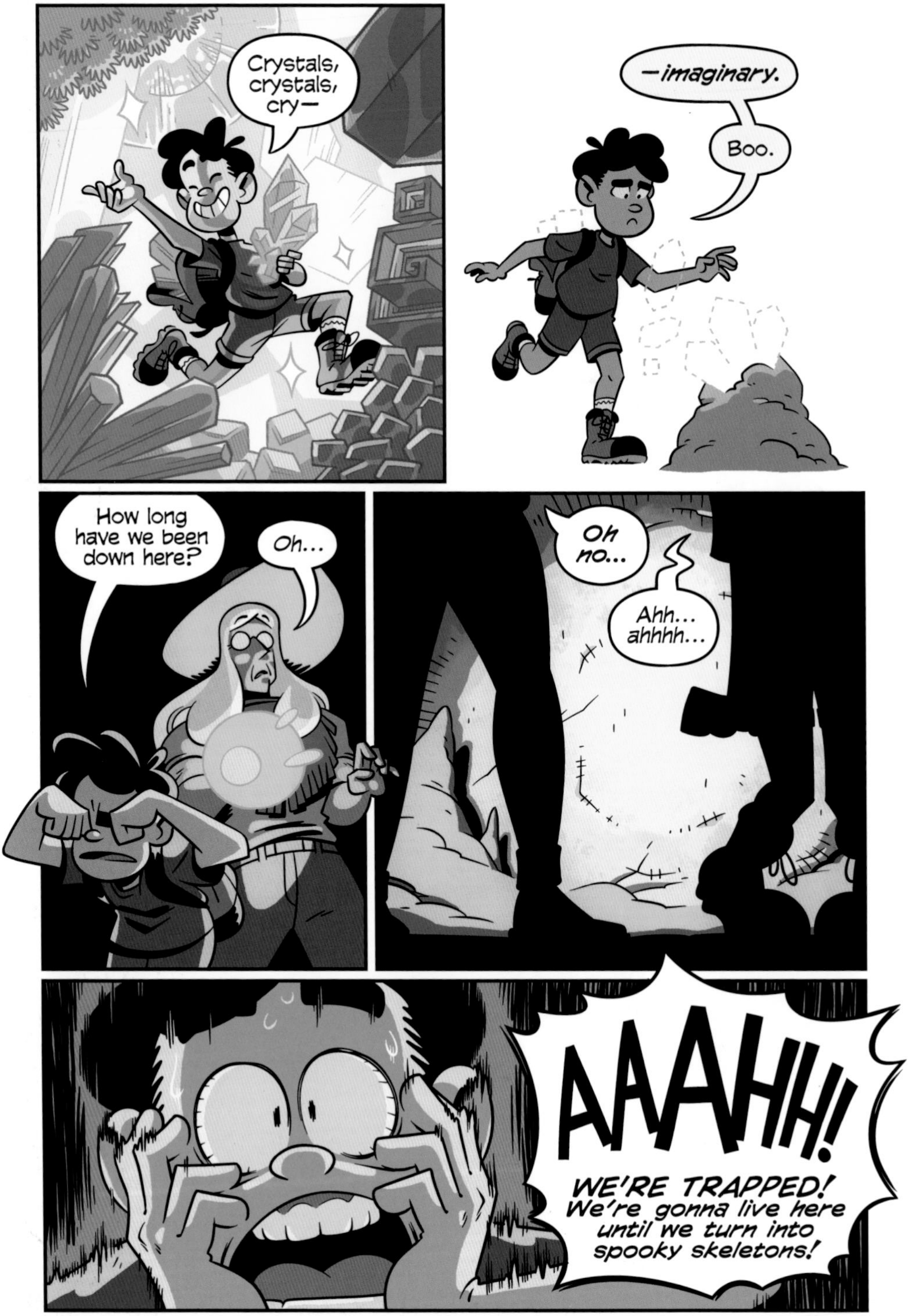
Crystals, crystals, cry—
—imaginary.
Boo.
How long have we been down here?
Oh...
Oh no...
Ahh... ahhhh...
AAAHH!
WE'RE TRAPPED! We're gonna live here until we turn into spooky skeletons!

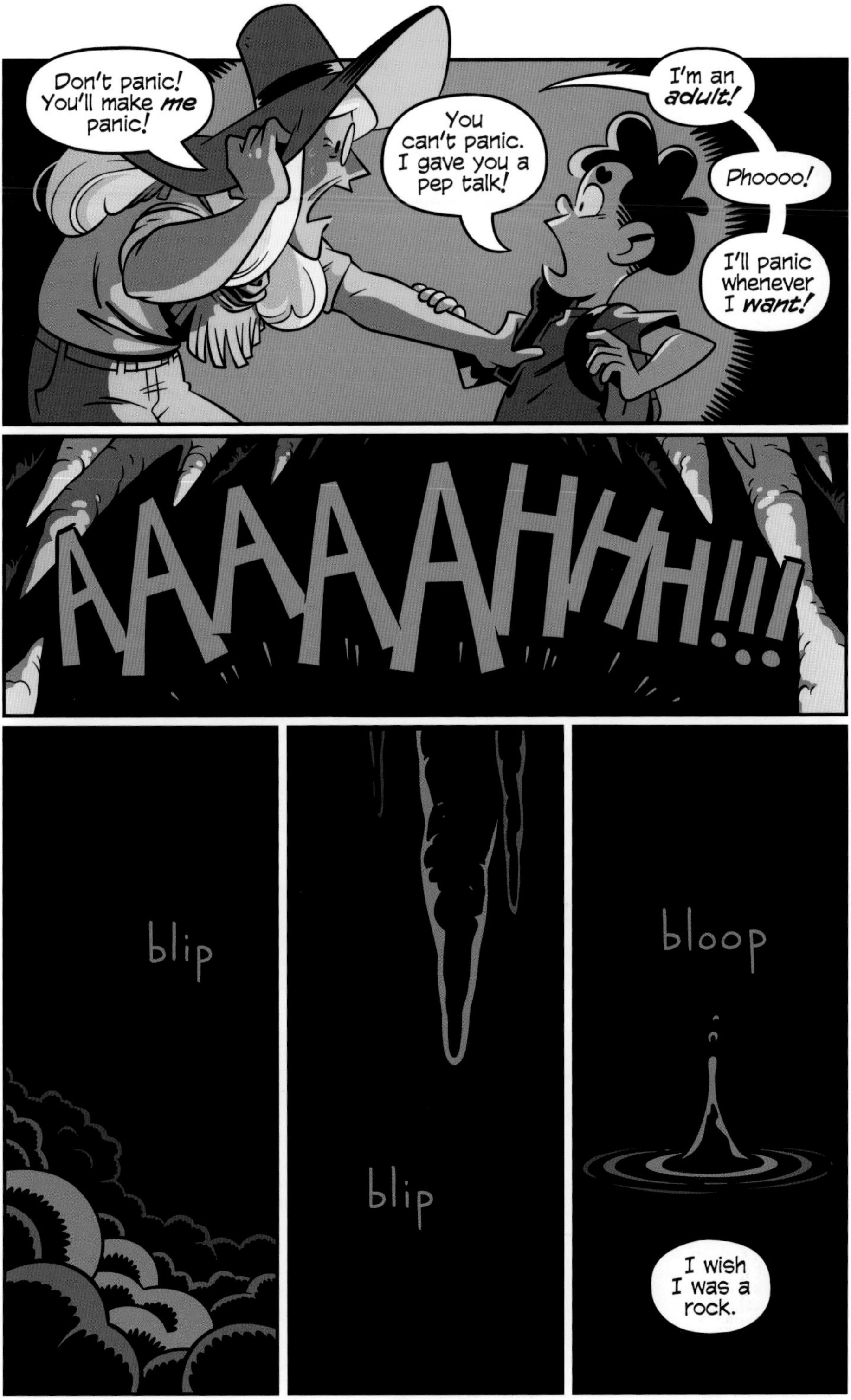
Don't panic! You'll make *me* panic!
You can't panic. I gave you a pep talk!
I'm an *adult!*
Phoooo!
I'll panic whenever I *want!*
AAAAAAHHH!!!
blip
blip
bloop
I wish I was a rock.

Rocks don't mind being underground. I bet they love it. Can't get enough.

They're probably all, "Cool, cool, I'll just hang out down here. Being a rock."

You know rock shifts at the surface, and you know it churns in the mantle. You don't know about what goes on in between there, though, do you?

Tell me. Anything to distract from our impending skeletonization.

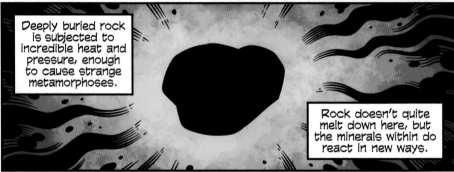

Deeply buried rock is subjected to incredible heat and pressure, enough to cause strange metamorphoses.

Rock doesn't quite melt down here, but the minerals within do react in new ways.

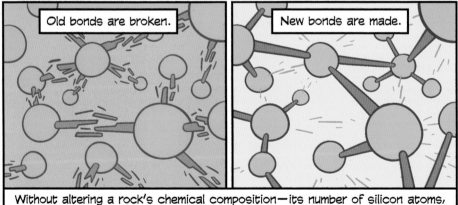

Old bonds are broken.

New bonds are made.

Without altering a rock's chemical composition—its number of silicon atoms, magnesium atoms, and so on—its mineral composition can change entirely.

The igneous and sedimentary rocks that were buried are gone; they've become *metamorphic rocks.*

The same initial rock will form different minerals depending on what depth and temperature it reaches, and the presence of certain minerals gives clues to these conditions.

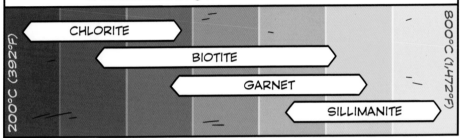

200°C (392°F)

CHLORITE

BIOTITE

GARNET

SILLIMANITE

800°C (1,472°F)

Burial metamorphism can occur over multiple stages. For example, mudstone becomes slate, then schist, and then gneiss as it's buried deeper and deeper.

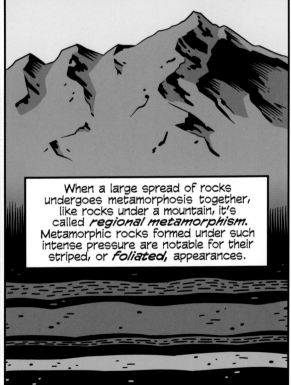

When a large spread of rocks undergoes metamorphosis together, like rocks under a mountain, it's called *regional metamorphism.* Metamorphic rocks formed under such intense pressure are notable for their striped, or *foliated,* appearances.

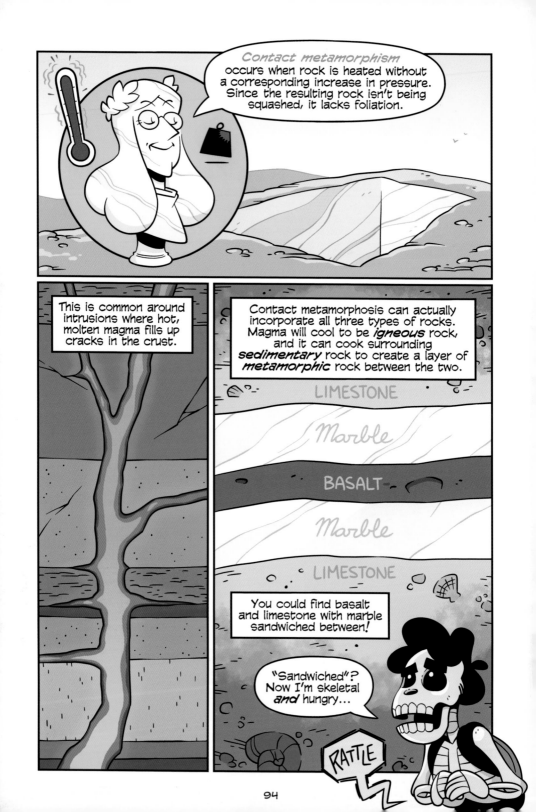

Contact metamorphism occurs when rock is heated without a corresponding increase in pressure. Since the resulting rock isn't being squashed, it lacks foliation.

This is common around intrusions where hot, molten magma fills up cracks in the crust.

Contact metamorphosis can actually incorporate all three types of rocks. Magma will cool to be *igneous* rock, and it can cook surrounding *sedimentary* rock to create a layer of *metamorphic* rock between the two.

LIMESTONE

Marble

BASALT

Marble

LIMESTONE

You could find basalt and limestone with marble sandwiched between!

"Sandwiched"? Now I'm skeletal *and* hungry...

RATTLE

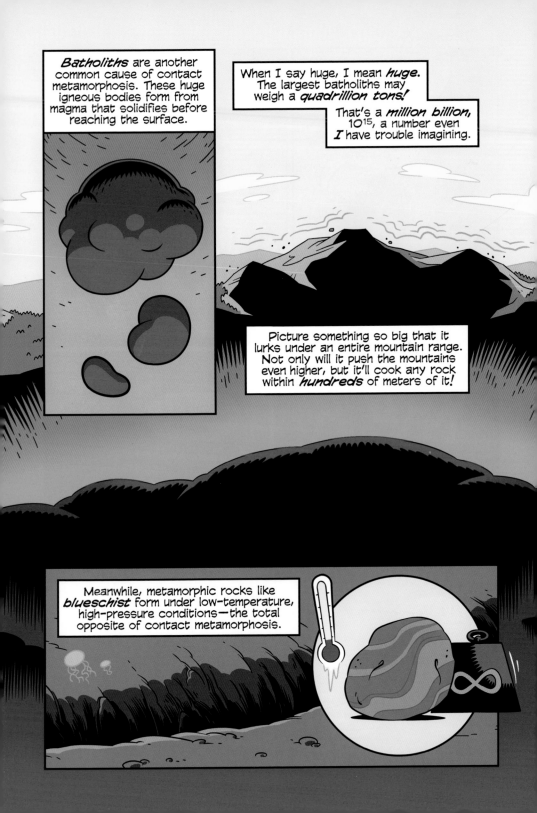

Batholiths are another common cause of contact metamorphosis. These huge igneous bodies form from magma that solidifies before reaching the surface.

When I say huge, I mean *huge*. The largest batholiths may weigh a *quadrillion tons!*

That's a *million billion*, 10^{15}, a number even *I* have trouble imagining.

Picture something so big that it lurks under an entire mountain range. Not only will it push the mountains even higher, but it'll cook any rock within *hundreds* of meters of it!

Meanwhile, metamorphic rocks like *blueschist* form under low-temperature, high-pressure conditions—the total opposite of contact metamorphosis.

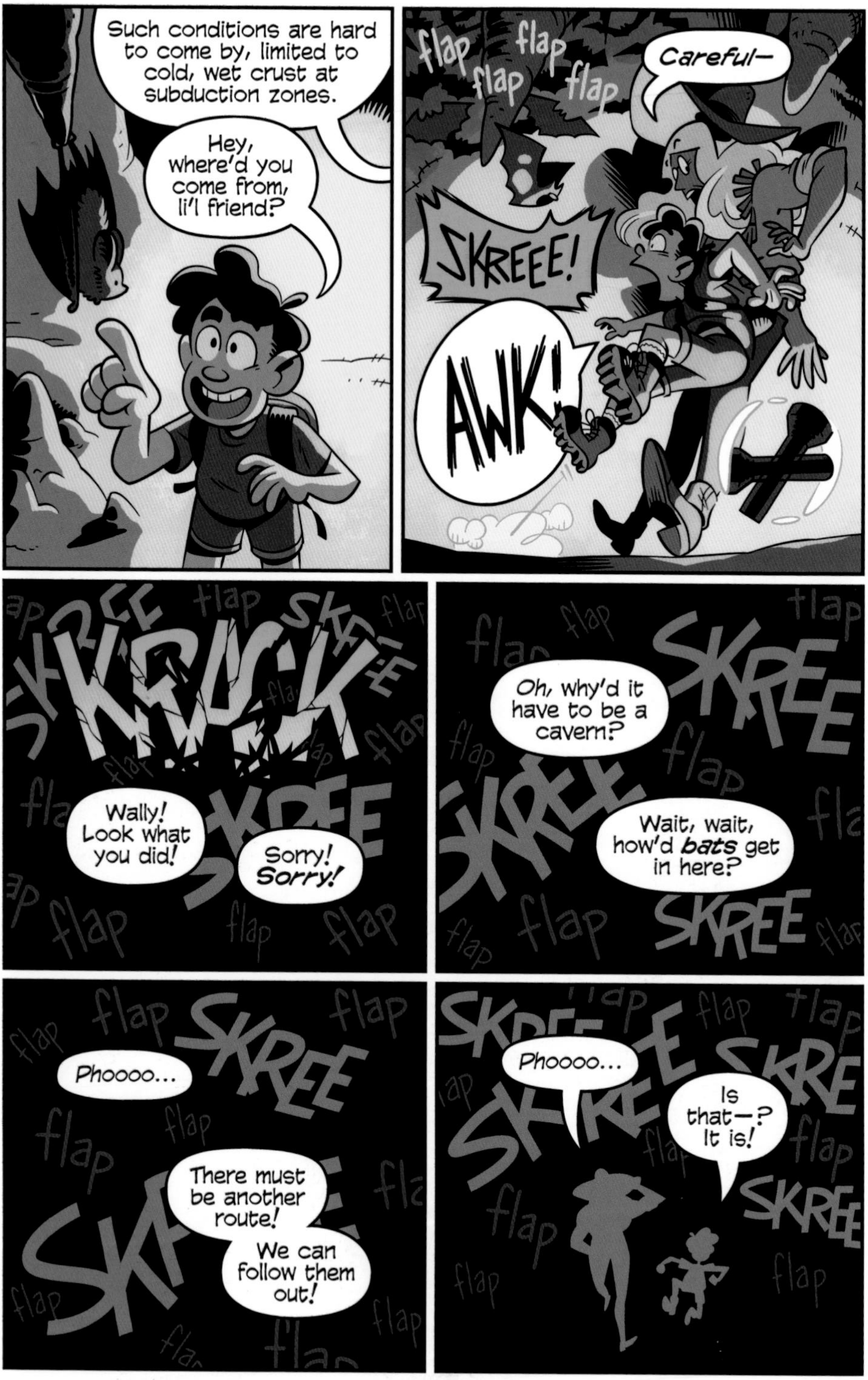
Such conditions are hard to come by, limited to cold, wet crust at subduction zones.
Hey, where'd you come from, li'l friend?
flap flap flap flap
Careful—
SKREEE!
AWK!
KRUCK
SKREE
flap
Wally! Look what you did!
Sorry! *Sorry!*
SKREE
flap
Oh, why'd it have to be a cavern?
Wait, wait, how'd *bats* get in here?
SKREE
flap
Phoooo...
There must be another route!
We can follow them out!
SKREE
Phoooo...
Is that—? It is!
flap

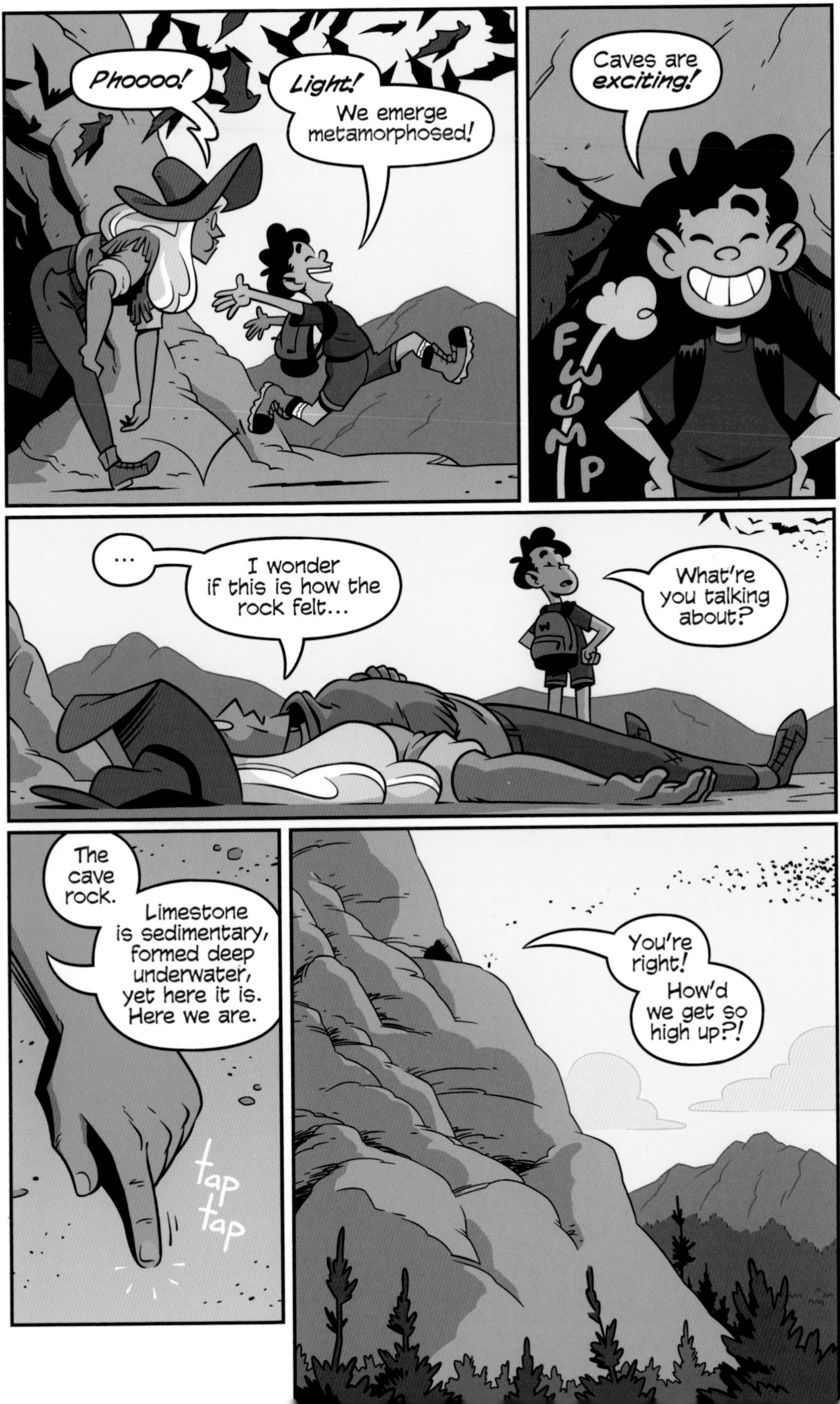

Phoooo!
Light! We emerge metamorphosed!
Caves are exciting!
FWUMP
...
I wonder if this is how the rock felt...
What're you talking about?
The cave rock.
Limestone is sedimentary, formed deep underwater, yet here it is. Here we are.
tap tap
You're right! How'd we get so high up?!

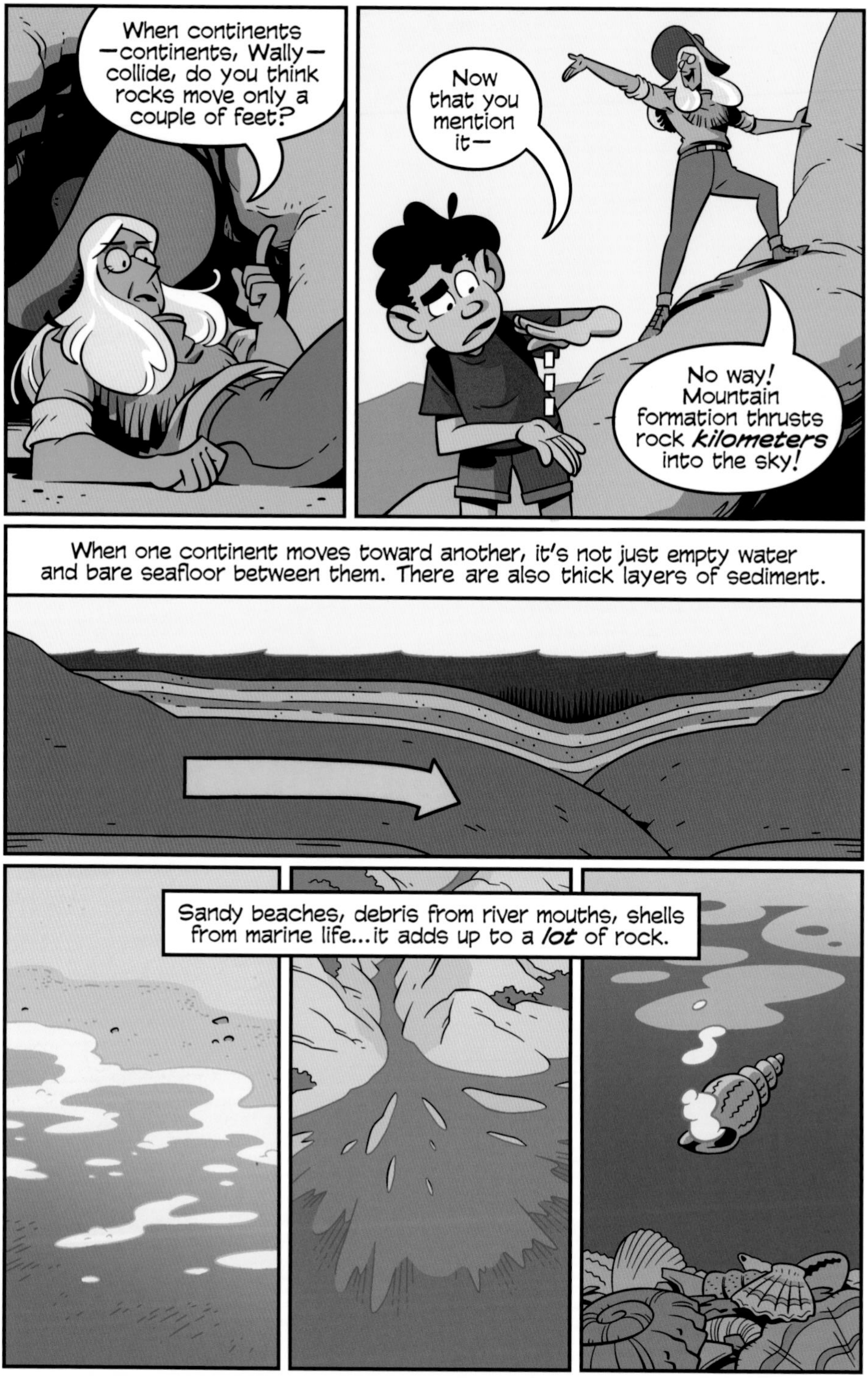
When continents —continents, Wally— collide, do you think rocks move only a couple of feet?
Now that you mention it—
No way! Mountain formation thrusts rock *kilometers* into the sky!
When one continent moves toward another, it's not just empty water and bare seafloor between them. There are also thick layers of sediment.
Sandy beaches, debris from river mouths, shells from marine life...it adds up to a *lot* of rock.

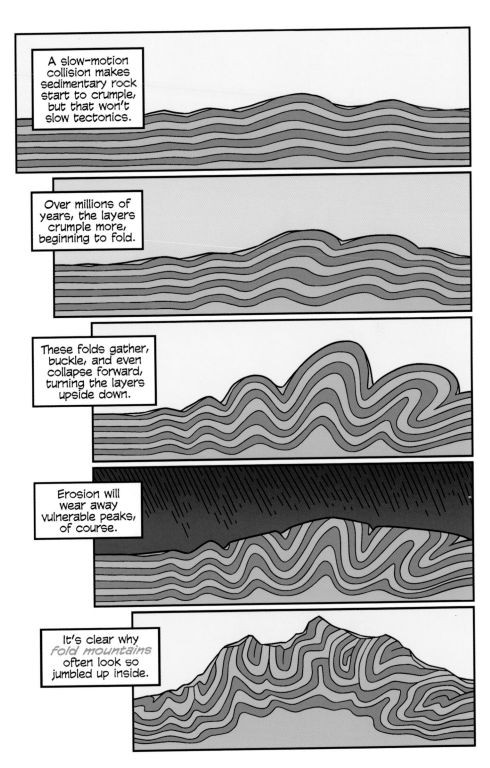

A slow-motion collision makes sedimentary rock start to crumple, but that won't slow tectonics.

Over millions of years, the layers crumple more, beginning to fold.

These folds gather, buckle, and even collapse forward, turning the layers upside down.

Erosion will wear away vulnerable peaks, of course.

It's clear why *fold mountains* often look so jumbled up inside.

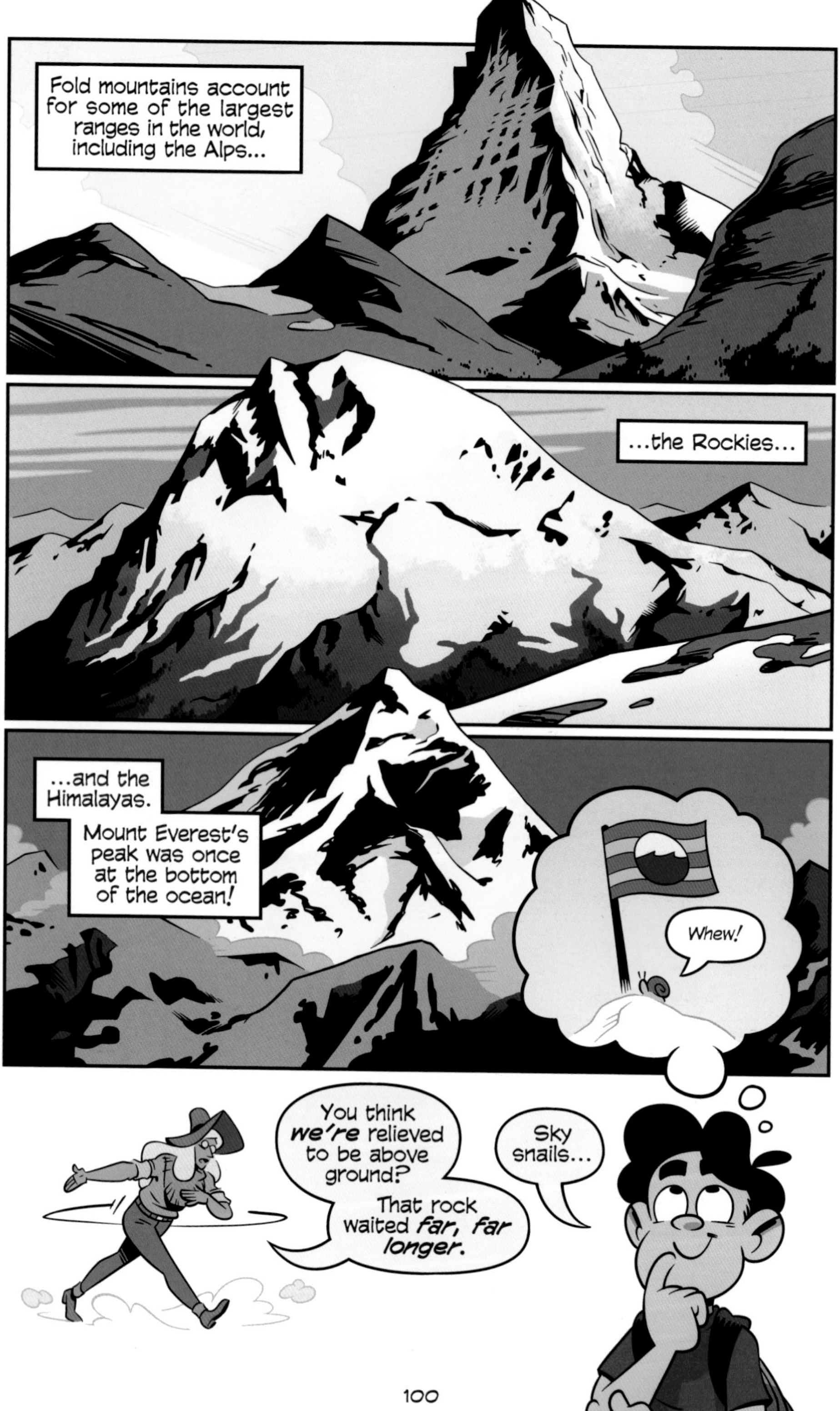
Fold mountains account for some of the largest ranges in the world, including the Alps...
...the Rockies...
...and the Himalayas.
Mount Everest's peak was once at the bottom of the ocean!
Whew!
You think *we're* relieved to be above ground?
That rock waited *far, far longer.*
Sky snails...

Some mountains aren't pushed up so much as tipped over.

When plates pull apart, extended crust breaks into irregularly shaped blocks.

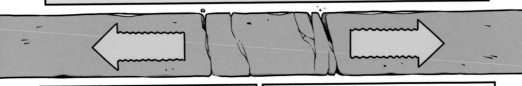

A perfectly squared-off block would balance nicely, of course.

But because of their awkward shapes, these blocks fall to one side.

EEP!

Sediment gathers on the low side, pushing it deeper to form *basins*.

The mantle swells to fill in the other side, pushing it higher to form *ranges*.

These mountains are long parallel stripes across Earth's surface.

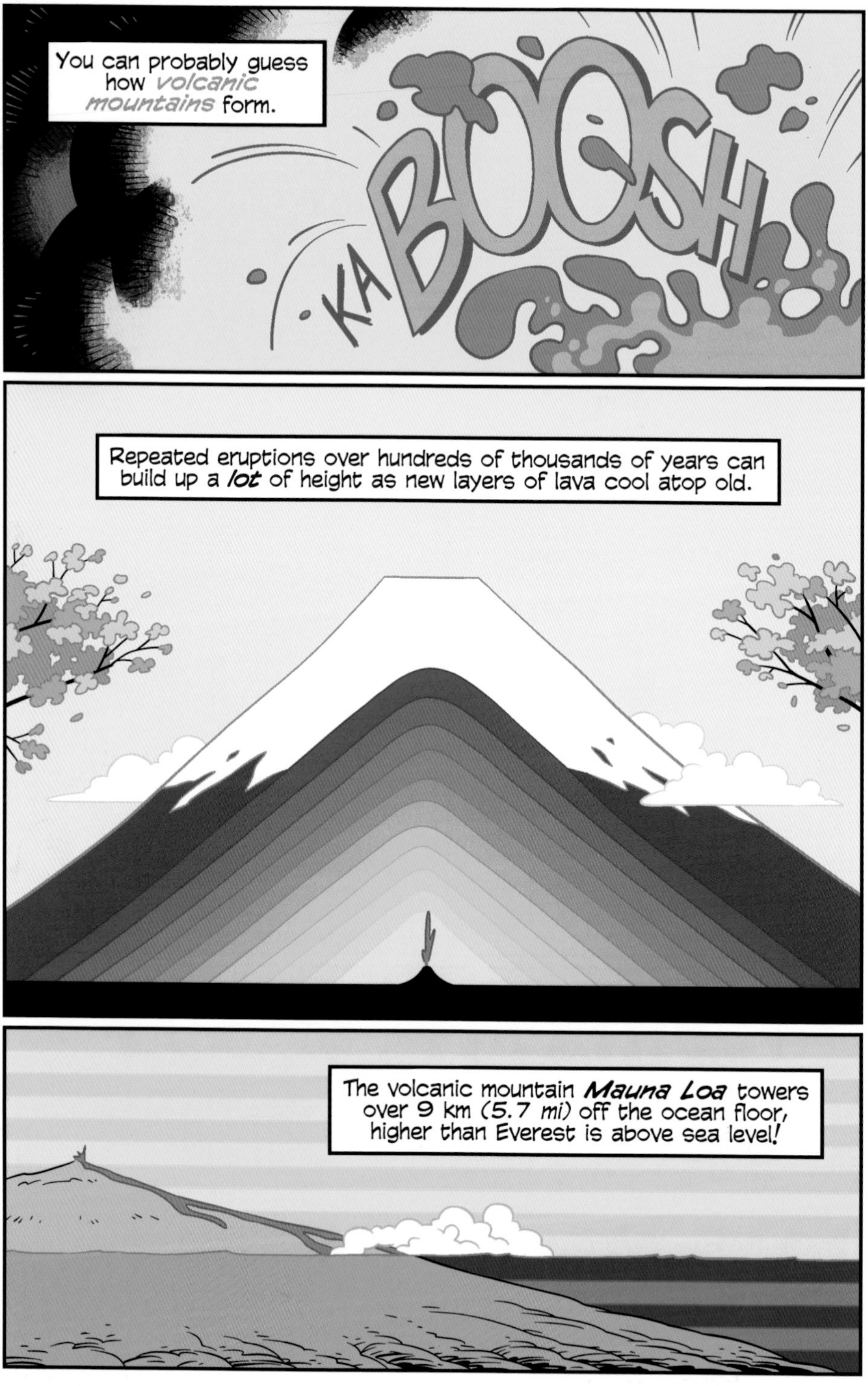

You can probably guess how volcanic mountains form.
KABOOSH
Repeated eruptions over hundreds of thousands of years can build up a *lot* of height as new layers of lava cool atop old.
The volcanic mountain ***Mauna Loa*** towers over 9 km (*5.7 mi*) off the ocean floor, higher than Everest is above sea level!

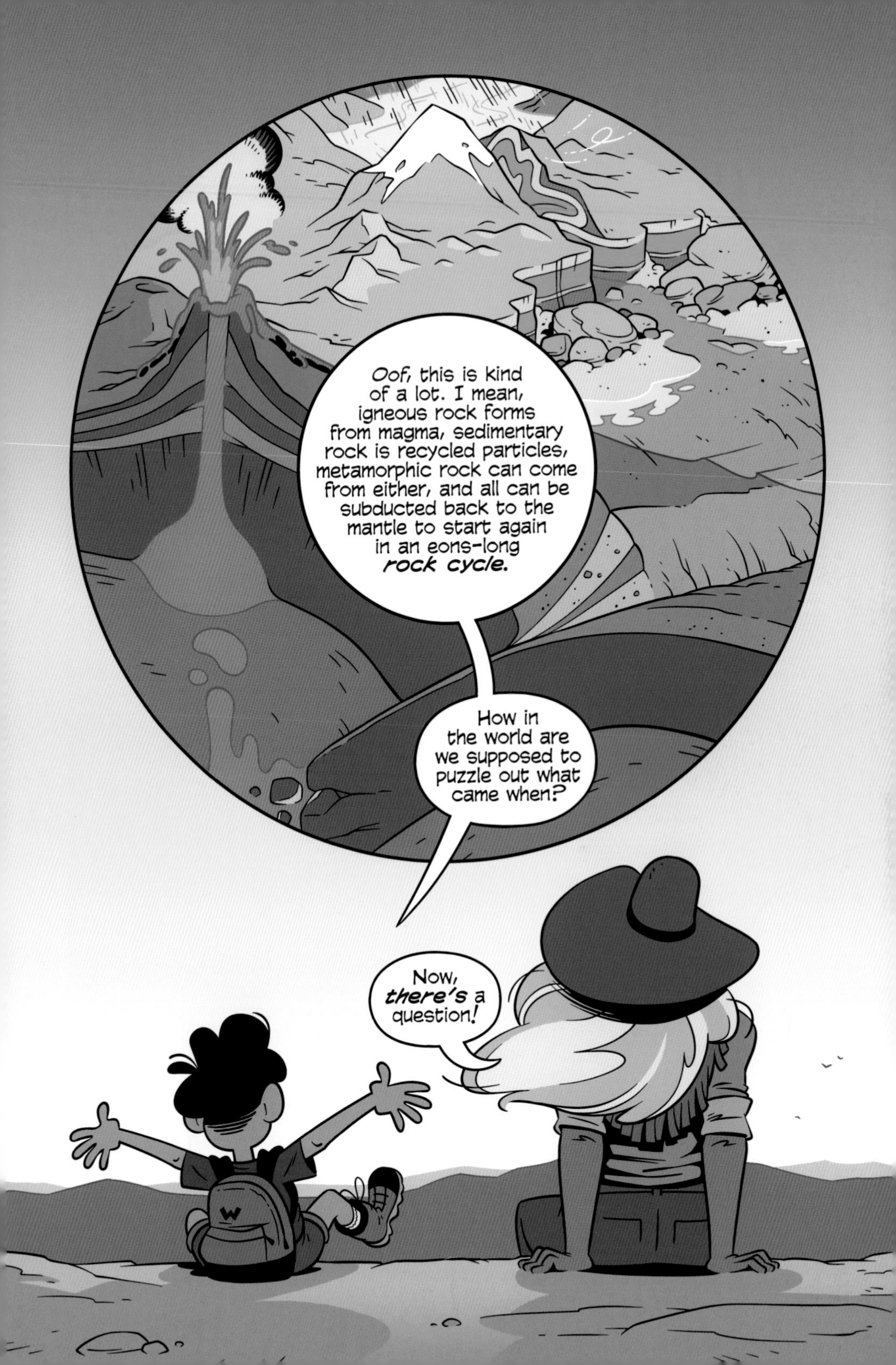
Oof, this is kind of a lot. I mean, igneous rock forms from magma, sedimentary rock is recycled particles, metamorphic rock can come from either, and all can be subducted back to the mantle to start again in an eons-long ***rock cycle.***
How in the world are we supposed to puzzle out what came when?
Now, ***there's*** a question!

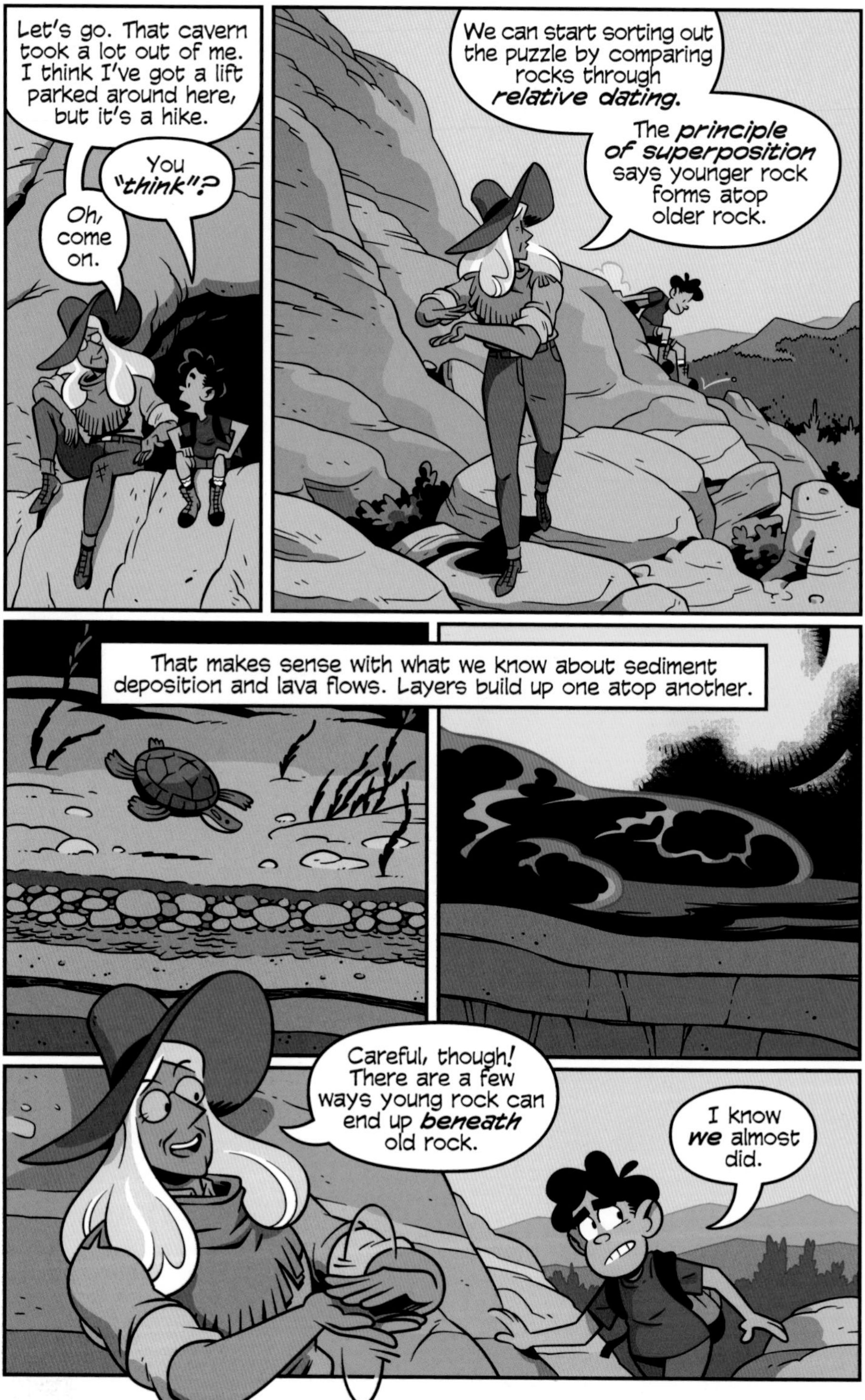

Let's go. That cavern took a lot out of me. I think I've got a lift parked around here, but it's a hike.
You "think"?
Oh, come on.
We can start sorting out the puzzle by comparing rocks through relative dating.
The principle of superposition says younger rock forms atop older rock.
That makes sense with what we know about sediment deposition and lava flows. Layers build up one atop another.
Careful, though! There are a few ways young rock can end up beneath old rock.
I know we almost did.

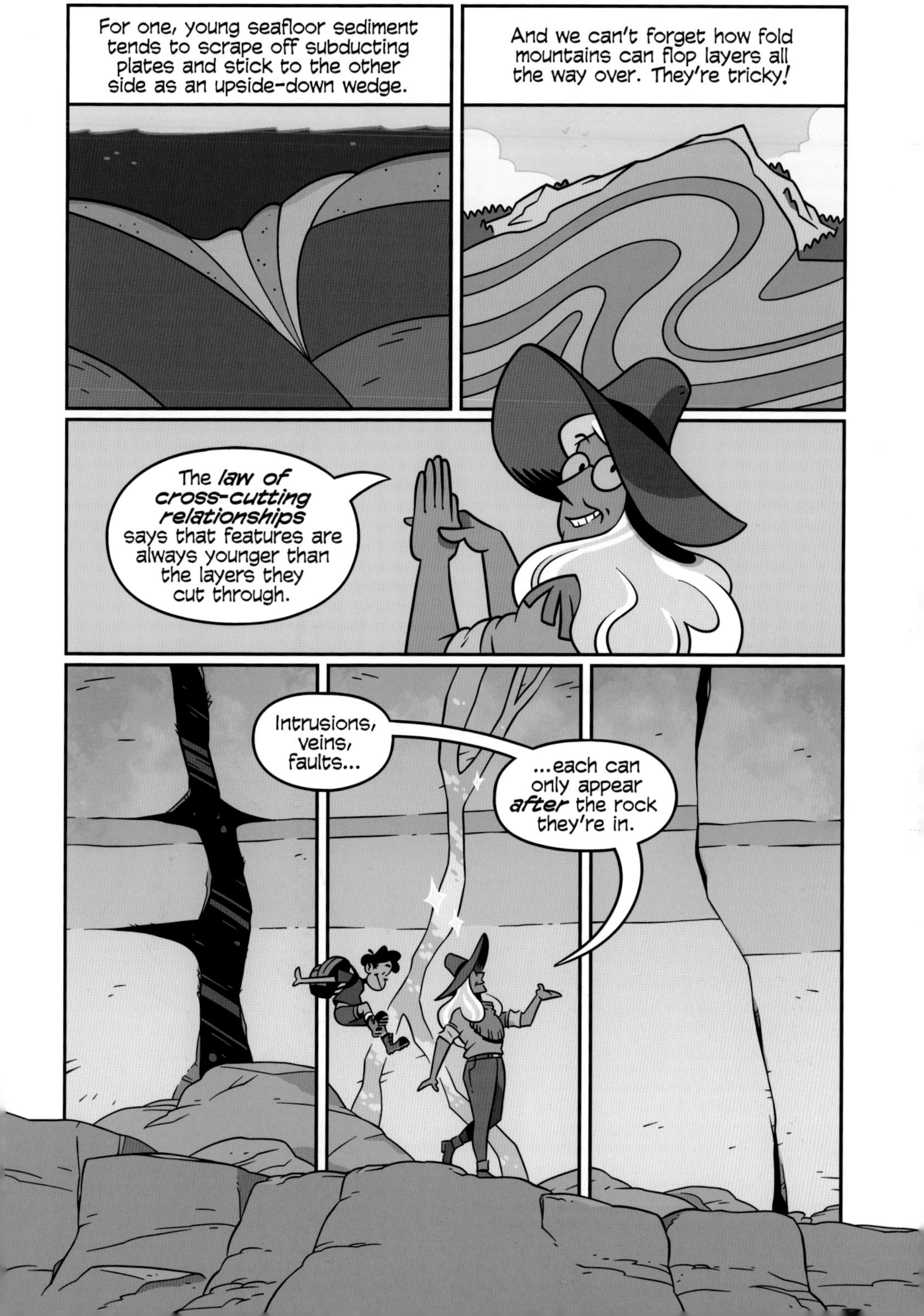
For one, young seafloor sediment tends to scrape off subducting plates and stick to the other side as an upside-down wedge.
And we can't forget how fold mountains can flop layers all the way over. They're tricky!
The *law of cross-cutting relationships* says that features are always younger than the layers they cut through.
Intrusions, veins, faults...
...each can only appear *after* the rock they're in.

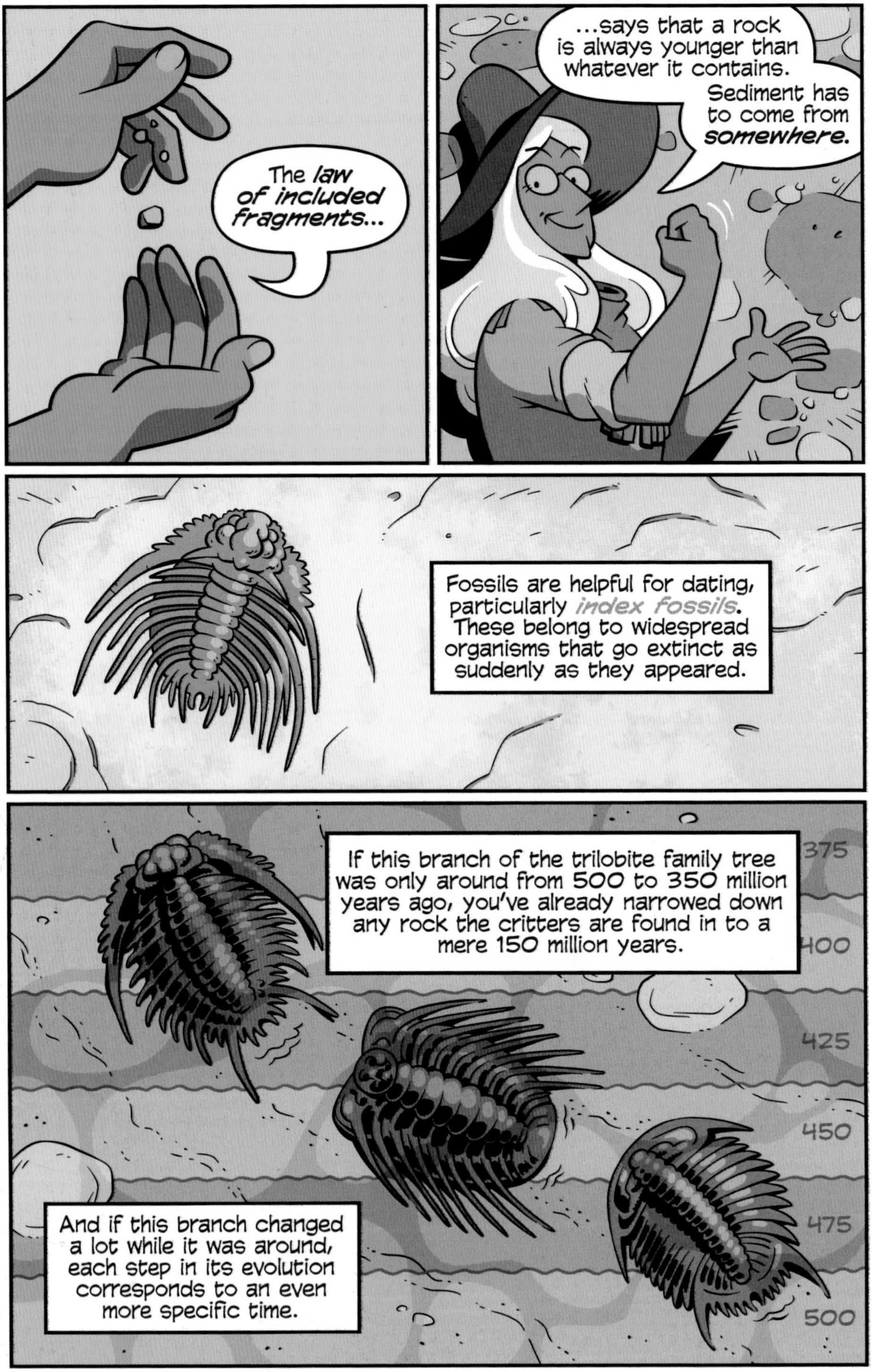
The *law of included fragments...*
...says that a rock is always younger than whatever it contains.
Sediment has to come from ***somewhere.***
Fossils are helpful for dating, particularly *index fossils*. These belong to widespread organisms that go extinct as suddenly as they appeared.
If this branch of the trilobite family tree was only around from 500 to 350 million years ago, you've already narrowed down any rock the critters are found in to a mere 150 million years.
375
400
425
450
475
500
And if this branch changed a lot while it was around, each step in its evolution corresponds to an even more specific time.

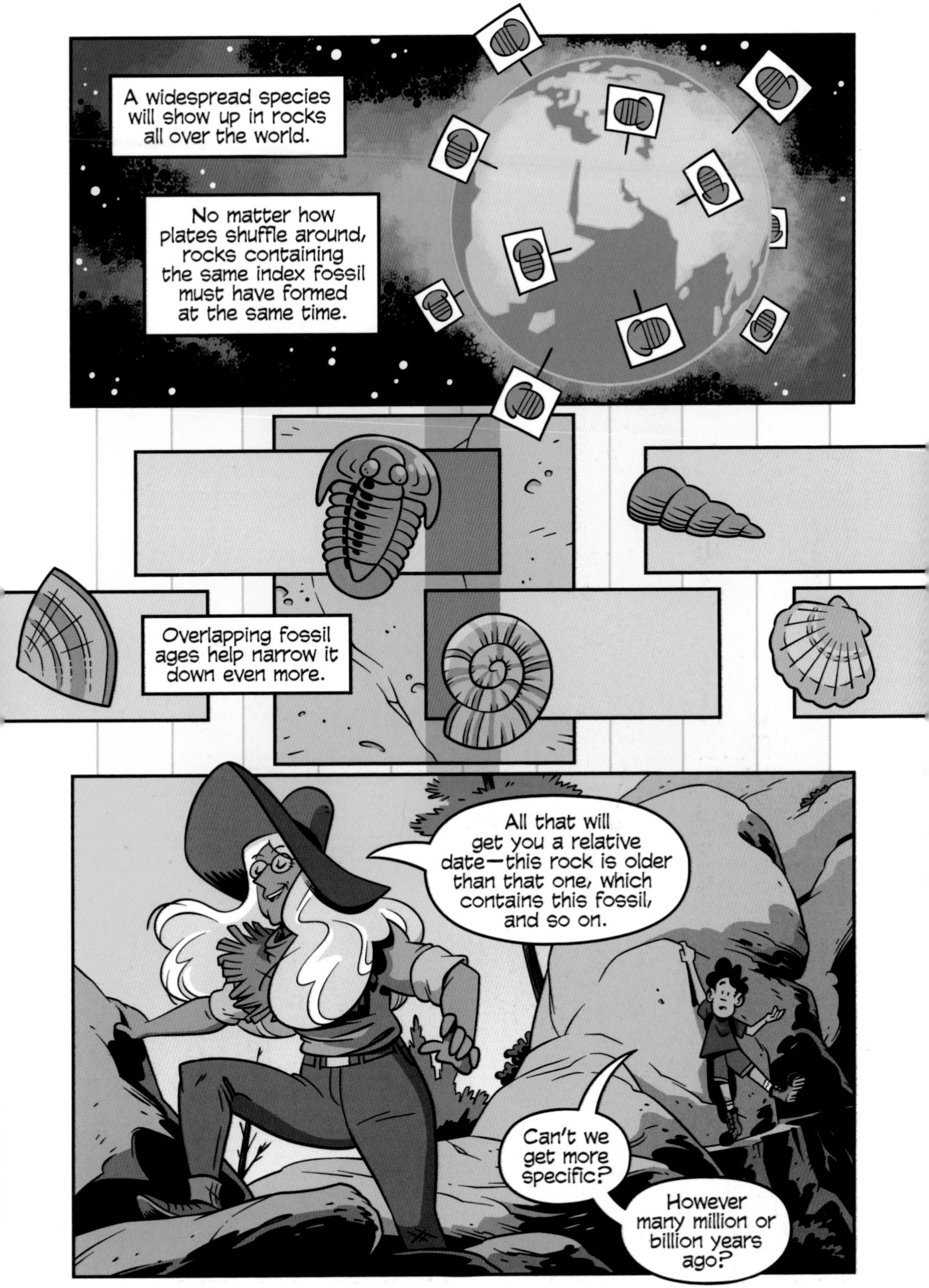
A widespread species will show up in rocks all over the world.
No matter how plates shuffle around, rocks containing the same index fossil must have formed at the same time.
Overlapping fossil ages help narrow it down even more.
All that will get you a relative date—this rock is older than that one, which contains this fossil, and so on.
Can't we get more specific?
However many million or billion years ago?

For that, we'll have to go way back and zoom all the way into a rock's atoms. Atoms of two elements in particular, *uranium* and *lead*.

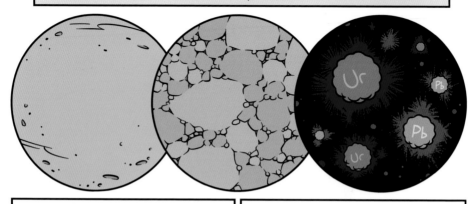

Uranium is radioactive. It turns some of its mass into energy!

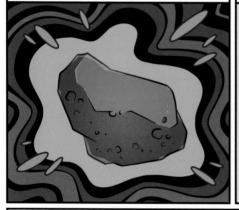

This one-way process leaves uranium atoms as tired, inert lead atoms.

We know how fast this transformation takes place, so we can measure the *tiny* amount of each element in a sample to discover how old it is.

This adds up to... 126%? That can't be right...

That wouldn't do us much good if we didn't know how much of each the sample started with, of course.

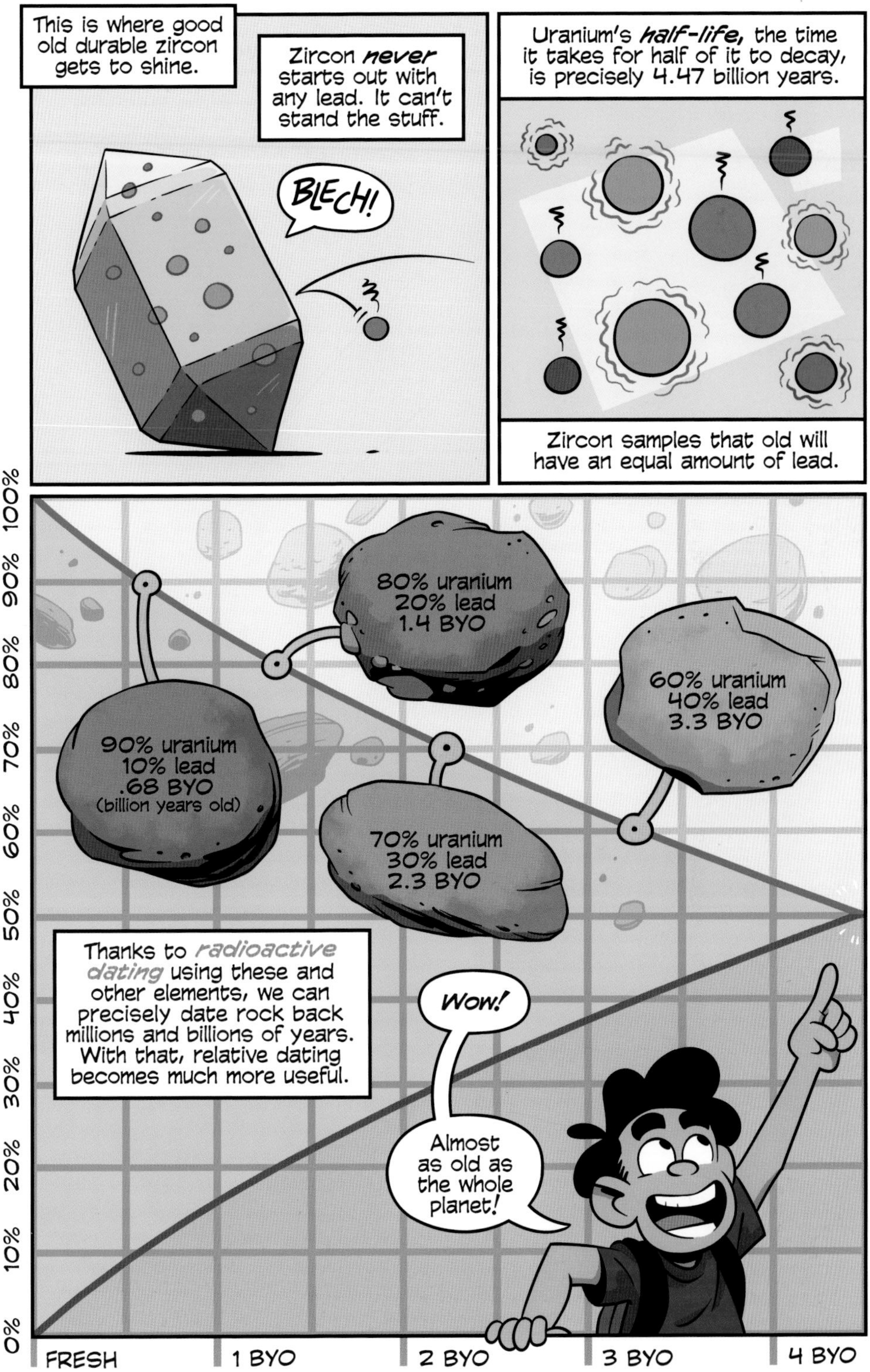
This is where good old durable zircon gets to shine.
Zircon never starts out with any lead. It can't stand the stuff.
BLECH!
Uranium's half-life, the time it takes for half of it to decay, is precisely 4.47 billion years.
Zircon samples that old will have an equal amount of lead.
100%
90%
80%
70%
60%
50%
40%
30%
20%
10%
0%
80% uranium 20% lead 1.4 BYO
60% uranium 40% lead 3.3 BYO
90% uranium 10% lead .68 BYO (billion years old)
70% uranium 30% lead 2.3 BYO
Thanks to radioactive dating using these and other elements, we can precisely date rock back millions and billions of years. With that, relative dating becomes much more useful.
WOW!
Almost as old as the whole planet!
FRESH
1 BYO
2 BYO
3 BYO
4 BYO

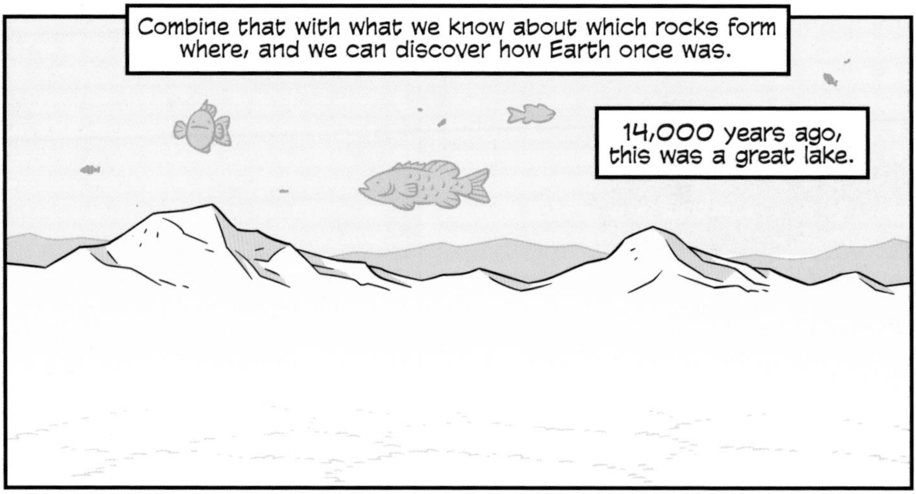
Combine that with what we know about which rocks form where, and we can discover how Earth once was.
14,000 years ago, this was a great lake.

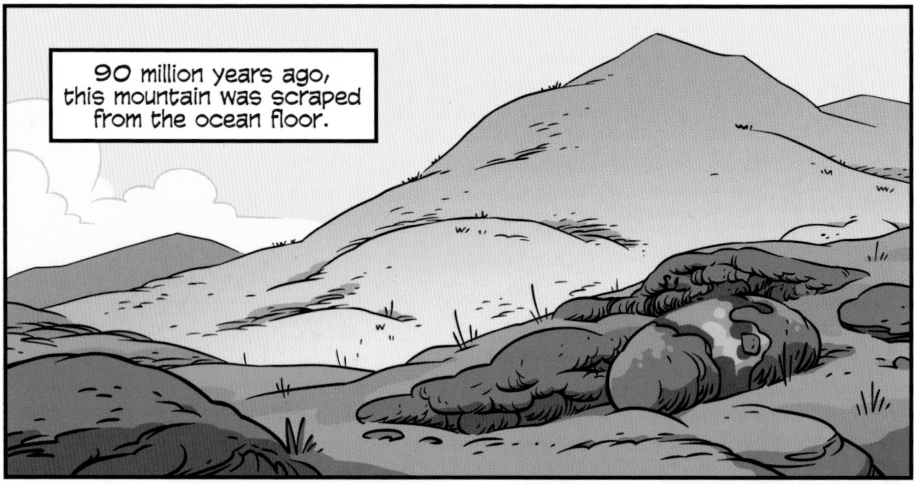
90 million years ago, this mountain was scraped from the ocean floor.

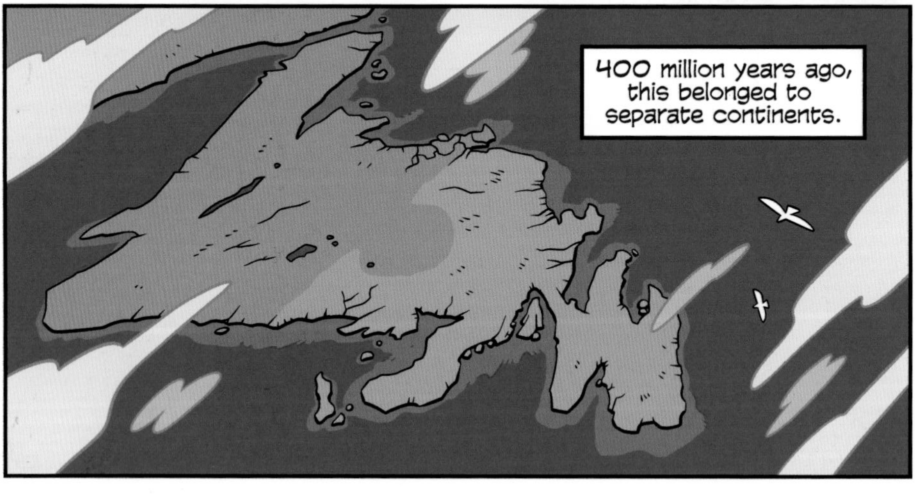
400 million years ago, this belonged to separate continents.

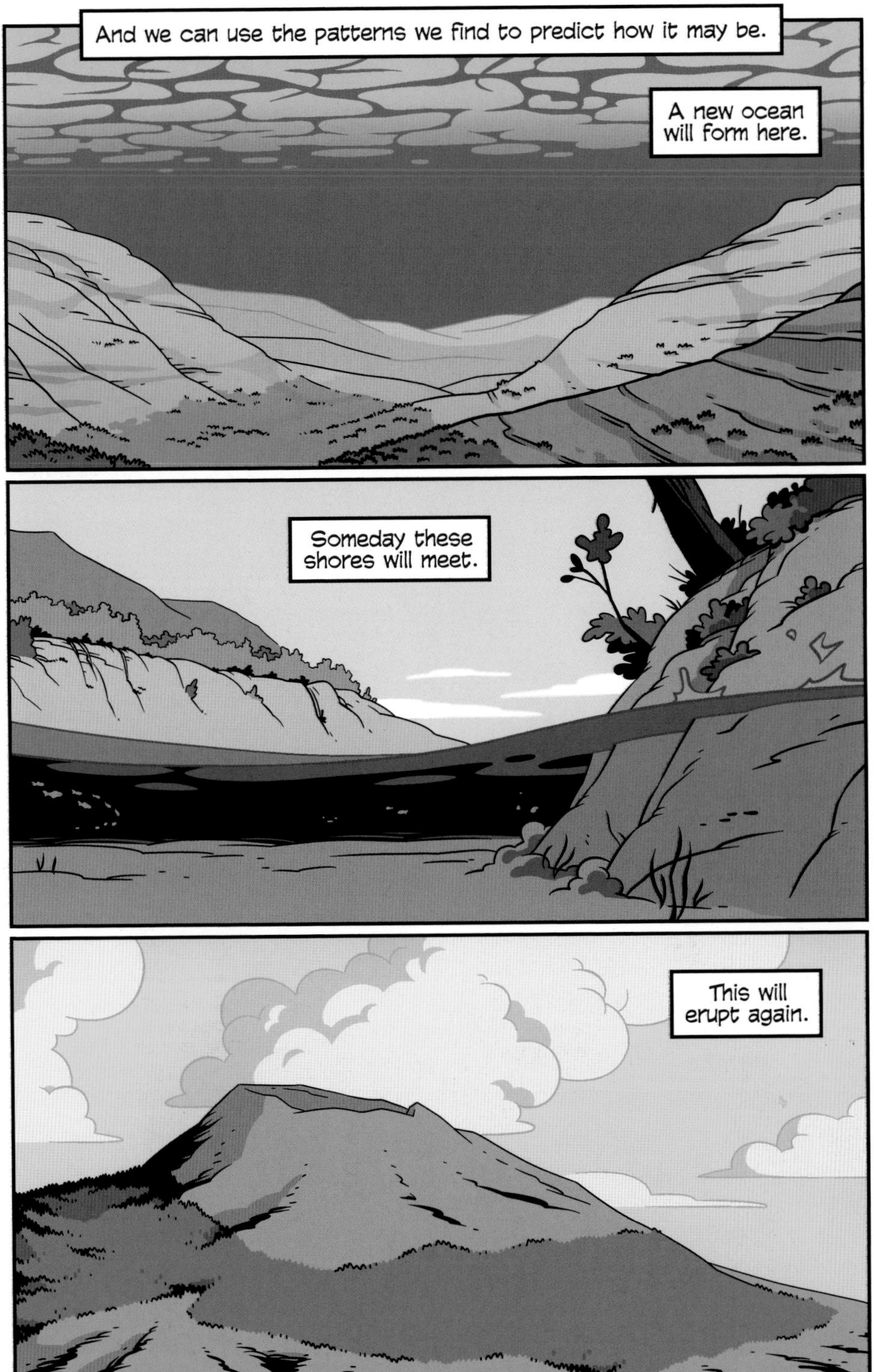
And we can use the patterns we find to predict how it may be.
A new ocean will form here.
Someday these shores will meet.
This will erupt again.

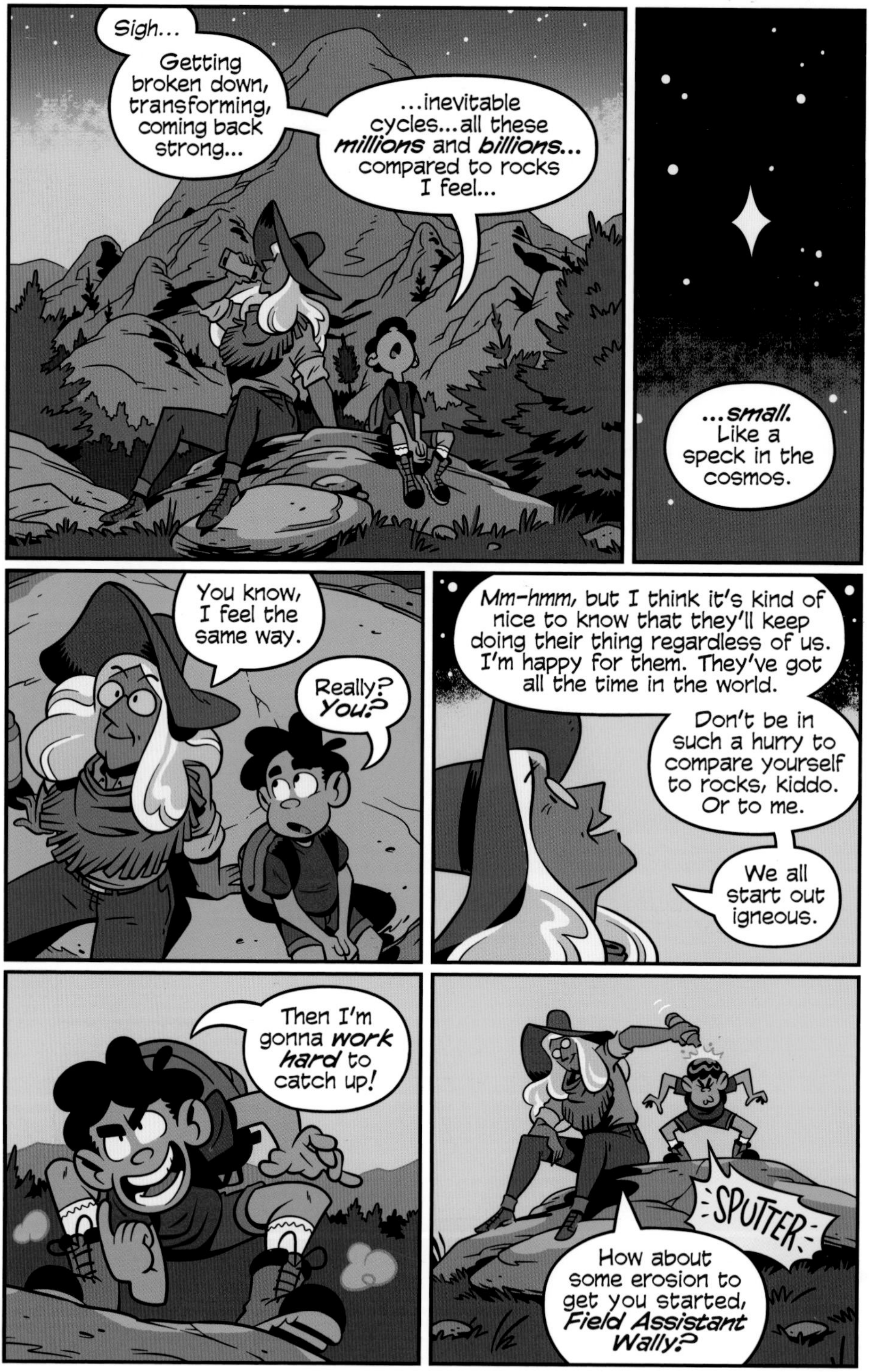

Sigh...
Getting broken down, transforming, coming back strong...
...inevitable cycles...all these *millions* and *billions*... compared to rocks I feel...
...*small.* Like a speck in the cosmos.
You know, I feel the same way.
Really? *You?*
Mm-hmm, but I think it's kind of nice to know that they'll keep doing their thing regardless of us. I'm happy for them. They've got all the time in the world.
Don't be in such a hurry to compare yourself to rocks, kiddo. Or to me.
We all start out igneous.
Then I'm gonna *work hard* to catch up!
SPUTTER
How about some erosion to get you started, *Field Assistant Wally?*

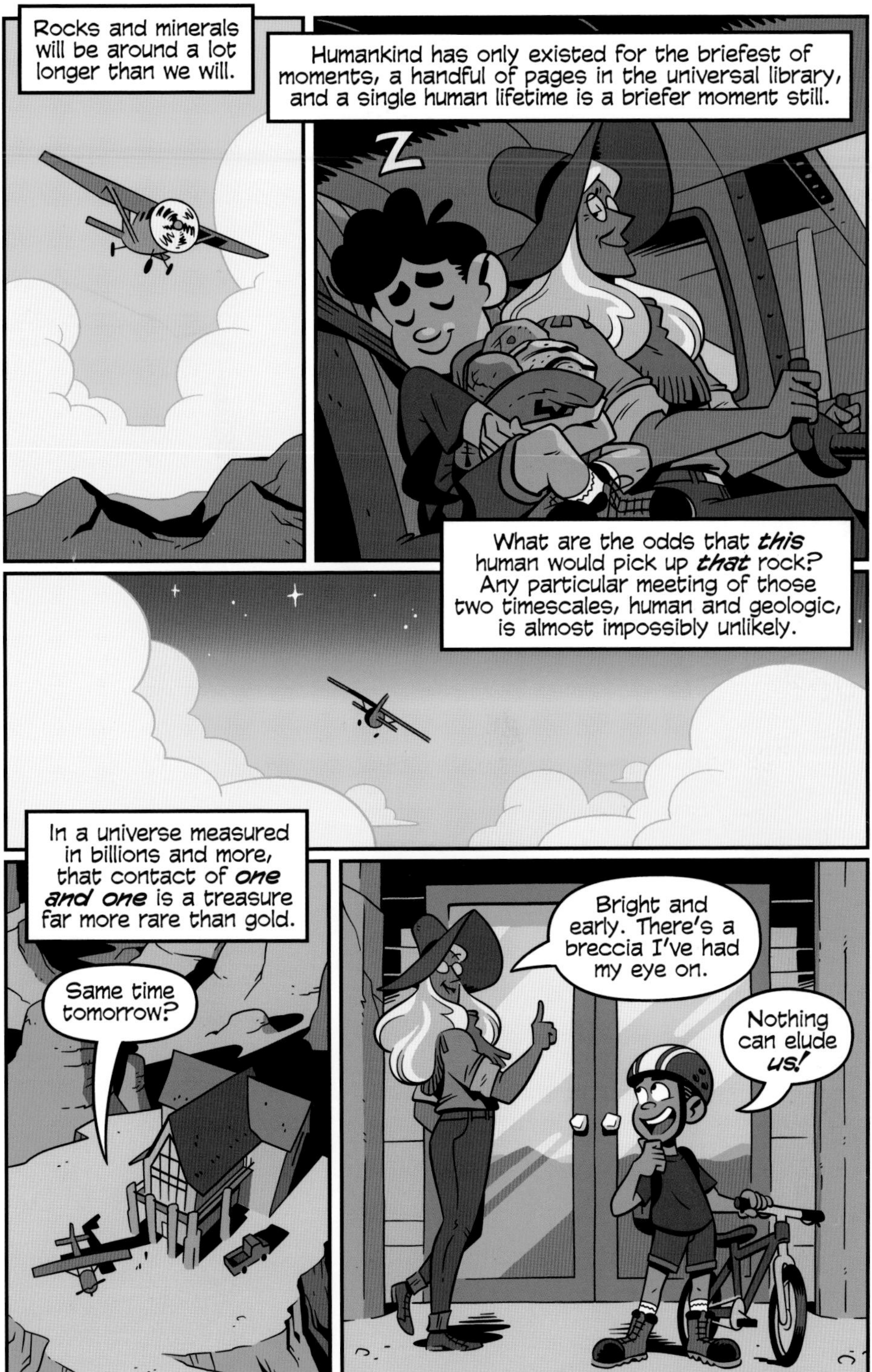

Rocks and minerals will be around a lot longer than we will.
Humankind has only existed for the briefest of moments, a handful of pages in the universal library, and a single human lifetime is a briefer moment still.
Z
What are the odds that *this* human would pick up *that* rock? Any particular meeting of those two timescales, human and geologic, is almost impossibly unlikely.
In a universe measured in billions and more, that contact of *one and one* is a treasure far more rare than gold.
Same time tomorrow?
Bright and early. There's a breccia I've had my eye on.
Nothing can elude *us!*

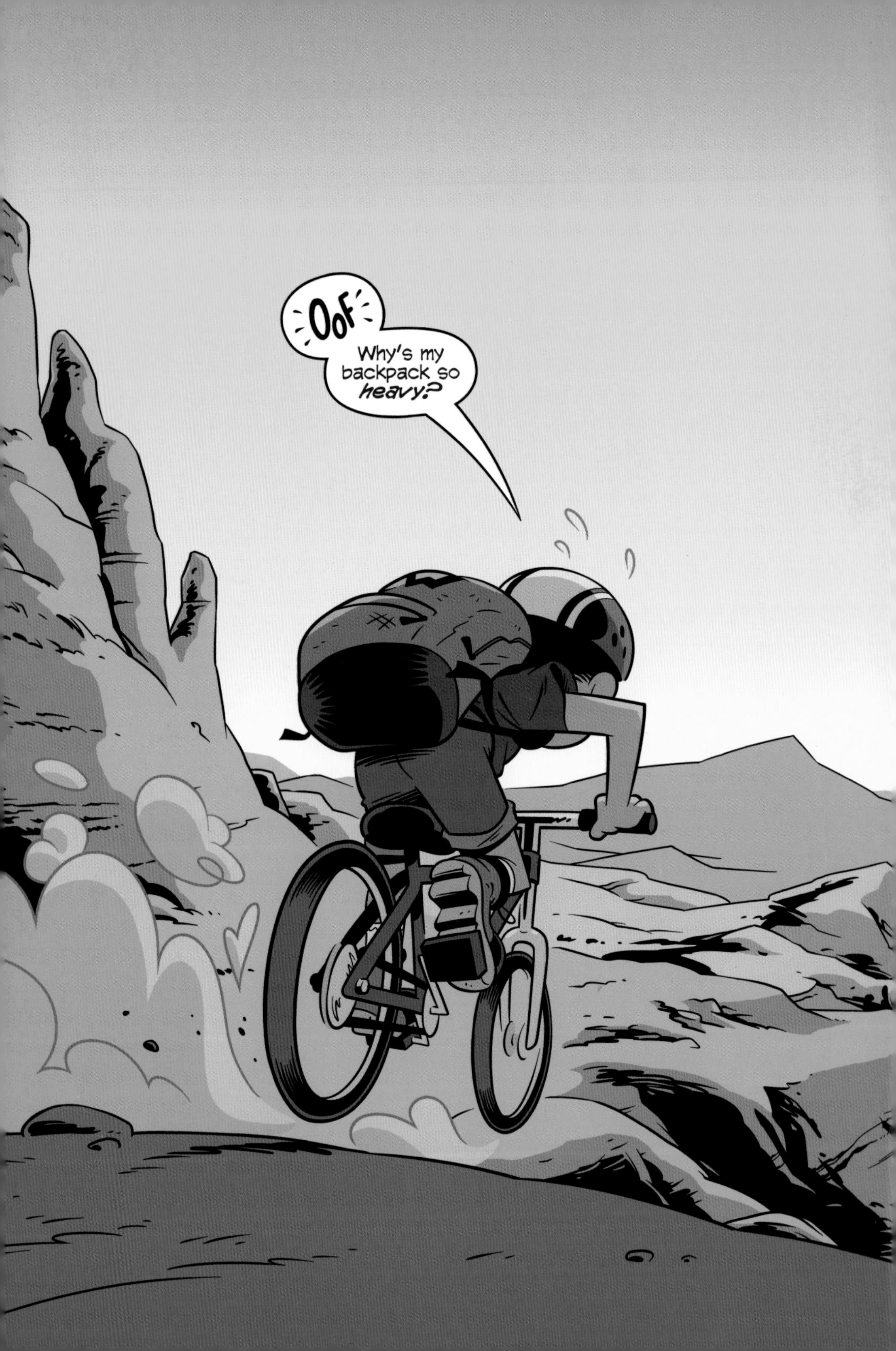
OOF
Why's my backpack so *heavy?*

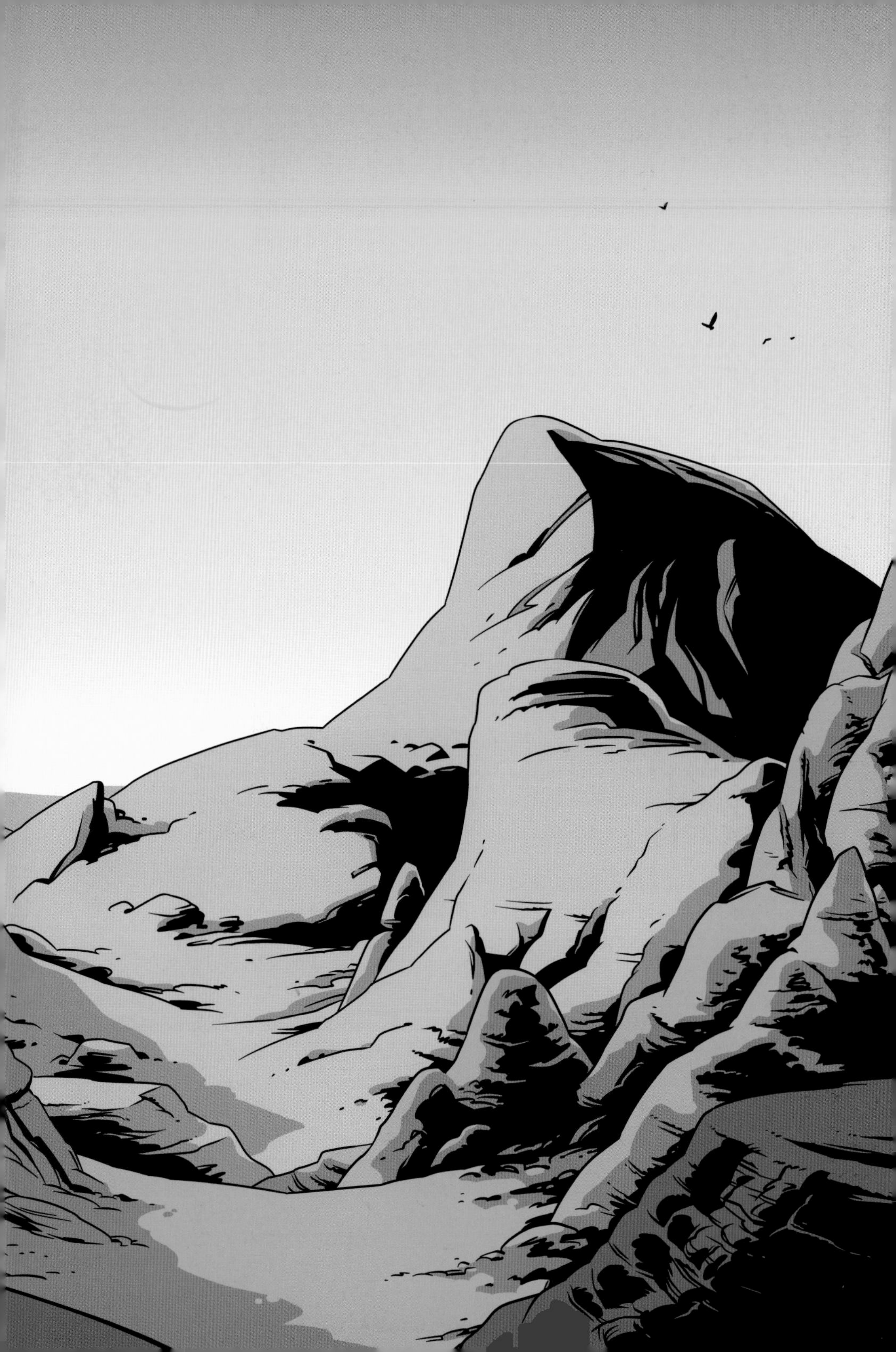

—GLOSSARY—

Cave

A sizable cavity in rock. *Caverns* are those formed by the chemical weathering of sedimentary rock, commonly limestone, and they may or may not be open to the surface.

Continents

Large areas of crust that rise above sea level. These correspond to plates and have collided several times in Earth's history to form a single *supercontinent*.

Convection

The cyclical churning of rising hot matter and sinking cool matter.

Density

The ratio of mass to volume. A little bit of stuff in a lot of space is not very dense, and a lot of stuff in a little space is very dense.

Element

An atom containing a specific number of positively charged particles. These are the basic chemicals that combine to create all matter. Copper, silver, and gold are elements.

Erosion

The wearing, breakdown, and dispersal of rocks. Different types can be caused by *wind*, *water*, *glaciers*, or *gravity*. Erosion caused by gravity is known as *mass wasting*.

Fault

A fracture in the crust. *Normal faults* are caused by crustal expansion and allow a section of crust to drop downward. *Reverse faults* are caused by crustal compression and push a section of crust upward. *Strike-slip faults* are caused by sideways movement. The sudden release of energy along a fault is an *earthquake*.

Fossil

Remains or traces in rock of living things from the past. *Index fossils* belong to widespread species easily assigned to a specific time period and allow us to track global plate movements.

Glacier

A large sheet of ice that can be kilometers thick and cover entire continents. They are the most powerful erosional force around.

Hotspot

Thought to be the top of a plume of extra-hot magma that rises from the core-mantle boundary. These create strings of volcanoes such as the Hawaiian Islands.

Layers of the Earth

The *core* is the innermost layer and has two layers itself: the solid *inner core* and the liquid *outer core*. The three-layered *mantle* accounts for most of Earth's mass. Its solid but flexible rock is the site of convection. The *crust* is the thin outer layer made of shifting, solid plates. It is the only layer of Earth that humans have directly seen or sampled.

Magma

Subterranean molten rock. This is called *lava* when it reaches the surface.

Mineral

A naturally occurring solid made of a single chemical compound arranged in a predictable way. Their orderly, repeating structures create *crystals*.

Mountain

A large, peaked landform that rises much higher than the surrounding surface. *Fold* mountains are pushed up by continental collisions, *volcanic* mountains are created by repeated eruptions, and *basin* and *range* formations are tilted segments of stretched-out crust.

—GLOSSARY CONTINUED—

Plate
> A section of planetary crust that rides atop the mantle. Earth has seven major plates and many more small plates. Their movements and interactions are *tectonics*. Boundaries where plates are spreading apart are called *divergent*, those coming together *convergent*, and those sliding against each other *transform*.

Radioactive Dating
> A method of determining the age of rocks. It relies on measuring the amounts of different radioactive elements within a sample.

Relative Dating
> A method of determining the age of rocks. It relies on comparing features of other rocks with known ages.

Rock
> A solid aggregate of minerals. *Igneous rock* forms either deep underground from magma—*plutonic* igneous—or aboveground from lava—*volcanic* igneous. *Metamorphic rock* is directly transformed from another existing type by intense heat and/or pressure. Metamorphosis can be by *burial* if the existing rock sinks deep beneath the surface or by *contact* if magma rises and heats it. *Sedimentary rock* forms from mineral deposits at the Earth's surface. These can be *clastic*, made of preexisting rock fragments; *biochemical*, made of the remains of living things; or *evaporite*, made of minerals once dissolved in water.

Speleothems
> Cave formations made of mineral deposits left behind by water. These come in many extraordinary shapes.

Subduction
> The process by which the old, cold, dense crust of the seafloor pulls itself beneath less dense crust at areas known as *subduction zones*. This can create kilometers-deep trenches.

Vein

A concentrated deposit of a mineral or element left by water circulating through cracks in rock.

Volcano

A hole in the crust that allows lava, ash, and gases to escape from underground *magma chambers*. Different mineral mixtures within the chamber result in different types of volcano such as *stratovolcanoes*, *shield volcanoes*, and *cinder cones*.

Weathering

The weakening and breakdown of surface rock. This can be *mechanical*, brute force like the freeze-thaw cycle and *salt weathering*; *chemical*, subtle changes from acid rain or oxidation; and/or *biological*, caused by living things like moss and roots.

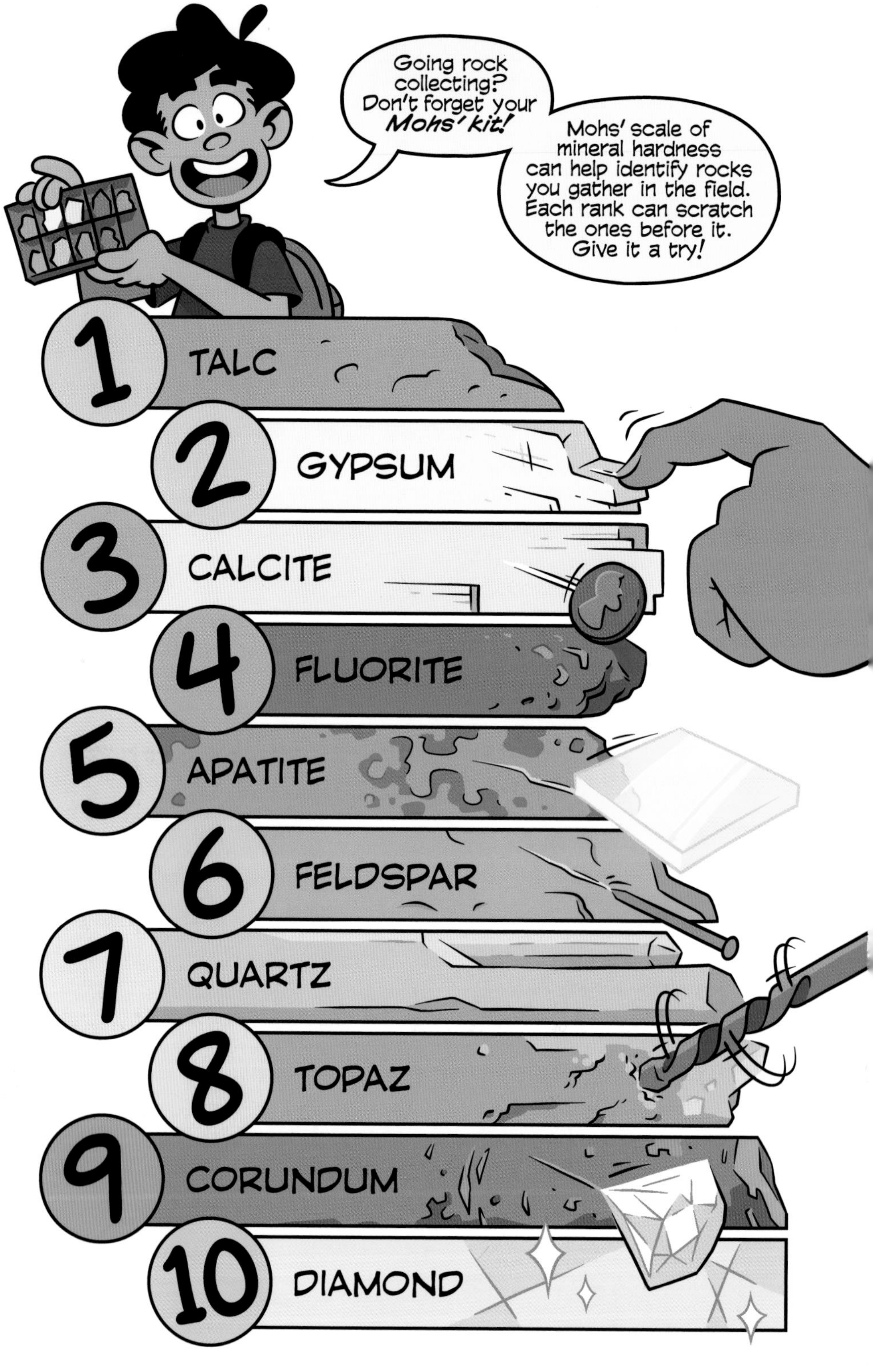
Going rock collecting? Don't forget your *Mohs' kit!*
Mohs' scale of mineral hardness can help identify rocks you gather in the field. Each rank can scratch the ones before it. Give it a try!
1 TALC
2 GYPSUM
3 CALCITE
4 FLUORITE
5 APATITE
6 FELDSPAR
7 QUARTZ
8 TOPAZ
9 CORUNDUM
10 DIAMOND